Abductions and Aliens

Abductions

What's Really Going On?

& Aliens

Chris A. Rutkowski
with a foreword by John Robert Colombo

THE DUNDURN GROUP
A HOUNSLOW BOOK
TORONTO · OXFORD

Publisher: Anthony Hawke
Design: Scott Reid
Printer: Transcontinental Printing Inc.

Canadian Cataloguing in Publication Data

Rutkowski, Chris
Abductions and aliens: what's really going on?

ISBN 0-88882-210-3
1. Alien abduction. I. Title.

BF2050.R87 1999   001.942   C99-932210-3

1   2   3   4   5   03   02   01   00   99

THE CANADA COUNCIL | LE CONSEIL DES ARTS
FOR THE ARTS | DU CANADA
SINCE 1957 | DEPUIS 1957

We acknowledge the support of the **Canada Council for the Arts** for our publishing program. We also acknowledge the support of the **Ontario Arts Council** and financial support of the Government of Canada through the **Book Publishing Industry Development Program** (BPIDP) for our publishing activities.

Care has been taken to trace the ownership of copyright material used in this book. The author and the publisher welcome any information enabling them to rectify any references or credit in subsequent editions.

J.Kirk Howard, President

Printed and bound in Canada.

Printed on recycled paper.

Dundurn Press
8 Market Street
Suite 200
Toronto, Ontario, Canada
M5E 1M6

Dundurn Press
73 Lime Walk
Headington, Oxford,
England
OX3 7AD

Dundurn Press
2250 Military Road
Tonawanda, New York
U.S.A. 14150

For Zachary ... may you never stop asking questions

TABLE OF CONTENTS

ACKNOWLEDGEMENTS

There are many people whom I would like to thank for their assistance, either direct or indirect, in the preparation of this book.

These include: Mary Anderson; my mentor Chester Cuthbert; Geoff Dittman; Lorraine, Sean, and Allison Fair; Geoff Green; my dear friends Jeff and Linda Harland; Jimmie Holman, Jim Melvin, and Sean Jones for Internet and computer assistance; Jon O'Quetwa, Pamela Sindriglis, Andrew Tugby, and Lorraine Welch from the IRC gang.

I would like to thank members of my writers' group (SDGE) for their support, encouragement, proofreading, and comments, not only on this project, but also my other writing efforts during the past few years. These include Katharine Carr, Fatima DeMelo, Susan Rocan, Kevin Russell, and Evelyn Woodward. I must thank Crystal Rocan for her special help, too.

Thanks are due to John Robert Colombo for his foreword, his comments, and his encouragement, and to my publisher, Tony Hawke.

A special thanks to louise sherman (lowercase but definitely upper echelon), who helped me a great deal during the preparation of the manuscript, to Kelley Grandmaison, and to Vladimir Simosko, who was always there with some wisdom and ideas.

... and a "thank you" to Nancy ...

FOREWORD
by John Robert Colombo

From the beginning of recorded history, our species has raised its eyes to the heavens and marvelled at the cycles of light and dark, considered the apparent movements of the sun, the moon, and the planets, and paused to wonder about the stars. Especially the stars, which are so incredibly distant and remote from us. The paradoxical stars, which seem to be fixed in the firmament and yet seem to twinkle and wink at us. These stars, so tiny in the night skies and yet so immense in space. We cannot help but wonder about the nature of the connection, if there is a connection, between the overpowering stellar array and the puny affairs of our species on this tiny planet we call Earth. We cannot help but wonder if there could be any "cosmic connection" at all.

To overcome this sense of remoteness in the universe, we have given some of the more prominent stars their own names. The ones that are visible to the naked eye have been grouped into constellations and christened with names taken from local mythologies. Constellations of stars fill the sky, visible by night, invisible by day. Eighty-eight constellations are known to astronomers, twelve to astrologers. The distances of the stars from Earth are so immense that the void and vastness of the cosmos are both chilling and bracing. The cosmos chills to the bone with proof that man is nowhere near the centre of all creation because there is no centre; the cosmos braces man for the fact that he may be alone in the universe, an orphan of the cosmos. He may be all alone, but then again he may not be. The French writer Albert Camus has one of his characters in the desert of North Africa raise his eyes to the night sky and feel "the benign indifference of the universe."

Is the universe benign? Is it indifferent to the human species? Or is there some "grand plan" that has assembled the stars — those distant suns — that influences and guides the betterment of the human species on the planet Earth? Is there life on the planets that are now understood to circle around many of those remote suns? Is that life at all Earth-like?

To try to answer such questions we must define what we mean by lifeforms. Earth swarms with life from the mosquito to the great whale, from the dinosaur to the kangaroo, from a blade of grass to a rose bush, from a virus to an enzyme, from a microbe to a bacterium, from a pterodactyl to a meadow lark, from a man to a woman ... there is no shortage of life on the planet Earth, though some unique species have been extinct for millions of years and others are endangered and on the point of extinction in our own time. Current opinion holds that none of the planets in our solar system (though possibly some of their moons) are likely to be the abode of life.

There may be lifeforms on the planets of other solar systems.

If there is life elsewhere in the universe, and if off-Earth life has evolved as has human life on the planet Earth, then it is as likely as not that there are non-human beings who live in those worlds and look up to the sky speculating about the forms that life may have taken on planets like Earth that are distant from them. These non-human beings are called aliens. We on Earth have always seen strangers as aliens, though in the past the strangers we have met on Earth have hardly been strange at all! Strangeness is not merely a matter of skin colour, cast of features, languages spoken, social customs, religious beliefs, cultural concerns, or civilized values that are taken for granted but seldom easily granted to "the other," to alien beings.

Aliens from distant planets would appear to us to be alien indeed! In the Earth's oldest scriptures—poetic works like the Vedas and some of the books of the Old Testament—there are descriptions of such beings, or at least there are scholars and popular writers who maintain that this is so. Such beings are the Elohim who descended to Earth where they married the daughters of man. What do we make of the Vision of Elijah, of "wheels within wheels," and of his assumption into the heavens? In the late Middle Ages in England, there is an account of the Green Children who seem to have emerged from a deep cave to visit a little English village. The Ojibwa of the Rama Reserve, near Orillia, Ontario , have a traditional story about "the Skyman" who descended for a three-day visit and then ascended in some sort of craft. Such descriptions are generally taken to be poetic expressions, not factual accounts of what might well have been.

Turning from scriptures and traditional accounts and searching the skies, could it be that the domain of these creatures is centred on the stars of the Milky Way Galaxy or the stars of galaxies even more distant? Early man has always seen "mystery lights" in the sky. Perhaps these are vehicles or craft of some sort to transport the denizens of distant worlds to our own skies. They crossed the void of space and entered Earth's atmosphere and then effected a landing of their craft on what science-fiction writer Robert A. Heinlein called "the Green Hills of Earth" — actually the planet resembles Carl Sagan's "pale blue dot" from space — to meet with the children of Adam and Eve.

I could continue with "cultural tracking," that is, with showing how we have projected onto the skies not only our hopes and fears but also our technologies. In the days of ships of sail, galleons were seen in the skies. In the days of hot-air balloons, "air ships" were described. In the days of sleek aircraft, sleek space craft were depicted. And in the days of radar-defying Stealth fighters, logic-defying starships are hypothesized. This is "cultural tracking." The wonder of it is that alien technologies lag so far behind earthly technology!

I am indulging in the Extraterrestrial Hypothesis (ETH) which equates the "visitors" with alien beings from space. Another equation (popular with marginalists and conspiratorialists) is that the "visitors" come from the interior of the Earth (perhaps through the Polar Opening) or, more likely, from our inner selves. C.G. Jung compared UFOs to bull's-eyes in the sky or, more elegantly, air-borne mandalas. He would see alien beings or MIBs (Men in Black) or "hybrids" as contemporary expressions of our own dehumanization, not the inhumanity of imaginary alien beings.

But I will indulge my fantasies no longer....

Chris A. Rutkowski is well equipped to write this book. As the country's leading researcher and investigator of UFOs, he has extensive experience working in the field and in the study. By profession he is an astronomer and past president of the Winnipeg Centre of the Royal Astronomical Society of Canada; by training he is a writer and communicator. In 1989, he launched the first of his annual tabulations of the previous year's UFO sightings province by province. These statistical accounts of UFO activity in Canada are reported by the media across Canada and are regarded as models of their kind outside the country.

Unnatural History: True Manitoba Mysteries (Winnipeg: Chameleon Publishers, 1993), his first book, is an admirable account of the flora of the supernatural and the fauna of the paranormal to be found in his native Province of Manitoba. "The one characteristic most people will readily admit to having is curiosity," he wrote in the preface to that book. "A sense of wonder leads to discoveries about the places we live in, the mechanisms of life and the universe itself."

An expression of that "sense of wonder" will be found on every page of the present work, Rutkowski's second book. It is concerned with the alien abduction experience and how it affects the population of Canada and also, by extension, the population of North America — indeed, the entire planet and perhaps even all the lifeforms of the cosmos itself! (One wonderful characteristic of ufology and of the alien abduction syndrome is that one can hardly limit it to Earth; it seems to burst forth and spill out across the cosmos!)

Rutkowski discussed in his first book some UFO sightings, contacts, and abductions. But the present book tackles the subject head-on. The author presents thirty-three accounts of reports of abductions and examines them from various perspectives. To my knowledge he has written the first in-depth study that considers abductions and aliens — the twin phenomena so characteristic of our times — from the angle of someone who is conversant with the subject and sympathetic to its witnesses and proponents but also committed to questions of common sense. Almost all other authors of books on alien abductions are parti pris: committed one way or the other to a given outcome, whether as believers or as scoffers, as credulists or as sceptics. It is an "easy out" for the authors of such books to introduce the notion that the phenomenon is so florid and free-flowing that we can throw restraint out one porthole and reason out the other and invoke the so-called Festival of Absurdities or the Oz Factor rather than attempt an explanation for the modest needs of the innocent bystander or devoted reader. This is not Rutkowski. He maintains a critical stance throughout. He shows compassion for the extraordinary suffering reported by "experiencers." He retains a heroic curiosity.

Like most of the readers of this book, I count myself a bystander. I hold no opinion pro or con the alien abduction experience, other than to feel that the reported experiences (in the plural) are so varied that the accounts of them need to be considered individually as well as collectively. I promise one thing: In our lifetime there will be no consensus as to the nature and cause of the rash of reports of alien abductions, reports that in the modern day seem to have begun with the abduction in 1957 of Antonio Villas-Boas in Minas Gerais, Mexico.

Since then, the phenomenon has been closely tracked, widely reported, and over-interpreted by the mighty triumvirate of contemporary abductionists: the padre-like advocacy of Budd Hopkins, the tenacious categorizing of David Jacobs, and the transformative and integrative hypotheses of John Mack. If I understand the books written by these authors, they are saying, collectively, that the alien menace is real, the alien menace is psychological, the alien menace is physiological, the alien menace is psychical, the alien menace is magical, the alien menace is spiritual, the alien menace is therapeutic, the alien menace is demonic the alien menace is not a menace at all because it is benevolent, the alien menace is indeed a menace because it is malevolent ... and so on!

The sense of wonder that we experienced when we initially imagined that "the flying saucers are real" was gradually diminished when the "contactees" related to us their lame and inane messages from the "space visitors" (whether "space brothers" or "space invaders") about the need for love and peace and warnings about the atomic madness of the human race bent on self-destruction. Any sense of wonder that managed to remain intact was finally dissipated with the dire reports that followed—incidents of capture, abduction, rape, and insemination fulfilling a masterplan of interstellar miscegenation!

The designation flying saucer dates from 1947, the description unidentified flying object from 1953. I wish I knew for sure when the term alien abduction was first used, but it was the case of Betty and Barney Hill, described by John G. Fuller in *The Interrupted Journey* (1966), that caught the public's attention. Today it is caught up in the conceits of Budd Hopkins's book *Missing Time* (1981) and its successors which have, as they say, "created the field." Between the 1940s and the 1980s, we enrolled in the "invisible college" and advanced from being freshman witnesses of "mystery lights" and metallic craft in the sky to being sophomore contactees who go on stellar journeys to being senior abductees who are witnesses to the hybridization of the human species. There are now graduate students — human-alien hybrids — among us, if we take to heart the later books of Messrs. Hopkins and Jacobs and the horror novelist Whitley Strieber.

My own work in the field has led me to the conclusion that the only compelling evidence that exists for the interaction of human beings with alien beings is anecdotal. Indeed, there is no objective proof that even one such encounter has occurred in all of recorded history, although there is much collateral evidence that suggests that "brushes" between the species have occurred in antiquity and are happening this very moment on a scale hitherto unanticipated, unprecedented, or unimagined. But evidence is not proof. By its nature no subjective report is able to constitute objective proof.

Undeterred, I continue to collect and examine first-person reports of human-alien interactions. In order to do so I have found it useful to take a term used in the study of folklore and apply it to these first-hand accounts. That term is memorate and it is a word used by folklorists to refer to a first-person narrative of an unusual event or experience. (In folklore the account need not be one that is supernatural, psychical, or paranormal in nature.) Memorates are texts and texts have distinguishing features. They have, for instance, formulaic beginnings and endings. The memorate commonly begins, "You won't believe me when I tell you what happened when I looked up the sky last night." In other words, the informant expects the listener to doubt his or her word. In the same way the memorate commonly ends with an admission and a confession: "That's what happened; I don't know what to make of it." The admission is that the hearer or reader will be puzzled by the foregoing account, and the confession is that the narrator himself or herself is also puzzled as to the reality of the experience. Faced with a memorate, a literary theorist (a deconstructionist perhaps) would have a fine old time demonstrating its structural incoherence or ambivalence. As the result of studying memorates, I have come to the conclusion that people who claim that they have seen a UFO (or a ghost for that matter) are as often as not people who disclaim any prior belief in the "existence" of UFOs (or ghosts). Some people are predisposed to believe, others to disbelieve; both report sightings and visitations. My position in a nutshell is that UFOs and ghosts belong to the category of experience, not to be the category of belief. Some day I plan to have a long discussion with Rutkowski about these matters!

When I make these points I am not sure that Rutkowski agrees with the weight that I grant them, but I do know that he is open to any number of new notions and that in this book he finds particular joy in describing the experiences of other people. This book is a lively brew that includes newly published accounts of experiences of informants known by first names alone (Dylan and Nellie, for instance) as well as a tried-and-true commentary on a genuinely puzzling event (the one described by Michalak). Stefan Michalak was the amateur prospector from Winnipeg who suffered in body and soul as the result of the Falcon Lake Encounter, a "classic case" of ufology, a Close Encounter of the Third Kind, about which Rutkowski is especially knowledgeable and insightful. (It is my prediction that one day Rutkowski will write an important, book-length study of the Falcon Lake Encounter.)

There is one dimension of ufology that has no connection at all with space — outer or inner — and that is the "entity experience," the seeing of beings that are not there or that should not be there. The term entity experience is identified with the English researcher Hilary Evans who in the 1980s in a series of well-argued books has described and analyzed the appearances of "entities" from apparitions of Satan to visions of the Blessed Virgin Mary, from encounters with goblins and old hags to visitations of devas and guardian angels. Such psychological mechanisms as projection and transference are called into play. Jacques Vallée in his ground-breaking book *Passport to Magonia: From Folklore to Flying Saucers* (1969) was among the first to draw attention to the continuum of "other-going" experiences from the "fairies at the foot of the garden" to the "little green men" of the planet Mars. Today's equivalents of the fairy-folk and the LGM (little green men) are visitors in craft from the depths of space, whether green-skinned Reptilians or silver-skinned Reticulian Greys (from Zeta Reticuli).

Rutkowski asks the question, "What's Really Going On?" He has a number of answers. It would be nice (or maybe not so nice!) if there were a single answer. But there are a number of answers and he offers a range of them. Caveat emptor!

Allow me to conclude with an interesting story that Rutkowski has told that is unaccountably absent from the pages of this lively and intriguing book. The story brings together his love for astronomy, his passion for ufology, and his friendship with the late J. Allen Hynek, astronomer and ufology's leading theorist and publicist.

"In 1979, there was a total eclipse of the Sun in North America," Rutkowski writes, "and the track went directly through Manitoba. Scientists from around the world descended upon the province, and a group tour was booked at Gull Harbour Lodge on Hecla Island, about 250 km north of Winnipeg. Among them were Dr. J. Allen Hynek and his family, and during that weekend, we spent some spare time together discussing ufology. At one point, we were sitting in his room, facing the patio doors which opened towards a clearing in the snow-covered bush. During our conversation, he suddenly paused and said, 'You know, if a UFO landed out there in front of us, we'd never be able to report it. No one would believe us, of all people!'"

John Robert Colombo is nationally known as the Master Gatherer for his compilations of Canadiana and also as Canada's Mr. Mystery for the dozen or so books that he has devoted to the study of the supernatural and the paranormal. Among them are UFOs Over Canada, The Little Blue Book of UFOs, *and* Close Encounters of the Canadian Kind.

PROLOGUE
An Exercise in Speculative Fiction

Again

I fidgeted on the cold metal seat.

"Why did you leave her?" Frank asked me.

I didn't answer right away. I knew he couldn't understand.

"Did you hate her?"

I sighed. They were annoying today, as usual.

"No," I finally said.

"Then, why?"

"Because,…" I searched for words, "it wasn't right."

I could see that confused them completely. Frank looked at Al with an expression I couldn't fathom. He turned and stared at me again.

"But you said she was attractive," Al tried. "You liked her face."

I really wanted out of there.

"I know I did," I stated. "But she wasn't my type, that's all."

"You are being difficult," Al said, obviously exasperated. He got up. "We are only trying to help you."

"Help me?" I shouted, standing. I bent down to meet his gaze. "How are you supposed to be helping me? Every time you do this, you're not satisfied with something."

I was getting mad, finally. It felt good. It was about time I started sticking up for myself. This had been going on far too long. Who did they think they were, anyway?

"You will stop acting this way," Sheila ordered from the corner of the room. At least, I thought it was Sheila.

"Not a chance!" I shot back. "I don't care how many nights you put me through this, it will never work!"

I could tell they were annoyed, but I couldn't figure out why they kept me this long tonight.

Frank was suddenly beside me. "You will continue to try with us," he stated decisively.

I felt the tingling begin again.

"It won't work!" I yelled. "Whatever your plans are, they're going nowhere. Why can't you understand that? I can't do it with just anyone!"

Everything was getting blurry. I was very, very tired.

"That in itself is interesting to us," I thought I heard Frank say. Maybe it was Al or one of the ones I never bothered naming. Their grey faces with those huge almond-shaped eyes all looked so much alike ...

I awoke in my bed again. The balls of light were already through my window, going up into the star-filled sky.

They'll be back for me again.

I wonder how many others they are doing this to.

But — they'll never understand.

INTRODUCTION
Alien on My Shoulder

Surveys and polls tell us that approximately 8 percent of all North Americans have seen UFOs.

To round it off, nearly one in ten people has seen a UFO.

(Not only that, but in 1992, a *Roper Poll* found that approximately 2 percent of the population has had an alien abduction experience — at least, according to Budd Hopkins, an abduction expert and director of the Intruders Foundation. The survey found that 18 percent of the population have woken paralyzed or with a sense of presence in their bedrooms, 8 percent have seen balls of light in their bedrooms while around 13 percent felt they were missing at least one hour in their lives. Combining these elements of abduction narratives, it sounds as if a very significant number of us have been abducted by aliens.)

It's no wonder, then, why so many people are interested in this subject. It's so pervasive in our society. We seem to be obsessed with the concept of extraterrestrial life and aliens. One can hardly turn on the television or go to a movie theatre without being exposed to a space theme of some sort, whether it be "Third Rock from the Sun" or *Independence Day*. Even Marvin the Martian is making a big comeback.

"Star Trek" still is immensely popular (although some are suggesting its popularity is finally waning), and science fiction is again in vogue. (Did it ever fall out of favour?) It seems as though we humans are becoming very blasé about the implications of extraterrestrial contact and willing to imagine the wondrous consequences of "What if?"

In general conversation, if the subject of unusual phenomena is mentioned, nearly everyone has a story to tell that includes some reference to the supernatural, whether it be aliens, monsters, or ghosts. That is the essence of the fascination with UFOs, in particular: they are good stories.

Over the years, I've been called a UFO investigator or a UFO researcher. Both are misnomers. This is because I don't actually investigate UFOs. Instead, I talk with people who say they have had UFO experiences. There is a big difference. Investigation implies some sort of rigorous legal or scientific procedure involving DNA testing of blood-stained gloves and cross-examination of people driving Ford Broncos.

Talking with people involves listening to their stories and sharing their tales of encounters, whether they be about grey-skinned aliens, ghostly apparitions, or giant hairy monsters in the Pacific Northwest. It's the fascination with such stories that got me interested in UFOs.

Mind you, I didn't have this in mind when I entered university. Oh, I always had a fascination about the night sky and stars and planets and galaxies — and all that space stuff. My parents took me to Houston during the early Apollo missions; I got to taste real astronaut ice cream, climb aboard lunar landers, and meet real astronauts (the "real ones" that were written about in Tom Clancy's book, not the ones who grow mould and breed ants aboard space shuttles).

Being young and foolish (as opposed to now being old and foolish), I went to university and obtained a degree in astronomy. If you haven't noticed, there are very, very few want ads in the newspaper which ask for degrees in astronomy. I committed the cardinal sin of college: I went into a field that is interesting.

I persisted in some graduate studies, however, and along the way became involved with the university's planetarium. I wrote and produced some shows there and generally hung around the planetarium office waiting for the phone to ring, hoping it would be the director of Mount Palomar calling to give me a job offer or something like that.

I remember one day, when I was standing in the hallway of the astronomy department reading a poster inviting graduate students to travel to an isolated mountain top in Chile and tend some telescopes there. One of my classmates was in the hall with me and we discussed the idea.

"Who would be stupid enough to spend two years on a cold, lonely, snowy mountain top in Chile?" I scoffed.

Well, *he* did. Perhaps you've heard of him: Ian Shelton. He went to Chile and discovered a supernova. It's named after him; his picture was in *Time* magazine. Lucky stiff. (Do I still sound bitter?)

No, my fate was to follow a different direction.

Something is out there

From time to time during my astronomy tenure, people would call the department, insisting that they had seen funny lights in the sky that they couldn't explain. Usually, the other astronomers and staff would take the calls and politely explain that the lights were not Martian spacecraft but in fact Air Canada 693 from Vancouver.

All went well until the time one instructor in the astronomy department was having a particularly bad day. (A bad day for an astronomer is when his or her calculation of the distance to the Moon is out by a few hundred kilometres. Well, I might have been responsible for my professor's miscalculation, but that's another matter.) His phone rang while I was in his office.

He answered, and after a few seconds cupped his hand over the receiver and said to me: "It's another one who's seen a UFO. You talk to her; I'm busy."

So, without any notice, I found myself talking with a person who was sure she had seen a UFO the previous night. I patiently tried to assure her that there were no such things as little green men and that it was probably a star or planet or plane or balloon or something.

She wouldn't be convinced. "I'm sure it wasn't an airplane," she insisted. "I see the airplanes fly over every night, and it wasn't a star because I live on a farm and know what stars look like."

She presented a fairly convincing argument as to why it could not possibly have been anything less remarkable than a UFO. Another classic example of the standoff between science and society.

There was something in her voice that intrigued me. Was it possible — just possible — that she had really seen something other than a plane or star?

Most astronomers are sure there is life out there somewhere. The recent media circus surrounding the discovery of the possible fossilized life elements inside Martian meteorites shows how seriously the idea is regarded. It's just that the distances between the stars are so great that getting here from there is impossible. (Well, almost impossible.)

How far away *are* things? If you shrank our sun down to the size of a pea and placed it somewhere in, say, New York, the next nearest pea (which would be the next nearest star to us) would be in ... Chicago. That's the next *nearest* star. It might be too much to expect that the star right next door (astronomically speaking) had life. Of course, most other stars are much farther away.

I should note, though, that there is a growing list of what are called extrasolar planets that have been discovered circling some stars in our general galactic neighbourhood. Astronomers are more and more convinced that planets are the norm for every star, and given the many millions of stars in our galaxy alone, it is looking like another planet similar to ours is out there somewhere.

It's that "somewhere" that is the problem. As the pea example showed, the distances between stars are very, very large. It takes a lot of energy, planning, money, and luck to engage in space travel, at least in our own experience. We were lucky to get to the Moon a few times, and it looks like we won't make it there again for a long, long time. So, travel between stars is virtually impossible. For us, anyway.

And there's the hitch: it's impossible for *us*. Right now. At this moment in our civilization. Assuming we don't blow ourselves up soon, we could be around for thousands of years to come. What will our technology be like in fifty years? One hundred? Can you imagine one thousand years from now? Why, we didn't have airplanes one hundred years ago, let alone rocketships!

We know that many stars in our galactic neighbourhood are thousands of years ahead of us in evolution. If there was a race of aliens on a nearby planet that was a few thousand years ahead of us, could they have conquered space?

Of course, that's science fiction. It's what I read as a teenager — that my teachers forced me to put down so that I could read proper things like great literature such as Milton or Joyce.

But W.O. Mitchell wasn't for me. I was attracted to names like Clarke and Bradbury and Asimov. I was less interested in stories about growing up on the Canadian prairie than I was about what life might be like on the Canadian prairie *five hundred years from now*, with robots tilling the fields and rocketships taking our grain to feed hungry refugees on Jupiter instead of some obscure Third World country. It all seemed more hopeful, somehow.

And that's perhaps why I was willing to take more phone calls at the planetarium. I was fascinated to hear the stories of mysterious lights in the night and encounters with *them*.

UFO stories

When a person tells me about his or her sighting of a UFO, it's a *story*. Stories aren't always meant to be believed or disbelieved — they are personal accounts of incidents in peoples' lives. As such, they give us glimpses into what we experience: how we perceive our world and how it affects our lives.

Science, however, moves in and tells us what can and cannot be, messing up particularly good stories at every opportunity. We have to give scientists some credit, after all. They gave us running water and telephones and digital watches, so they can't be all bad. But when it comes to aliens and UFOs, why do they have to be such spoilsports?

Not all scientists dismiss UFO stories, however. There are a growing number who are seriously interested in the phenomenon and actively study the reports. These are the people who are part of the Steven Spielberg generation and whose minds are filled with possibilities. Some of them now publish books about alien abductions and others speculate about a shift in cosmic awareness.

I just enjoy the wonder of it all.

At a reception for authors during a literary conference in British Columbia in 1994, a woman sought me out to explain why she had bought a ticket to my presentation. She confessed: "I'm a believer, you know, ever since my brother told me what happened to him."

Then she told me his story. (I hope I'll relate it correctly.) He was living in Northern Ontario many years ago, working with a railroad crew. One night, everyone's attention was drawn to a brilliant object moving in the sky. He didn't recognize it as an airplane or anything else familiar. Having signalling equipment handy, he tried to communicate with the UFO by shining a light at the object, using Morse Code. The workers were startled to see the object respond by shining an intense beam of light back at them, scaring them. What's more, this woman said her brother's hair turned white as a result of the experience!

That's just *one* story that was related to me at the conference. You can't imagine how many stories I've heard over the past few decades. The stories range from fairly dull encounters, like observations of distant lights moving in the night sky, to the extraordinary, such as actual abductions aboard alien spacecraft.

Some of the stories that interest me the most are UFO sightings by devout skeptics — people who don't believe in UFOs. They proclaim: "I'll never believe in UFOs until I see one myself!" ... and then they see one.

Such a case occurred in western Manitoba in 1988. In the fall, I received a call from a man with a gruff-sounding voice, demanding that I listen to his story. He insisted that he "didn't believe in those things" (UFOs) and that he used to always make fun of people who told stories about "seein' saucers." But this time, he had changed his tune. "I ain't makin' this up!" he said. "I know what I saw!"

He told me that the night before, he and a few friends were "jack lighting" in their favourite location, hunting deer. Jack lighting is a generally illegal sport where you hunt late at night and use a bright spotlight to startle deer and other quarry into a frozen state of panic, then shoot them with your rifle. The man sounded like quite a tough character, so I wasn't about to point out to him that his efforts could land him in jail.

He and his buddies had some success that particular night, and had bagged several animals. They packed up their gear and their trophies just before midnight, and drove off on their usual back road to avoid the Mounties. But this time, when they followed the road over a hill, they were shocked to see what they thought was a roadblock in the valley below. Bright red flashing "cherry" lights were directly in front of them.

"We were going pretty fast," the man told me, "and we'd had a few by then, so we didn't want to stop and get caught by the police."

The driver did what would have seemed natural in such a position: he sped up and tried to smash through the roadblock.

But much to their surprise, as they barrelled towards the lights, the lights stopped flashing, rose up off the ground and flew away across a field.

"We believe other people now," the man told me. "We've seen a UFO, too."

One of the most intriguing Canadian UFO cases is that of Stefan Michalak. He returned home from a prospecting expedition with serious ill effects that he claimed were a result of an extraordinary UFO encounter.

On May 20, 1967, in an area near Falcon Lake, Manitoba, Michalak had expected to enjoy a quiet weekend of prospecting. At 12:15 p.m., with the sun high and clouds gathering in the west, Michalak was startled by the cackling of some geese, which were obviously disturbed by something. He looked up and was surprised to see two cigar-shaped objects with "bumps" on them, about forty-five degrees in altitude, descending and glowing red. As they approached, they appeared more oval, and then disc-shaped.

Suddenly, the further of the pair stopped in mid-flight, while the other drew nearer and appeared to land on a large, flat rock which was later

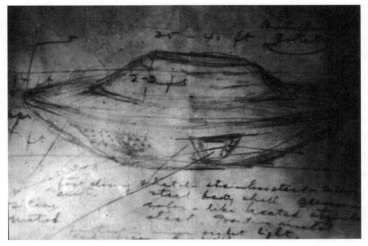

Stefan Michalak's sketch of the object near Falcon Lake, Manitoba, in 1967.

determined to be about 160 feet away. The one in the air hovered for a short while, then departed as well, flying into the west, where it disappeared behind the clouds. Turning his attention to the object on the ground, Michalak saw that it was the colour of "hot stainless steel," surrounded by a golden-hued glow. For the next half hour he knelt near a rock, making a sketch of the object and noting various features. The craft was saucer-shaped, about forty feet in diameter and approximately ten feet thick. Its upper cupola or dome was an additional three feet high. Michalak became aware of waves of warm air radiating from the craft, accompanied by the "smell of sulphur." He also heard the whirring of what sounded like a fast electric motor, and a hissing, as if air was being taken in or expelled.

A door had opened in the side of the craft, revealing some lights inside. This door was about two by three feet in size. Michalak approached to within sixty feet of the craft, and heard two humanlike voices, one with a higher pitch than the other. He was sure that the craft was an American experimental test vehicle, and walked closer to it, sarcastically asking, "Okay, Yankee boys, having trouble? Come on out and we'll see what we can do about it." Getting no response (the voices had subsided), and becoming flustered, he asked cautiously in Russian, "Do you speak Russian?" There was still no answer, so he gave greetings in German, Italian, French, and Ukrainian, then once again in English.

At this point, his curiosity got the best of him, and he walked closer to the craft, ending up directly in front of it. Poking his head into the opening, he saw a maze of lights on what appeared to be a panel, and beams of light in horizontal and diagonal patterns. There was also a cluster of lights flashing in a random sequence "like on a computer."

As Michalak stepped away from the craft, he saw that the wall of the craft was about eighteen inches thick. Suddenly, three panels slid over the opening, sealing it "like a camera shutter." He examined the outside of the craft and touched the side of it with his gloved hand. There were no signs of welding or joints; the surface was highly polished, and appeared like coloured glass with light reflecting off it, and made "silvery spectra" out of the sunlight. Drawing his glove back, he saw that it had burned and melted when it brushed the side of the object. Unexpectedly, the craft shifted position, and he was facing a gridlike exhaust vent which he had seen earlier to his left. This vent was about nine inches high by six inches wide, and contained a uniform pattern of round holes, each about 1/16 inch in diameter. A blast of hot gas shot from these holes onto his chest, setting his shirt and undershirt on fire and causing him severe pain. He tore off his burning garments and threw them to the ground. He looked up in time to see the craft depart like the first, and felt a rush of air as it ascended.

Michalak was physically injured, and over the next few years was examined and treated by a number of physicians in both Canada and the United States. Radioactive pieces of metal were found at the site, and Michalak's chest displayed a bizarre pattern of round burns which later left deep scar tissue. The United States Air Force labelled the case "unexplained" in its scientific study of UFOs published in the late 1960s. Recently, two different explanations were proposed by experts; a Canadian military researcher believes the saucer was actually a secret government test vehicle, whereas an American involved with the USAF study suggests it was all a hoax. Michalak, however, sticks by his story even today, and it is difficult to imagine what he would have gained from an elaborate hoax.

Although Michalak never actually encountered any "aliens," his case at least has some physical evidence to back it up, unlike most abduction cases. In fact, one could ask, if aliens really are capable of doing what is claimed of them — such as blocking memories, becoming invisible and so forth — then why did Michalak remember anything at all? After all, abductees are "remembering" alien abductions which occurred in their childhoods, long before 1967 when Michalak had his experience. Were the aliens in Canada technologically advanced, but simply not omnipotent?

(Michalak *was* hypnotically regressed, by the way. This took place in the late 1960s, well before its modern common usage by abduction experts. Even back then, the infant research tool was viewed as a possible, but limited way of recovering blocked memories. However, a tape of the hypnosis that I have in my possession shows that Michalak did not recall any details other than those he consciously remembered.)

Now, some readers might be thinking: "Sure, a couple of hunters and a prospector have seen UFOs, but certainly no people with trained eyes have ever had anything happen to them!"

Or, maybe, you're thinking that people only make up these stories to get attention and get their name in the paper. I can assure you that I also have reports from doctors, lawyers, police, airline pilots, butchers, bakers, and candlestick makers (you get the idea). Virtually none have wanted their names made public. In fact, I have been threatened with serious consequences if I was ever to make certain witnesses' names public.

On guard for them

I was in my office at the university one day, unhappily slogging through paperwork, when a military officer and his wife walked in.

He was good-looking, about 35, and with close-cropped dark hair. She was quite attractive, slightly younger, with a cherubic face surrounded by brown hair.

"We're looking for Chris Rutkowski," the man said. "The guy who's involved with UFOs."

I gratefully put down my pen. "That's me," I volunteered.

"My wife and I would like to talk to you about some things that have happened to us," he began.

That is how I met Dylan and Nellie. Over the next few months, I met with them several times, often in the company of Roy Bauer, an associate and co-researcher.

Dylan is in the Canadian Forces. He believes there are some things he simply cannot tell his military friends and officers. Since he was a young boy, he has had many unusual experiences that appear to involve aliens, poltergeists, ghosts, and various other entities.

His wife, Nellie, has shared many of these experiences. They are both convinced that someone — something — is watching them, controlling them, and influencing their lives.

During his teenage years in southern Alberta, Dylan recalls one day that he was with some friends in a wooded area not far from town. He says that he wandered away from the group, walking down a road with his knapsack on his back. He was shocked to see a glowing, disc-shaped object appear suddenly above the road in front of him.

He remembers being "very scared and fearful" upon seeing the object. In a panic, he ducked down in the short brush along the road. But then he started feeling very tired and sleepy ...

His next memory is of waking up in the dark on the opposite side of the road. His backpack lay opened with its contents spewed out in the dirt. The disc-shaped object was nowhere to be seen. He walked back home to find his family and friends worried about him. He had been missing for several hours, even though they had been up and down the road several times in their search. He could not remember what had happened during those missing hours.

Dylan says that the next morning the newspapers and radio were awash with stories of other peoples' sightings of UFOs the night before. I made inquiries at the town's news media, but no one could recall the case.

That incident started Dylan's history of experiences. Since then, it seems that "they" have been watching him and directing his life. Dylan is convinced that some entity or entities are keeping close watch on him.

This is carried to the point where he can get a "visit" from an entity at any time, day or night, and receive guidance or advice about choices he will be making. Indeed, Dylan was cautioned by this entity about discussing his experiences with me, for fear of some unfortunate incidents that might occur. He did not heed the warnings.

One particularly curious incident that was shared between Dylan and Nellie occurred early in their relationship. They were living in Edmonton and had gone for dinner one evening. For some reason, they found themselves walking home on a route that was not familiar. As they walked, they began to tire, but continued into a park. Their next recollection was of waking up huddled together on a park bench, covered in snow. They had no idea how long they had been there, or why they had fallen so soundly asleep that the falling snow did not wake them. What's more, they had a shared feeling that they had been transported somewhere else and had an encounter with entities during this missing period.

Nellie has a history of unusual events in her family. Her mother spoke of large, basketball-sized globes of light that would occasionally appear before her and float with her in a kind of teasing dance as she hung laundry or gathered wood near her home in rural Saskatchewan.

Nellie has dreams in which "beings of light" come to speak with her. She feels she has been directed to go on a shamanic journey and to share her insight with others. It is because she is fearful of the malevolent and seemingly omniscient entities that she has been exploring ways to halt the onslaught.

She appealed to me for help. I suggested that she try to keep a daily diary of her experiences. However, she rejected this because she knew that "they" would know that she was keeping the diary and would somehow intervene; she was very scared of inviting them to appear.

The experiences of Dylan and Nellie also have some sexual aspects. Once, when Dylan had considered disobeying the entities, a lesion developed on his penis. This was most unsettling to Nellie, and she was convinced that the entities also wanted to control their bedroom activities.

As I sat in their apartment, listening to their story, I glanced around. Their living room was adorned with books on shamanism, mysticism, psychic phenomena, and, of course, UFOs. Nellie reads as many books as she can on these subjects and discusses them with her husband at every opportunity.

Finally, they mentioned an issue of great concern to Nellie. She was concerned that their children were starting to have the same experiences. From listening to the things the children said and the dreams they retold, Nellie worried that they, too, were being visited by the entities. Both parents insisted that they had not told their children about their own encounters.

To this day, Dylan and Nellie still have regular contact with "them." Dylan sometimes gets up in the middle of the night and has telepathic conversations with the entities about the next day's events. He and Nellie believe they have been imparted with keen insight into the universe, transcending scientific knowledge.

Who these entities are is anyone's guess. Are they alien beings from an advanced civilization? Are they ghosts or supernatural creatures? Are they the products of active imaginations? Are they "screen memories" of traumatic incidents in the past?

Emily's crisis

It was clearly a cry for help.

"I need to talk with you. It's urgent," she said. "Please help me."

That afternoon in March was very busy for me, and I had little time to spare. But her plaintive cry gnawed at me.

"Can you tell me what's wrong?" I asked, trying to calm her.

"It's really something you won't believe," she said, "but I was told you might be able to meet with me. Do you ever go to the University of Winnipeg?"

"Not often," I replied. "Is there a way you could come to the University of Manitoba sometime?"

Without hesitation, she picked up on my offer.

"I can get on a bus right away," she told me.

I thought about how I could rearrange my schedule so I could meet with her. Something about this woman's tone suggested some urgency, so I gave her directions on how to take a bus between the universities.

"Is there a place to smoke there?" she asked. "I'm so nervous, I need to smoke."

That complicated things, since the University of Manitoba is mostly a smoke-free environment, but there was one coffee shop that still had a smoking section, so I thought I would take her there when she arrived within the hour.

On impulse, I called Cliff Noble, an associate who is a psychologist. He had worked with me on several previous occasions when abductees seemed to need some attention beyond anything I could provide. He had hypnotically regressed some abductees and was relatively familiar with the phenomenon.

I asked him if he was willing to see another abductee on short notice. He agreed, and I breathed a sigh of relief. I had an uncomfortable feeling about this woman.

She arrived sooner than I expected. She came to my office and I quickly took her across campus to the smoking area.

Emily was in her late forties, with short, permed dark hair. As she sat at the tiny table with me, she lit cigarette after cigarette, rolled and with filters crudely attached. She had six in her package when she started talking.

"I don't know where to start," she said, nervously. She glanced around at the other tables nearby. "I wonder if they can hear me."

I assumed she had been talking about the other people at the surrounding tables. They were all indulging in deep, smoke-clouded discussions and watching the video screens hanging from the ceiling.

"Don't worry," I told her.

Emily proceeded to tell me about *them*.

"Have you ever had anyone tell you about the Reticulians?" she asked.

I assured her that I had, which was quite true.

"Good," she said, and began her story.

She had been living an uneventful life, raising a family and working odd jobs until about seven years ago. At that time, her life "seemed to fall apart." She had separated from her husband and she admitted she was in something of a spiritual crisis.

She says she had been very distressed, and was laying in bed, sobbing. She confided that she had even considered suicide.

That's when *they* came to her.

"Suddenly, they were there, in my room," she explained. "They just materialized."

"They" were alien beings from other planets, as she soon found out. They had decided to help her during her time of need because they knew she was "right" for their work on Earth. What work this was, exactly, she was unsure.

But help her they did. With their support, Emily overcame her depression and began functioning again in society. She even became interested in news events and in other subjects she had always avoided.

"I became smarter," she said. "I enrolled in university so that I could get a better education."

Emily in fact began taking courses towards a bachelor's degree in science. She studied hard, began piecing together her family life, and everything seemed to be getting very positive.

"The grey ones were my friends," Emily noted. "They would walk with me on the street and only I could see them. We would talk about everything. I tried telling my ex-husband about them, and he said he had been visited by them, too."

But then, the "toast-coloured" aliens came.

"I don't know why they started to come," she lamented. "They were always just confusing me with the things they said and told me to do."

The original aliens were small, grey-skinned creatures with large heads and a "delicateness" about their demeanour. But these "browns" were taller and looked more like humans. And they had a different agenda for Emily.

"The brown ones always made me do things, whereas the others would only help me."

One example of the browns' control took place during one of Emily's science classes.

"I was supposed to make a class presentation," she said, "but they had been bothering me all night and I couldn't prepare for it. So, when I went to the university, I didn't know what I was going to do. When it was my turn, I was just going to apologize, but I blacked out. The next thing I remember is that I was in the hallway after class and everyone was telling me what a great presentation I had given. But I didn't remember anything about what had happened! Later, the beings told me that they had taken control of my body and mind and had done the presentation for me."

"I was really angry at them for doing that," she added. "It wasn't right."

Emily was very nervous during our discussion. She kept looking around to see if anyone was staring at her. She smoked cigarette after cigarette and her hands shook every time she lit up.

"Can you help me?" she pleaded.

I didn't know what to say. What *could* I say?

"Why did you call me?" I finally asked.

"Because they told me to," she replied.

I was taken aback. Aliens knew about me and were referring abductees to me?

"What did they say?"

She paused to borrow a cigarette from a person at the next table. "I had gotten mad at them for making me so upset, so I told them to stop it."

She continued, "They told me to talk to someone about them, someone who knew about their presence. I asked them for a name, and your name popped into my head. I found out you were at the university and I found you that way.

"Do you understand what I'm going through?" she implored. "Is there anything you can do to help me?" She began sobbing, and I tried my best to comfort her.

"Perhaps," I said, as reassuringly as possible.

"My family won't talk to me now, and I can't concentrate on my studies," she cried. "Is there any way to stop them?"

I thought for a minute, then carefully suggested, "Have you thought of going to a clinical therapist? I have a friend who has helped me with people like yourself who were experiencing similar problems."

She sobered up immediately. "What's he like?" she asked. "Is he one of those scientists who doesn't believe in these things?"

"No," I replied. "He is a psychologist and he has helped several UFO abductees before. If you want, I can take you to him right away."

Tears welled in her eyes. "Can he see me right now? I have to talk with someone who can help me!"

"He can see you right now," I said. We left the campus immediately and I took her to see Noble. I last saw her being led into his clinical office, just before the door closed.

Much later, I discussed her situation with him.

"She was extremely delusional," he told me. "I referred her immediately to the psychiatric unit at the hospital downtown. If she went in through the emergency entrance, she could be seen right away."

"But what was really happening to her?" I asked.

"I have no idea," he replied.

Alien Abduction Syndrome (AAS)

Emily was a very extreme case of what I am calling *Alien Abduction Syndrome* (AAS). She was absolutely convinced that several types of alien beings (there was a third kind that had visited her as well) had invaded her life and were manipulating her mind and body to suit their will. No one else could see them when she did, yet they were almost always present and "watched over her" throughout each day.

It must be noted at this point that few other abductees I have met were as emotionally and mentally troubled as Emily. However, I include her case because it illustrates one of the most common explanations for AAS: delusion.

Many years ago, before alien abductions were as much in vogue, I came across a book by Barbara O'Brien, titled *Operators and Things: The Inner Life of a Schizophrenic* (Signet, 1976). Its author is a former schizophrenic who somehow spontaneously recovered from her illness without direct treatment.

What is fascinating about the book is that O'Brien relates almost exactly the same story as Emily. In fact, her book begins with the following analogy:

> Let us say that when you awake tomorrow, you find standing at your bedside a man with purple scale-skin who tells you that he has just arrived from Mars, that he is studying the human species, and that he has selected your mind for the kind of on-the-spot examination he wants to make.
>
> While you are catching your breath, he walks casually to your best chair, drapes his tail over it, and informs you that he will be visible and audible only to you. Fixing his three eyes sternly upon you, he warns you not to reveal his presence; if you attempt to do so, he threatens, he will kill you instantly.
>
> You may wonder, perhaps, if you are sane. But the Man from Mars is standing before you, clear and colourful, and his voice is loud and distinct. On the basis of what you can so clearly see and hear, you accept the fact, astounding as it is, that the stranger is what he says he is.
>
> (O'Brien, p.1.)

O'Brien's *operators*, as she calls them (or, rather, as they call themselves) do not look like Martians. But her analogy is interesting in the light of what abductees are reporting today, nearly forty years after the book was written.

O'Brien's operators have complete control over her mind and body. They instruct her to leave her job, dissociate from her friends and take a bus to another city. They make her more paranoid by suggesting that other people she meets are humanlike operators who know what she is thinking and are monitoring her activities. They tell her what to say, how to dress, and where to go each day. When she finally admits herself to a hospital (only after they allowed her to do so), she is told precisely what to say in order to avoid being subjected to shock therapy and other invasive treatments that might harm their relationship with her.

When she finally "comes out" of her delusional state of reality, she realized that the operators were actually mental constructs that allowed her to survive while going through a nervous breakdown. In effect, they were her brain's "defence mechanism," which allowed her to escape from an emotional stress (from her job and other things) while appearing to anyone watching her as a completely functional, normal being.

After having counselled Emily that afternoon, I have no doubt that she was experiencing exactly what O'Brien describes. Instead of human operators, Emily had aliens to guide her and protect her. They took her mind and body over when she was under more stress. And, when the mental breakdown was reaching critical proportions, they guided her gently towards help: me. I was chosen because I was not a "typical scientist" who would lock her away in an institution. I was sympathetic to her understanding of aliens, and therefore could aid her in her subconscious search for help.

In a way, I feel that I did not live up to her expectations. If I had been an abductee therapist such as those who practice in the United States, I might have hypnotically regressed her in order to uncover hidden memories and other information placed in her brain by the aliens. I might have had her x-rayed in order to locate an alien "implant," which would have been necessary in order for them to find her wherever she went.

I did none of these things. I referred her to a clinician. What else could I do? Her experiences were beyond the scope of UFO research. There was no supporting evidence to back up her claims, and the aliens bore little resemblance to anything other than delusional entities.

The question is, then, how much of a delusional disorder can be read into other abductee accounts? Is it really a justifiable explanation for abduction experiences, or is there another way to interpret the stories? Or, is it possible that some people really are having encounters with aliens?

The trouble with dismissing all AAS cases as delusions is that not all are as simple as that of Emily. Some abductions are one-time events, without any ongoing or residual effects. Many abductees do not report being under the control of alien beings, nor do they express any paranoia, fear or distress. Many do not exhibit any particular stress or emotional discord. They simply report the fact that they had an unusual experience that may or may not have been a waking dream — or encounters with alien beings.

Another complicating issue is that UFO reports themselves are not at all unusual. Most UFO sightings are of lights in the night sky. These are called nocturnal lights (NLs) and may have a variety of explanations, including fireballs, aircraft, balloons, stars, and planets. As mentioned earlier, surveys have suggested that as much as 8 percent of all North Americans have seen a UFO. This means that being witness to a UFO is a very common thing — so common, in fact, that it has to be considered a "normal" part of daily life.

If this is the case, then some abductees' experiences could be simply an indication of "normalness."

But this leaves us with a problem again. If some experiences are "normal" and Emily's was not, how can we possibly differentiate between the two? Why is one "normal" and the other "delusional?"

Suppose

Although observing a UFO is common, seeing aliens or finding physical evidence of their passing is very, very rare. The actual rate of occurrence of close encounter cases is approximately one in five hundred. Furthermore, the sighting of a UFO does not in itself imply alien invasion. We must remember that the definition of a UFO is, simply, an *unidentified flying object*, and has no implication of extraterrestrial intervention. It is the *interpretation* of the sightings that is so controversial.

To those who believe that alien visitations are occurring today, UFOs are the proof that they are here. To those who do not hold that belief, a UFO is simply "one of those things."

To adopt a truly objective and unbiased attitude towards UFO reports is difficult, but not impossible. I personally prefer to sit on the fence and be unconvinced by stories of aliens in bedrooms but open to the possibility that alien encounters could be occurring.

Some skeptics suggest that many abductees are probably suffering from low self-esteem and may be creating alien abduction imagery to make themselves feel important and "chosen" to help save the human race. Others say abductees are unable to cope with repressed sexual abuse or unhappy marriages and are calling out for help through their subconscious.

What we know for sure is that many people *think* they have been abducted or contacted by aliens. Others simply have a period of missing time in their lives that they cannot account for, and feel that "something" happened to them.

The trouble is that many of the people who talk to me about their experiences don't fit into any of these neat categories. They have happy lives, good marriages, challenging jobs, and generally good heads on their shoulders.

Recent studies have shown that people who report seeing UFOs are perfectly normal — as normal as you or I. (Perhaps I should rephrase that.) Young and old, women and men, from all countries and cultures, people continue to report having experiences that do not appear to have conventional explanations.

Most UFO reports (about 95 percent, to be exact) are not classified as "unknowns." People *do* make mistakes and errors of judgment. It's that other 5 percent that is the "interesting stuff."

That stuff is the source of the stories we have as a legacy of awe and wonder about our place in the universe.

Suppose there was a race of advanced alien beings on a planet circling a star that was one hundred light years away from Earth. This is so far away, it would take a radio signal from them one hundred years to reach us, and vice-versa. It would take a typical NASA space probe hundreds of thousands of years to reach there, at top speed.

They haven't heard of us yet, because our early experiments with radio one hundred years ago weren't really powerful enough to be noticed. Our real transmission of radio and radar didn't begin until several decades later, so if they were pointing their satellite antennas in exactly our direction, they might detect a faint signal from us in twenty or thirty years. Their first knowledge of us might be an *Amos 'n' Andy* radio show.

Intrigued by such signals (and curious as to who Gracie Allen might be), they assemble an alien conclave to review the situation. It is decided that they will investigate the signals. Their own version of Congress is much more efficient and exploration-sensitive than ours and approves a major space expedition. They send a large interstellar spacecraft in our direction, equipped with a number of smaller scout craft for zipping around our atmosphere.

Not wishing to announce their presence, they hide their ship inside the asteroid belt and send smaller ships in, being careful to avoid the brilliant electromagnetic glare of our radar systems. From their vantage point in space, they learn everything they need to know about the denizens of the blue planet. They map our surface, monitor our transmissions, and test our environment.

But the anthropologist on board wants to get a good look at the life forms, so they send him down to gather a few specimens. They land in an isolated area where they can be selective about their prey. The bag a few different species, examine them, and let them go.

This is a bit simplified, but is one general scenario that could explain some aspects of the abduction phenomenon. It's rather far-fetched, but in terms of speculation, it's all fair game.

But what scenario is the actual explanation for abductions? Are aliens really invading our lives and treating us like test subjects? Are they trying to guide us into a better understanding of our universe? Or are abductees simply imagining their encounters? If the latter, I'd still have to ask the next logical question: why?

CHAPTER ONE
What the Experts Think About Abductions

Abductees and contactees: What's the difference?

Ask any UFO buff about abductions, and he or she will fill your ears with stories about women levitated out of their apartment blocks through solid walls into hovering spaceships, one-armed men who take pictures of flying saucers, and microchip implants discovered in abductees' big toes. The stories are as varied as they are plentiful. Some have taken on lives of their own, growing and changing with each retelling in print, at UFO conferences, or on the Internet.

When someone is described as a medical expert, it's usually safe to believe that he or she has a medical degree or is employed in a hospital. A culinary expert may have worked as a chef at a string of exclusive restaurants. But a UFO expert is — well — anything you can imagine.

There is no "UFO University" where one can get a degree or training in ufology. *Anyone* can call himself an expert in UFOs, without much quibbling from the sidelines. The reality is that no one knows with certainty exactly what is being experienced by the typical UFO witness, let alone abductees. If anyone claims to really know the "truth" about UFOs and their alien pilots, you can be assured that he or she knows no more or no less than any other ufologist.

In fact, this is the fundamental problem in ufology. Each unexplained UFO report and each abduction case is different in some way from the mass of other reports and experiences on record. This is very obvious when one looks at the small collection of abduction stories just in this book. Although there may be a kind of general similarity in the witnesses' belief they were being watched or had an experience aboard a spaceship, the details of the accounts vary substantially. Some report aliens with round eyes, some with almond-shaped eyes, and some eyes that are human in appearance. Some aliens are grey-skinned and small in stature, while others are tall, blond-haired, and lanky. Some aliens give abductees unpleasant medical examinations while others take them on tours of heaven. Some pilot flying saucers while others are spiritual travellers and appear not to need any physical transportation.

Because of this, it is hard to come up with a satisfactory and coherent explanation for the entire abduction phenomenon. Even if we accept that aliens are indeed abducting people, we have to try to make sense out of the large number of abductions reported, the varied nature of the experiences, and the mixed-up "wisdom" imparted to abductees and contactees by the supposedly omnipotent extraterrestrials.

One of the persistent myths in ufology is the colour-coding of aliens who are visiting us. Remember the phrase "little green man?" It was coined somehow following the publication of a science-fiction novel titled *The Green Man*, written by Harold Sherman in the mid-1940s. (There was also a sequel a few years later.) In the story, a tall, benevolent, green-skinned alien in an egg-shaped craft used ray guns to stop automobiles and effect paralysis on humans. Amazingly, such actions are claimed of aliens and UFOs today.

However, the green skin has rarely been reported by UFO witnesses. The grey-skinned variety is most common, although the blonds (or Nordics) are quite popular as well. In the 1950s, contactees almost exclusively described contacts with humanlike aliens, most often with blond hair. Indeed, these aliens were usually benevolent, taking people on trips to Mars and Venus but also commissioning contactees as their intergalactic ambassadors. Their messages for mankind were often admonishments about our pollution of the environment or our inhumane treatment of one another. Chastising us for our nuclear tests was also high on their agenda.

Aliens of the 1950s also gave contactees brief glimpses of idyllic planets where war had been eliminated, there was plentiful food for all, and all races could live in peace and harmony. Their technology had advanced beyond our wildest dreams and manual labour was a thing of their past. Machines and/or robots served them completely.

Despite their superiority, the aliens were unable to give contactees a single clear photograph of their spaceships or impart some useful knowledge such as a cure for any specific disease or a new kind of rocket fuel. Contactees were left to spread the word through appearances at conventions and on the lecture circuit throughout North America. Some became so popular that they went on speaking tours around the world. One, George Adamski, even had an audience with the Pope. Other contactees claimed they were themselves aliens incarnated in human form so as to live and work among us.

Perhaps it was the Cold War or postwar expectations of a better life that attracted people to contactees in the 1950s. The motivations of most contactees usually resolved into hawking their wares, telling their stories, and gaining some notoriety. Most faded into obscurity after their stories grew old and the crowds at conventions dwindled. By the mid-1960s, contactees were on the way out.

Or so it seemed.

In 1961, Betty and Barney Hill had their infamous UFO abduction in New Hampshire. It took a few years before it reached public attention, but when it did, it revolutionized ufology. Up until this point, stories about actual physical contact with aliens were generally taboo among serious researchers. It was one thing to have witnesses claim they observed a landed flying saucer, but entirely another when it came to accepting stories about aliens taking humans aboard a UFO. In retrospect, this was perhaps the next logical step in the evolution of UFO reports, but it seemed to have caught many researchers off-guard.

"Classic" UFO abductions

Over the hills and far away

It was September 19, 1961. Betty and Barney Hill were driving south on U.S. Highway 3 through New Hampshire. They were returning from a bit of a vacation in Quebec and were near the town of Groveton. As they drove, they noticed a bright light in the southwestern sky. Although they thought it might have been an airplane or satellite, they became uneasy. Betty's sister had seen a similar light in 1957 and since their car was the only one on the highway, they worried that the flying object had an interest in them. So worried, in fact, that Barney stopped the car and retrieved his pistol from the trunk.

They drove slowly, keeping a close watch on the object as it appeared to descend slowly among the trees and mountain peaks. Soon, the object had approached to the point where it looked like a flattened, circular disc, hovering an estimated one hundred feet away. Barney stopped the car and got out. He watched the object through binoculars as it slowly moved across the road in front of them and stopped in a field on the other side.

Through binoculars, Barney could clearly see creatures of some sort through the windows of the craft. He became unnerved and jumped back into the car, shouting, "They're going to capture us!" He gunned the engine and sped away, and they kept a close eye on the object. Suddenly, a beeping sound filled the car.

The next thing they knew, they were hearing another set of beeps and were quietly sitting beside each other as Barney drove along. They reached home without further incident and started unpacking, but felt odd and clammy, and very disoriented. They seemed to recall seeing "the Moon" sitting on the road as they drove, but didn't have much more recollection than that.

The next day, Betty called and reported their sighting to the U.S. Air Force. It was explained as an observation of the planet Jupiter.

But Betty started having very vivid dreams about their experience. She was deeply troubled by what had occurred for some reason, and became obsessed with finding out more about flying saucers. She began writing down what she remembered about her dreams.

In her dreams, she and her husband were surrounded by small, grey-skinned men wearing bluish "uniforms." The men had barrel-shaped chests, big noses, black hair, and dark eyes. The men led the Hills into a disc-shaped craft where they met the "leader" of the group. He informed them they would be examined separately and Barney was led away down a corridor. Betty was confronted by a gentle "doctor" who took samples of her hair and fingernails and scrapings of her skin. He gave Betty a "pregnancy test" by inserting a long needle into her belly-button.

At one point, some crew-members ran into the room and excitedly conversed with the leader in a strange language. The leader then looked in Betty's mouth and examined her teeth. He was puzzled as to why Barney's teeth came out and hers did not. Laughing, Betty explained that Barney had dentures.

Betty asked the leader where he was from and he replied by asking her if she knew much astronomy. She admitted she didn't know much about it, and he pulled a map out to show her. It was a star map, with dots and circles of various sizes connected by lines. He asked her if she knew where the Earth was on the map, and she of course said she didn't.

He curtly told her there was no point in telling her where he was from, then, since she couldn't read the star map.

Soon, Barney came out of his own examination room and the two were led out of the ship and placed back in their car to continue on their way. They had no memory of what had occurred because the leader had told them they would forget what happened, and no one would believe them, anyway.

Betty's dreams became more worrisome and Barney's old problem of alcoholism resurfaced. They sought help and were referred to several psychiatrists to treat them for their anxiety. In the course of their treatment, the story of their experience was brought out, although none of their therapists or physicians thought the story was real.

Finally, in 1964, they were referred to Dr. Benjamin Simon, a psychiatrist in Boston. He was the first psychiatrist to consider hypnosis as a course of action in their case. Although Betty was more anxious, Simon first worked with Barney. He had reservations about being hypnotized, but agreed to the treatment. Barney's account was not as detailed as Betty's, perhaps because he admitted he kept his eyes closed throughout much of the experience since he had been frightened. Both Barney and Betty remembered their experiences, though under hypnosis, their abductors were still grey-skinned but were bald, didn't have large noses, and had huge, almond-shaped, penetrating dark eyes which to Barney "pushed into my eyes."

This latter point has been a bone of contention among debunkers and believers in this case. There has been considerable debate concerning the fact that an episode of *The Outer Limits* television show featuring aliens with such eyes had aired shortly before Barney underwent hypnosis, and that this could have been the source of that image. However, Betty insists that they rarely watched those kinds of programs, and besides, Barney said in 1961 he was bothered by the creatures' stares.

Another interesting aspect was the star map that Betty saw on board the craft. Under hypnosis, Betty was asked by Simon to draw the map if she felt she could do so with any accuracy. What she drew showed some dots connected by lines which Betty explained were "trade routes" or "expedition routes." The map was published in *The Interrupted Journey*, John Fuller's book on the case, and in 1968, an amateur astronomer named Marjorie Fish decided to see if the star pattern matched any known pattern of stars in the sky. She selected only sunlike stars within about fifty light years of Earth (effectively, our local "neighbourhood") and found the main stars indicated the aliens' origin was likely Zeta

Reticuli, a pair of stars visible from the southern hemisphere. Ever since then, several abductees and contactees have said that their alien visitors claimed to hail from this planet, and are widely called Reticulians or Reticulites.

The map has been debated many times, and it is the contention of most skeptics that the patterns are random and that any collection of such stars will show the pattern if you look at it long enough. Supporters of the Reticulian interpretation point out that Fish considered only sunlike stars, a minority in the galaxy, and that the coincidence of them forming the pattern is highly unlikely. But the identification of the stars is linked rather precariously on the accuracy of Betty's drawing in the first place.

Until this time, aliens belonged only to speculation and to the contactees. In science fiction literature, aliens were anything imaginable, from giant robots and talking insects to hairy monsters and disembodied brains. For contactees, the aliens either were human or assumed human form for various reasons. But once abductions began being reported, we had a third category.

The archetypal alien, according to abduction literature, is the *grey*, a humanoid entity that is short in stature with a bulbous head, almond-shaped eyes and a slitlike mouth. Greys are said to be studying or experimenting upon humans for various reasons, thus explaining abductions as a scientific endeavour. In effect, the greys embody the challenge of ufology in its quest to go beyond science fiction or contactee literature. The greys are, by definition and creation, a possible scientific explanation for UFO abductions.

(For the science purists, I should clarify that statement. When calling them "scientific," I mean in the sense that one can form a science-based scenario in which life on other planets has evolved to produce intelligent species that developed space travel and are visiting Earth using some undiscovered technology. This is not to say that ufology is *itself* a science. Ufology can make use of scientific principles and ufologists can use scientific methodology to study the UFO phenomenon, but it likely is not a distinct science in the sense that geology is different from biology.)

Once ufology had accepted the possibility that the flying saucer occupants could exit their ships for whatever reason and interact with humans, the stage was set for the new round of cases. From time to time, there emerged new stories of alien encounters, with a few specific characteristics.

First of all, the aliens acted like humans. In the Hill case, the aliens seemed like diplomats, treating their captives with respect while examining them in detail. They were careful with their medical procedures, as we probably would be under similar circumstances. They were courteous enough with Betty, displaying a star map when obliging her request to tell her where they were from. And, they seemed to have distinct classes, whereby one was clearly the "leader."

Secondly, the aliens seemed physically real. They piloted spaceships and appeared to break a few laws of physics, but they were still controlled with technology such as dials, levers, and steering wheels. The ships all needed some kind of power source, which is variously described as "antimatter," "element 115," or "crystals." And even in the medical examinations, there were surgical instruments that may not seemed like standard AMA issue, but were tools, nevertheless.

Putting out fires

Unusual medical examination played a prominent role in the 1975 case of Travis Walton, who was "zapped" by an apparently physical saucer and who subsequently disappeared from the face of the Earth. He was missing for several days, and when he was returned, he described an incredible story of abduction aboard a spaceship, encountering Hill-type aliens and touching interesting gadgets such as a holographic star projector of some sort.

Walton's encounter was witnessed by four companions who were working with him, clearing a forest as part of a logging contract. But when Walton was "taken," his buddies took off in fright and did not see the departure of the craft. In fact, his disappearance was considered a homicide and his co-workers were under suspicion for the crime. When he finally appeared, he had only fragmented memories of his ordeal. Hypnosis was used to recover some of his story, and he and his friends were administered polygraph tests to determine the story's truthfulness. Not surprisingly, the conclusions of the polygraph tests and the hypnosis have been subject to much debate and consternation.

The Walton case was made into a Hollywood movie, which also created some controversy. *Fire in the Sky* chronicled the story, and the renewed interest created another phenomenon unto itself. The movie spent a lot of time conveying details of the investigation, fairly accurately chronicling the actions of police and UFO investigators as they tried to unravel the mystery of Walton's experience. However, towards the end of the movie, scenes depicted a rather bizarre interpretation of what Walton slowly recalled had happened.

Walton was depicted on board the alien spaceship immersed in brown goo as a result of evil alien experimentations. Walton's original description of a sterile, antiseptic alien spaceship and operating room had given way to an interior that attempted to outdo the *Alien* series of flicks. Membraneous pods, ET-like aliens and slimy honeycombs populated the ship's interior. This was somewhat at odds with his original description, which had more resembled an airplane hangar.

Walton's aliens were described as very much akin to the Hills', with large eyes and small, delicate bodies. At one point during his abduction, he successfully fought off a group of them, who had tried to restrain him. Walton said he also encountered a humanlike alien who led him through the ship and eventually to another room where he was overpowered and rendered unconscious.

The movie's storyline, which followed the social and public effects of an alleged UFO on a community, was actually very good. The police interrogated Walton and his associates at length, and arranged for lie-detector tests for several of them, which unfortunately produced mixed results.

A Hollywood executive later explained to me that the original screenplay was relatively straight and didn't include the fantasy sequence that ended up in the movie. It seems that other movie execs got upset when *Intruders* and other UFO abduction movies were promoted and released about the same time, showing more classic abduction sequences. They wanted something *different*, so they rewrote the script ending to include the "brown goo" scenes.

Well, that's showbiz.

Sex and the single abductee

It happened at a time long before the media exploitation of abductees on sensational news programs. It was shocking, remarkable and certainly bizarre. But what on Earth occurred?

On October 15, 1957, at 1:00 a.m., Antonio Villas-Boas was driving a tractor as he plowed a field on the family farm in the Brazilian state of Minas Gerais. He noticed a red "star" was moving towards him and soon revealed itself to be an egg-shaped object. It hovered over him, shining a bright beam of light on the ground. It moved over field nearby, and as its tripod-like landing gear extended down to the ground, his tractor engine quit.

Terrified, he jumped down from the tractor but suddenly found himself in the grasp of a small creature whom he managed to escape, only to find himself surrounded by three more. Together, they managed to drag the struggling Villas-Boas inside the ship where he was placed in a room with polished metal walls.

These aliens were much different from either those encountered by the Hills or by Walton. They wore helmets with goggles to protect their eyes and wore tight-fitting grey uniforms that covered their entire bodies. In addition, they "growled" to each other quite a bit, obviously discussing their captive.

Soon, they moved on him, making him remove his clothes. One of them sponged him down with a thick liquid and two others held him while they used some rubber tubes to withdraw some blood from his neck. After they left, he noticed a foul smell in the room and saw a grey gas of some kind entering the room through some vents in the ceiling. Nauseated, he threw up.

Suddenly, a naked woman entered the room. Even though she wasn't quite human (she had almond-shaped eyes, white skin, and very blond hair, and made animal-like growls instead of talking), Villas-Boas was extremely aroused and immediately had intercourse with her twice. After the second time, she pushed him away and walked to the door. Before she left, she pointed to her belly and then to the sky, possibly indicating that she would take their offspring to the stars.

Shortly thereafter, Villas-Boas was given his clothes and then escorted out of the ship. He suffered no ill effects, though over the next several weeks, he had more bouts of nausea and was unable to sleep.

It was more than a month before be contacted a Brazilian journalist and told him the story. Unfortunately, he was told his story was too bizarre to be published. (A far cry from 1999, when it seems anything goes!) It was five years before he met some ufologists and his story eventually came out.

Today, Villas-Boas still insists his experience actually happened, despite its incredible details. One must remember that for its time, his story was practically unique in the annals of serious ufology. Many UFO buffs simply refused to accept it and didn't want to talk about it, even when it was published in a major UFO magazine in 1965. It is hard to accept that he was influenced by movies, TV, or books about flying saucers and aliens because his village was isolated and insulated from such things. An abductee in the 1990s might be influenced by TV and movies, but in 1957 that was hardly a consideration, and Villas-Boas' story contains many elements that were not common to abduction scenarios until recently.

These three cases — Hill, Walton, and Villas-Boas — present conflicting and confusing images of the aliens at work on our planet. There are differences in the appearances of the aliens, differences in their ships, and differences in their methodology and actions. One can argue that humans are very different and that we have different styles of carrying ourselves, but the differences in just these three popularized cases show us *how* different the aliens must be from one another.

Aliens and their activities

In one sense, aliens portrayed in early abduction accounts were not "magical" in their existence or abilities. They were space travellers visiting Earth. They may have had technology vastly superior to ours, but they were certainly not godlike in their abilities.

However, this changed somewhat as the abduction phenomenon evolved and really took flight. Today, abductions often seem to occur in a different reality than that with which we are accustomed. Witnesses are often levitated right through solid walls, and aliens can appear and disappear at will. Some abductees have even reported alien encounters while in the presence of other people who were not aware or sharing that same experience.

This step in the development of abductions creates a definite connection between "old" and "new" ufology. In effect, contactees are back, supplanting simple UFO abductions with complex, reality-bending stories that are clearly a throwback to the fifties-style encounters. Indeed, the line between abductees and contactees has been blurring so much it is hard to tell the two classes apart.

This has been solved by some abduction experts who ignore the categories entirely. To them, it is completely possible that aliens have evolved so much that they are, indeed, capable of "Star Trek"-like matter transmission through walls and in complete control of time in order to better experiment upon humans. It's not that this is not a possible scenario; aliens might very well have evolved to a point where they are almost godlike, but we would then be quite justified in asking questions such as, "What do they need spaceships for, then?"

In fact, recent abductee/contactee cases dispense with UFOs entirely. Many abductions begin in an experiencer's bedroom, where he or she is transported directly to "another place" that may or may not be inside a spaceship. Perhaps the basic abduction experiences occur on Earth but the complex physical exams need to be done on board a "mother ship."*

The trouble is that abductions are starting to sound a little too much like contactee stories, and this is making some researchers uncomfortable. For a while, when the abduction phenomenon was still in its infancy, it looked as if ufology could be studied completely scientifically. Reports of nocturnal lights and daylight discs could be statistically analyzed and "landing traces" could be sampled and tested for radiation (assuming that interstellar spaceships would be built shoddily enough that they would leak radiation).

As abduction stories became more and more elaborate, ufology ran into problems. How can an abduction experience be physically verified? And, since some abductees under hypnosis recall experiences that may have occurred weeks, years, and even decades earlier, how could someone physically pinpoint the locations and times of the abduction events? It began to look like abduction encounters were dreamlike in their imagery. It was time for psychologists and psychiatrists to get involved.

The psychology of abductions

Once some ufologists started to accept elaborate abduction stories as true, there was a need to quantify the experiences somehow. Some abductees remembered their alien encounters while others did not until they were

---

*There is another viewpoint, too, that is gaining momentum among some UFO researchers. In this scenario, popularized by the science fiction novel *Fastwalker* by ufologist Jacques Vallee, what we assume to be alien intervention is actually a covert operation directed by humans for nefarious purposes. Eve Frances Lorgen, another abduction researcher, describes the malevolence as quite dastardly, indeed:

> ... the abduction phenomenon exhibits, in my opinion, basic warfare tactics on many different levels: physical, mental, emotional and spiritual. In order to fully understand the alien abduction programme, one must look at it through the lens of an intelligence operative.
> (www.soft.net.uk/staffs/ufoesp/pov.html.)

In her view, the evil is that of real aliens, although there is thought to be some kind of human/alien collaboration, much like as portrayed on the "X-Files" television series.

hypnotized to unlock their "missing time" episodes. Psychologists and psychiatrists gingerly began to get involved with abductees. Still a generally taboo subject within the medical profession, a few medical professionals ventured to offer their opinions on what was really happening.

One of the first to openly study abductions was Leo Sprinkle, a clinical psychologist in Wyoming. He was a consultant to the famous Condon Report, advising the USAF/University of Colorado team on the psychology of UFO witnesses. Sprinkle's interest in the subject was related to a UFO sighting of his own in the early 1960s. His curiosity about the nature of the UFO phenomenon was heightened when he was called in to help investigate some early UFO abductions, particularly that at Pascagoula in 1973 and the case of Sandy Larson in 1975. In the 1980s, Sprinkle founded the Rocky Mountain UFO Conference, at which abductees could find solace and support from each other and from abduction therapists. The yearly event has a definite New Age bias, and this is reflected in the personalities and beliefs of the abductees that attend. (Later, Sprinkle himself revealed that he was probably an abductee.)

The Larson case was remarkable in that it contained the incredible imagery found in abduction cases today. Sandy Larson had been driving through North Dakota when she and her daughter were abducted aboard a UFO. On board, they were given medical examinations and the aliens even seemed to operate on Sandy's brain. When probed further by Sprinkle's hypnosis, Sandy also recalled being levitated through solid walls and having had a series of bedroom visitations earlier in her life. Moreover, her experience seemed to have no foundation upon which to draw. She was relatively uneducated, and abductions had not yet been thrust into the public eye. (The Hill case was not brought to public attention until 1966, and neither it nor the Pascagoula case had the dreamlike qualities that Larson described.)

In effect, the Larson case was the turning point in ufology. It brought together two disparate groups within ufology: those who approached the UFO phenomenon from a scientific perspective, and those who did not.

A stunning example of how the borderline between scientific and lay ufology has been erased is found in the current ufological literature, specifically that related to abductions. The work in question is that of John Mack, the Harvard psychiatrist who has begun devoting his time to counselling and studying abductees.

Mack risked his professional reputation by indulging in this particular subject, and indeed his status at Harvard was challenged by a review committee which seemed to be concerned about his public support of abduction ufology. In the end, the committee found no reason to suspend Mack and it appears as though academia is grudgingly accepting the idiosyncrasy of one of its own.

Mack's book *Abduction* details case after case of abductees and comes to the conclusion that something very unusual is occurring to these people. In fact, he makes it clear that he believes none of the abductees' experiences can be attributable to mental illness. Despite this, the case histories he presents show an incredible display of bizarre behaviour and incredible descriptive testimony that stretches belief. Furthermore, many of the case histories include observations that the abductees had been in abusive domestic situations, been abused themselves, were leading difficult lives, or had other experiences that might suggest they were in need of psychological counselling. Some were deeply involved in New Age beliefs and it could be that their "abductions" were a consequence of a desire to improve their personal well-being through an imagined experience. (One abductee told Mack he was "spiritually attached to deer" because it was his "totem animal.")

For example, in Mack's book, an abductee named Jerry is described as "an ordinary housewife." Through Mack's counselling and therapy, she recalled an incredible series of medical examinations by aliens who gave her a gynaecological examination when she was only thirteen years old. Since that time she had "an aversion to sex." Her parents were divorced when she was 8. She married her first husband when she was 19 and pregnant, but this marriage ended quickly, partly because she "never loved him" and because he "played sexual games" with the children.

Another abductee named Joe was himself a psychotherapist who worked with people to overcome their fears of the dark and other ailments. Joe remembered under Mack's hypnosis how aliens had similarly experimented upon him and inserted a painful needle into his neck behind his ear. But Joe came from a family who were "dysfunctional," "emotionally tight," and he "wasn't hugged or kissed much." As a teenager he experimented with LSD, and later in life he retreated into northern Maine where he lived by himself for a year. He was on a "personal quest" and sought "spiritual understanding," even joining a spiritualist church. One of the memories unlocked through Mack's hypnosis was when an alien "baptized" Joe; he said the aliens were

giving me strength and knowing, just knowing, that I'm not alone.
I'm loved and I'm connectable ... I don't know where I belong.
(Mack, p. 182.)

It's not hard to interpret that Joe's lifelong spiritual quest had something to do with his personal angst, and that the compassionate aliens filled a desperate need for acceptance and reassurance in his life. In short, the cases presented by Mack show that while the abductees were not officially diagnosed with any mental illness, there were many signs that they had troubling lives, needed some positive reinforcement, and were looking for some hope.

In his speculations as to why the aliens are abducting humans, Mack goes as far to postulate that in cases where abductees did have a history of sexual abuse, the aliens were led to "intervene in a protective or healing manner." In other words, abductees have alien encounters because the aliens are compassionate, not because the abductees are traumatized and are imagining the aliens as saviours.

Mack seems to accept some very strange elements within the abductees' experiences. One woman said that after her abduction, she was returned to Earth wearing underwear that was not her own. The interpretation? Alien fallibility.

Mack has dismissed his critics on various grounds and has suggested that abductees' incredible experiences and memories "are experientially true but didn't factually happen in this reality." But what does *that* mean?

The trouble with disagreeing with Mack's findings is that very little unbiased and truly objective scientific research has been done on the abduction phenomenon to date, and one would need such data to refute it. Vocal debunkers of abductions, such as Philip Klass, who calls abduction therapy a "dangerous game," claim they don't have the time nor resources to spend on the issue in order to produce a consistent rebuttal.

However, one thing we can say with certainty is that there is widespread disagreement among ufologists as to the nature of abductions. Some, like Mack, are convinced of alien benevolence. Others such as David Jacobs, who writes of the "threat" of alien abductors in our midst, see a more dark purpose. To Jacobs, the abduction phenomenon is due to the aliens' breeding of human/alien hybrids. They have now bred several generations of hybrids who have human emotions but are second-class citizens on board the aliens' spacecraft, performing menial tasks and suffering oppressive conditions. In fact, hybrids are the reason we know about the aliens' ultimate plan: "to take over the world" ("The same thing we try to do every night, Pinky!"). The aliens have slowly been replacing us all with a hybrid population, and soon, within no more than a generation, the world will be theirs. (In fact, during my own public talks and presentations, I note this very fact. It must be true that aliens have been taking over the minds and bodies of certain selected humans. How else can we possibly explain politicians?)

It seems that the hybrids are bored and are starting to rebel against their masters, to the point of telling abductees about the aliens' secrets. However, because the hybrids are not quite human, they feel no remorse for occasionally sexually abusing female abductees.

Jacobs feels that his "competent hypnosis" style is able to sort out the difference between truth and fact in abductees' stories. Those who describe disparate details from his scenario likely do not understand proper abduction research methodology.

Regarding the conflicting views of alien abduction experts, a cynic has noted:

> One group, represented by Dr. Richard J. Boylan among others, claims that the aliens are all benevolent and that experiencers who report negative experiences are either disinformation aents or victims of mind control experiments by rogue intelligence agents. Another group, of which Dr. David Jacobs is the outstanding example, claims that the aliens are all evil and that those who report positive experiences as victims of mind control by the aliens and need to see a competent hypnotist who will convince them of that "fact."

He added:

> ... the experimenter's theoretical perspective determines what he or she will see. I strongly suspect that ufology will achieve no respect as a disciplined inquiry until this experimenter bias can be greatly reduced.
> (www.ufomind.com/ufo/updates/1999/feb/m08-015.shtml.)

As for the "rogue intelligence agents" at work, one of the most vocal proponents of that theory is Helmut Lammer, of the Austrian Space Research Institute. In a treatise published on the web and often cited and reproduced, he explained:

> MILABs [the acronym for Military Abductions of Alleged UFO Abductees] could be evidence that a secret military intelligence

task force has been operating in North America since the early eighties, and is involved in the monitoring and kidnapping of alleged UFO abductees.... They monitor the houses of their victims, kidnap and possibly implant them with military devices shortly after a UFO abduction experience.... they are searching for possible alien implants ... [and] alien-hybrid embryos ... [and are] using advanced mind-control technology....
(www.alienjigsaw.com/milab.html.)

Most ufologists recognize the fact that there is usually no physical evidence left after an abduction. This contributes to the uncomfortable feeling that the experiences have at least some element of illusion and subjective perception. Other researchers, such as English scholar Terry Matheson, point out that the absence of hard evidence forces the abduction phenomenon into the realm of a literary process. Abductees and abduction experts have created a myth which is self-perpetuating because there is no way to absolutely verify any of the claimed details.

Implants

Two exceptions to the problem of evidence are impressive at first sight. One is that some abductees *have* found "implants" within their bodies and some seem to have memories of aliens placing them there. These implants have been collected and examined by some researchers and reported in the UFO literature. If these objects are in fact of alien origin, then there would be no question that clandestine examinations of humans were actually taking place.

The trouble is that the implants appear to be anything but devices for tracking or monitoring abductees. Each one is different, with different shapes and sizes and made from differing elements. They have been removed from behind ears, in wrists, noses, shoulders, and, in one celebrated case, a toe. Some of these implants are encased in organic membranes and display no sign of rejection by the body.

While abduction experts excitedly point to these artefacts as proof of alien intervention, others candidly note:

This is baffling, since one would assume that the greys who reportedly have inserted these implants in humans would use devices made of the same elements. There may be other reasons for the use of varying elements in implants. We do not know what they may be. And that's all we can say at this point. (Fenwick, 1995.)

One implant was found to be composed of aluminum, silicon, and titanium. It was noted that such an object "would be a transducer and can be used to transmit signals." But radiologists who had seen copies of one abductee's x-rays said they were similar to those of patients who had stepped on a needle or metal fragment that later migrated to another location, becoming encapsulated in mineral deposits and tissue. Furthermore, what could be said about an alien tracking program with methodology varying from subject to subject? Wouldn't it at least make sense to put the implant in the same part of the body on each individual?

The main proponent of implant research is Derrel Sims, an investigator for the Houston UFO Network (HUFON). In 1995, he worked with Dr. Roger Leir, a podiatrist who has removed several implants including three from a woman's toe and one from a man's hand. Sims is a former military police officer with no degree from any major accredited institution, but several from various hypnotherapy and personal growth institutes. His obsession with proving the extraterrestrial origin of implants has been shared with many others.

In a paper published in a major UFO journal in 1994, Sims made an extraordinary statement:

The well-documented recovery and study of physical evidence supports reports of physical abduction and of individuals being the unwilling subjects of medical examinations or research, in some cases including being the surrogate host to embryo or fetal implants for a few weeks. Judgement of the overall motives and the benefit or detriment to the abductee of CEIV (Close Encounters of the Fourth Kind) happenings can not be evaluated at present. (Sims, D. & Florey, M.J. "Evidence for, and Implications of, Medically Unexplained Iimplants in Abductees." *HUFON Report.* September 1994, 6-8; January 1995, 3-5; February 1995, 6-8.)

Virgil Priscu, an Israeli anaesthesiologist specializing in emergency room medicine, had an opportunity to meet and talk with Sims when the latter was giving a presentation to a group of believers. Priscu was not at all impressed. In a post to a UFO-related Internet mailing list, he noted:

I am afraid that all claims made by Mr. Sims or his associates have not been confirmed or underwent a peer review process. Therefore, I personally have serious doubts as to the veracity of these claims.... I know a thing or two about what we call "Foreign Bodies" (FBs) found quite often, especially in the feet of some unsuspecting patients by an incidental x-ray made for another purpose. They get there by various methods: walking or playing barefoot on the beach, grass, etc., and not noticing when the FB gets in. (During a fall, running or getting hurt by some other bigger object from which a small splinter can get into one's foot and remain there for many, many years under the skin — until sometimes they are discovered by chance while some other physician or medical practitioner — like a podiatrist — is examining the patient for another, unrelated complaint — and sometimes x-ray their feet!) If it is a substance that degrades slowly, after years only a small notch of "reaction" tissue remains in place of the former FB. It is composed of human tissue components. No mystery, no "implants."
(*UFO Updates*, 14 August 1997. Subject: Re: UFOR: Skywatch: UFOR: Bedouin "Alien" Murder.)

This is completely at odds with comments published by Eve Frances Lorgen, another abduction expert and a profound believer in extraterrestrial intervention. In a published paper on alien implants, Lorgen notes:

The alleged implants removed ... were studied by two different pathologists, and then sent to various independent laboratories for extensive scientific analysis. The tests performed on these alleged alien implants were: a pathology/tissue evaluation, laser induced breakdown spectroscopy (LIBS), extensive metallurgical testing involving a density immersion test, x-ray energy dispersive spectroscopy, scanning electron microscopy, x-ray diffraction pattern analysis and electron/magnetic and fluorescence property analysis. Isotopic range tests are also in progress. Tests were conducted by the National Institute of Discovery of Science (NIDS), New Mexico Tech, and other independent sources.
(Lorgen, E.F. (1998). *Alien Implant Removals*. Website: http://users1.ee.net/pmason/el.html.)

However, in a report from one of the independent labs, the mystery was less obvious:

> The results do not prove that there was anything unearthly *per se*, but there are certain characteristics of the elements found that could imply a possible purpose for the implantation.
> (Fenwick, Lawrence. (1995). Implant probed in Canada by scanning electron microscope. *CUFORN Bulletin*, 15(1).)

Specifically, the "implant" was found to be composed of aluminum, silicon, and titanium. And, because it was noted that these metals are used to manufacture transistors and semiconductors, and because they resist corrosion, conduct heat, and electricity, "we can then extrapolate from that knowledge and form the obvious conclusion." Implants are therefore alien transponders.

On the other hand, other experts have not been so generous with their interpretations. One debunker, Trevor Jordan, is a medical professional with significant knowledge regarding foreign bodies underneath our skin. He didn't think the claims of Sims and Leir were particularly accurate. He believed the tissue surrounding the implant was

> no more than the tissue which develops around any retained foreign matter in the body, and I can't see how [Sims] substantiates his claim that this combination of elements has never been seen before. The lack of any "fresh or resolved" inflammatory or rejection process in the surrounding tissue suggests that the foreign body had been there for some time.
> (*Abduction Watch*, Number 15, November 1998.
> www.magonia.demon.co.uk/abwatch/aw15.html.)

Recently, Sims has been loaning some implants to selected individuals with scientific alliances and associates. This is encouraging, but the results of the tests have mostly been either inconclusive or have indicated that the implants were inert orts composed of a variety of materials. One interpretation offered by implant proponents is that the implanted objects are passive devices which must be scanned by alien sensors in order to be detected. This is possible, considering we have no way of understanding truly alien technology. However, it seems more reasonable to assume the "implants" are nothing more than what they appear: bits of glass, metal, and wood from old injuries long forgotten by abductees.

Nevertheless, the scientific testing of implants is a positive step towards verification of such a phenomenon. To date, such tests are done in relative secrecy and the methodology communicated only within a small circle of insiders. One reason for this is because mainstream science frowns on such frivolities as alien implants and would come down hard on a staff scientist who was identified as being interested in the subject, let alone using valuable research time and equipment for such an endeavour.

However, a few brave individuals arrange such testing as part of their professional development and personal curiosity. Canadian ufologist Nick Balaskas has assisted with several "implant" tests, with minimal results. Among the first things he looked at were x-rays of a UFO witness whose x-rays appeared to show an implant inside his head. Even though several other independent physicians and radiologists asked to examine the x-rays could not explain the mysterious object in the images, Balaskas' radiologist easily found the object could be positively identified as an elastic hair band.

American ufologist and multiple UFO experiencer John Velez asked one medical professional what would be required by scientific researchers before any implant was considered mysterious:

> An x-ray featuring a "foreign body" in someone's body does not constitute evidence for an "implant" (with the implication attached to such an object). It is what it is: a FB (foreign body). It must be considered within the whole context: a detailed history of the patient should be taken by an experienced medical practitioner, in an effort to determine the possible accidental origin of any FB.
>
> A careful physical exam should be made (by a medical practitioner with experience in treating such patients — like an orthopedic surgeon, general surgeon, plastic surgeon, etc. — according to the nature and situation of the FB in the patient's body). Sometimes, and with the elapse of a long period of time, FBs migrate in surprising ways to surprising places. Finally, a better understanding of the nature of the FB could be made by extracting it from the patient's body and submitting it to the right kind of examinations (a forensic lab could be a good choice — usually they are best at this).
>
> If a person chooses to perpetrate a hoax by utilizing a very common FB that he could have got in a very common way (like

running barefoot and getting stuck with some small object in the foot, or a car accident, or a blast injury or a war/weapon injury), he could cause quite a stir in the all "too-willing-to-believe UFO community" (by sticking to an abduction/aliens/UFO story). (*UFO Updates*, September 4, 1997.)

This does not daunt Sims, however, since he has some contacts within the scientific community. Does he have to approach mainstream scientists with his work? As one of his supporters noted: "He doesn't need to; he has his own consulting agencies and professionals on his team." In other words, a profound distrust of the scientific community, coupled with the expectation that the implants might be found to be less than mysterious, will effectively block their acceptance by the scientific community while fostering the popular belief that the implants are anomalous according to "researchers."

The other seemingly tangible evidence of alien experimentation is the presence of "scoop marks" found on abductees' bodies following their experiences. Unfortunately, the history and date of creation of such marks often are frustratingly difficult to establish.

This is not, however, the way such physical scars are portrayed in popular UFO literature. Scoop marks are now an accepted part of standard abduction fare, and most pro-UFO writers mention them as factual components of many abduction experiences. Some abductees have memories of being subjected to painful experimentation at the hands of aliens, and scoop marks — small horseshoe, triangular, or bowl-shaped scars on various parts of their bodies — are proof of their tortures.

The assumption is that the aliens require some of our DNA or must take biopsies of humans in order to proceed with whatever programs they are undertaking at our expense. It is true that puncture biopsies are one way in which terrestrial physicians obtain tissue samples for study. However, hair strands can provide DNA, too, and are much less intrusive and painful to procure. Saliva can give alien researchers more microbial life forms than they can count on one tentacle. Puncture biopsies also don't make much sense, if the aliens are really as omnipotent as is claimed. After all, if, as reported by abductees, the aliens can walk through walls, levitate cars, slow down, time and manipulate our memories, why should they need to perform such minor operations?

The scars are problematic in other ways, too. Abductees with scoop marks sometimes claim that the marks appeared overnight or that they had no recollection of ever being injured in that part of their bodies. Documented proof of such claims is elusive. How do we *know* that a particular scar on a knee was not present before an abduction, other than taking the abductee at his or her word? Further, some marks vanish with time, too. In *Abduction*, by John Mack, an abductee named Catherine saw "an odd light in a cloud moving across the horizon" and then discovered "a small straight scar under her chin for which she could provide no explanation." Catherine believed her brother Alex

> may have had abduction experiences but doesn't know it. He had an unexplained mark on the side of his left hand that has the same horseshoe shape as two scars Catherine has on her left hand that she believes are abduction-related. This mark has since disappeared. (Mack, J. 1994. *Abduction: Human Encounters with Aliens*. New York: Scribner's, pp. 144-145.)

This hardly constitutes proof of anything, much less an incredible abduction by aliens. What's worse, the mark is now gone, and there is no way to examine it for structure or clues to its creation. This in itself is odd, since other abductees have reported being subjects of alien operations, immediately after which there were no scars whatsoever!

One case of this kind involved Olive, a Canadian woman whose encounters with aliens included being operated on to remove a cancerous cyst from inside her arm. I invited Olive to my home to give a presentation to me and my colleagues one evening in 1977. She told us that the aliens possessed highly advanced technology, including interstellar drives, mind-reading devices, matter transporters, invisibility, and advanced surgical techniques. When asked for proof of her claims, Olive unabashedly explained how, while on board the main ship high above the Earth, the aliens had used an amazing x-ray device on her that indicated she had a cancerous cyst in her arm that had gone unnoticed by terrestrial physicians. She then rolled up her sleeve to show us all that she did not have any trace of a scar from the aliens' operation on her, during which they removed all trace of the cyst and repaired her arm completely. We were, of course, astounded by the stories of her experiences.

Another case is the Sandy Larson case mentioned earlier. Larson, you'll recall, was abducted with her daughter while driving from Fargo to Bismarck in North Dakota in August 1975. During hypnotic regression by an investigator, Larson, one of the earliest reported abductees, seemed to have a memory of aliens actually opening up her skull and operating on her brain. She was stitched together again without any visible scarring.

Why would some alien surgeries leave scars and others not? Perhaps some abductees' stories are false and others true. Perhaps the aliens have learned new techniques over time. Perhaps one race of aliens has perfected scarless surgery and has not shared the knowledge with their kin.

Larson's case is particularly interesting for another reason. While her therapist, Leo Sprinkle, was caring and deeply concerned with Larson's psychological well-being and that of her daughter, he himself may have had some conscious or unconscious bias in his investigation. Sprinkle is well-known within ufology, and has been involved in many noted UFO cases as well as cases involving other bizarre phenomena such as cattle mutilations and psychic events. Since Sprinkle believes he is an abductee, one can wonder if his experiences have influenced his treatment of abductees — or the other way around.

Sprinkle's investigation and hypnotic regression of Larson has been published in several forms. In 1976, an article in a popular UFO magazine documented Sprinkle's approach. During one of his many sessions with Sandy and her daughter, Sprinkle may have accidentally helped along the conscious recall of Sandy's experience. She seemed to recall that on board the spacecraft, an alien, which looked like a six-foot-tall "mummy" with a miner's light on its head, had "operated" on her brain. One published transcript reads:

Sprinkle: Do you have a feeling of what kind of experiment it is?
Larson: I feel like I breathe different ... It's like somebody took a knife and made the inside of my nose sore.
Sprinkle: Made the inside of your nose sore?
Larson: Scraped it.
Sprinkle: Did you see anybody touching your nose?
Larson: Uh huh.
Sprinkle: Could you see hands?
Larson: No.
Sprinkle: Could you see an instrument of some kind?
Larson: Yeah.
Sprinkle: Can you describe it?
Larson: I would say it was like a little knife or like a cotton swab.
Sprinkle: Not very big, but something that was placed inside your nose?

Here we see that, according to the published article, Sprinkle *himself* seems to have suggested that something was put inside Sandy's nose. In fact, since this article was published in 1976, this could be an original source of the popular abduction story element where an "implant" is placed in someone's nose. The point is it may have been the therapist and not the abductee who had suggested something being placed into the nose, even if it was simply an inaccurate quote.

The mystery seems to completely evaporate later in the article when it is noted that

> Curiously enough, some time before, Sandy had undergone a very similar operation performed on her by a local physician, who was treating her for a sinus ailment. The operation proved quite painful and its effects lasted for more than a couple of months. Sandy was scheduled to undergo further treatment but, remembering the extreme discomfort, chose not to pursue the matter. Before long, her sinuses ran as freely as they ever had. She claims, however, that in the months since [her abduction], *she has had no trouble whatsoever.* (emphasis in original)
> (Clark, Jerome. (1976). "The Sandy Larson UFO Abduction." *Saga UFO Report*, Vol. 3, No. 3, August 1976.)

It seems more than probable that Sandy's bad memories of her sinus operation may have spilled over into her dreams, "creating" the memory of the alien's sinus operation, rather than the possibility that the alien had been responsible for the cure.

As for her brain, she thought that it had been removed later in the operation.

> Sprinkle: Is there anything else you can recall about the examination?
> Larson: It feels like they're separating me ... Feels like they reached their hand on the top of my head and took the brain out and set it beside me.
> Sprinkle: Do you remember looking and seeing at that time?
> Larson: No.

The point here is that Sandy had no physical signs of brain surgery, let alone another sinus operation. So, if the aliens are capable of such advanced surgical techniques that they can perform brain surgery without any clinical indications, scoop marks on abductees' legs and forearms seem rather trivial.

With this background, it appears possible that both implants and scoop marks have their origins in UFO literature outside of actual cases. Furthermore, the confusion and lack of incontrovertible evidence for either implants or scoop marks being definitely linked to abductions makes their use as "proof" of alien intervention subject to doubt.

They who *know*

In 1994, during the preparation of one of my analyses of Canadian UFO reports, I discovered that I needed additional files from the National Research Council of Canada (NRC) in Ottawa. I had been in touch with a number of individuals there, and I had been informed that the files I required were only going to be available for a month.

In preparation, I went on the Internet and connected to the National Capital Freenet in order to talk with people on the UFO SIG (Special Interest Group) there. The SIG covers a broad spectrum of ufology, from crackpots to serious students of the subject. There are lots of questions from people interested in the phenomenon, unfortunately usually answered by people with limited background in the subject. The questions range from: "Has anyone heard of a book by a guy named Ruppelt?" to "Are UFOs propelled by antigravity?"

I entered into correspondence with some of the Freenet people, and one person, Patrick Milloy, was particularly interested and willing to do some legwork in checking out sightings. I copied down phone numbers of some others, and thought I could phone them if ever in Ottawa. The opportunity arose sooner than I expected.

I coaxed Milloy to go to the NRC and take a look at the 1994 cases to date. While there, he noted that the 1993 cases still had not been transferred to the National Archives. Since I needed the 1993 cases for the annual *Canadian UFO Survey*, a study I compile each year, which analyzes the numbers and distribution of UFO reports in the country, I asked him to try and go through them before they were removed. Unfortunately, he couldn't make it before the deadline, so it looked like we'd have to wait until the cases showed up in Archives — in April or May, and at much more expense.

As it turned out, I was able to find the resources and time to book an immediate flight to Ottawa. Denise Cardinal, the NRC UFO records keeper, (bless her soul!) promised the files would still be waiting for me, and that I could view them before they were sent away.

I arrived around midnight on February 17 and was met by George Kriger, a longtime friend and Ufology Research of Manitoba (UFOROM) associate. The next morning at the crack of dawn, we went to the NRC. We met Denise and quickly went to work on the 1993 and 1994 reports. It took an entire day to read through the hundreds of pages of documents, copying down the data needed for the analyses. We celebrated our hard work by going to sleep by 8 p.m., because ufologists are not always party animals.

My flight out wasn't for another few days, so I had time to check out bookstores and various other attractions in the Nation's Capital. There was a one-man band in the Market, and some good deals in the Glebe, as usual. The line-up for beaver tails was too long, so we just opted for some fast food.

While at the NRC, I had found a copy of a recent article from the *Ottawa Citizen*, in which a local hot-air balloonist had claimed that an infamous UFO video from Carp, very near Ottawa, might have been of his own balloon during a night flight, since he flies with a strobe and light sticks. It sounded like a reasonable possibility, and I thought I'd check into it if I had a chance.

I tried tracking down the balloonist, with no success, though a rival balloonist told me that the strobes on balloons didn't match the one in the video, confirming my own recollection of the last time I saw such lights on night flights.

I gave up my quest and decided to pursue other avenues. Just before leaving Winnipeg, I had received some information about an abduction therapist in the Ottawa area, so I contacted him. We had an excellent chat on the phone, and had started to settle on a time when we could alter our schedules to meet when he mentioned the Center for the Study of Extraterrestrial Intelligence (CSETI), an American contactee-oriented UFO group founded by Dr. Steven Greer. Some don't find that particular group's activities convincing (they have been known to telepathically "vector in" passing interplanetary spacecraft), but this therapist was vehemently in favour of their approach.

During our discussion, the therapist made a good case for the distinction between "proactive" and "reactive" ufology. The latter is what most ufologists do: investigate cases after they are reported. The former involves going to an area where UFOs are being reported, and wait to see if any come by. The idea isn't particularly new; Project Starlight International ran in the 1970s, Project Hessdalen is more recent, and there are UFO buffs' skywatches along Lake Ontario, Gulf Breeze, and near Groom Lake. In Manitoba, ufologist Grant Cameron and his assistants stalked a red-coloured nocturnal light bobbing and weaving about in the night sky in 1975 and 1976. Watching and chasing the light literally every night, they were witnesses to what became affectionately known to the local community as "Charlie Redstar."

CSETI goes a little bit further, and that is what gets many people rankled and leery. They claim communication with the aliens via strong flashlights and less traditional methods such as telepathy. The CSETI group is denounced by other groups, and this could be viewed as a kind of "jealousy" in some ways.

Despite our differences, this Ottawa UFO researcher agreed to meet with me to explain CSETI's position a bit better. So, while I was still in Ottawa, George and I visited him at his office in the basement of his house.

I asked him if I could be blunt with my questions, and he said he'd be open to anything. I started by discussing our backgrounds, then went right for the abduction jugular. I asked if he had any trouble with criticisms of his objectivity in treating abductees ("experiencers") given that he believes aliens are definitely involved.

He was almost surprised. "No," he said. "They're definitely here."

He informed me that a "select" group of scientists "definitely have physical evidence" of alien intervention, including tissue samples from EBEs, pieces of crashed saucers, and various photographic evidence.

"Who?" I asked.

"I can't tell you," he replied.

"Why?"

"Because."

"Does Friedman know? Stringfield? Clark? Andrus?"

"They may or may not."

And so it went. He told us that his secret group (which may or may not be CSETI) is keeping this information from the public "until the right time."

"When?" George asked.

"Soon."

"How soon?"

"Sooner than you think."

"Today?"

"No."

etc.

He then showed us a video which included both a video from Gulf Breeze and the one in Carp that I had been investigating.

"If you don't believe already, then these videos won't convince you," he told us.

The Gulf Breeze video was supposedly one of four views from separate cameras. Two of the views were copyrighted by others in the group and we were told they could not be reproduced freely. The screen showed a triangular formation of whitish lights which seemed to move in tandem but changed perspective as if they were in fact on a large deltoid object that was not illuminated. Accompanying the video was a running commentary by people including Steven Greer who were saying things like: "Oooh!" "Aaaaah!" and "Look how they're moving together!"

George thought they were lights on balloons. I didn't bother asking our host about the tethered balloon theory.

The Carp video is one that has been seen on television repeatedly. If you want to believe it's an alien spaceship, that's your right. What was on TV before us was the alleged video of a landed saucer from 1991. The original Carp "crash" dates back to about 1989. The 1993 sightings in the area are another matter entirely. I gleaned several UFO reports in the region from the NRC files from about that time.

The reality is that Clive Nadin, an Ottawa researcher, went to the alleged site of the crash, interviewed many witnesses, and surveyed the area. There was *absolutely no evidence* of any crash or close encounters. All local reports that I read were of "funny lights in the sky," plus one where the witness was "chased by a UFO following my car until I turned into my driveway — then the UFO was gone."

The video itself started with what looked like a fire in a field, near a lighted object. To us at the time, it looked possible that the object was a fire truck responding to a brush fire. Its structure was partly illuminated on the underside, where the hose connections need to be lighted. I've seen a fire response team in a field at night, and it looked very similar to what was on the video.

However, West Carleton, where Carp is located, is a large rural township. A field on fire would be (1) *big* news, much bigger than a mere UFO, (2) well reported in the local paper, and (3) a major topic of conversation. The long-time locals (four or five generations in some cases) still talk about a major fire that took out farms and forests over one hundred years ago. So while it might look like that in the video, it was an unlikely explanation.

Of course, there was no evidence the video was actually filmed in

West Carleton. The only connection is that one alleged witness said she saw a "similar" object in 1991 in the area.

Through the determination and hard work of Tom Theofanous and other UFO researchers in Ontario, the video was conclusively shown to be that of a pickup truck surrounded by flares and filmed in such a away as to obscure its identity. This is disputed by some UFO buffs, especially those who were accused by investigators of having a hand in the hoaxed video, but the explanation seems reasonable given the evidence presented by the two groups. Suffice to say that there is a difference of opinion about the Carp affair.

As for the Ottawa abduction expert, he said he had no trouble "knowing" about the reality of ETs and treating experiencers ("abductees"). He told us that he was more concerned with "healing" his clients rather than deconstructing their memories. He told us that CSETI members in Ottawa had gone out to the West Carleton region already and that they would return to the area to "make contact" in 1994.

We know for sure there was a string of UFO reports from the Carp area in the 1990s (including a crop circle in 1993). The NRC files have a half-dozen or so cases from the area for 1993, and there is a history of observed UFOs in the region. One can easily conclude that the area is prime for UFO spotters wanting to do some proactive ufology.

Perhaps CSETI is on the right track, after all.

Being "normal"

In one recent book about UFOs, another expert offered her own assessment of the abduction problem, although she approached the topic in a unique manner. The author, Vicki Cameron, admitted her lack of experience and background in the subject in the first few pages, and even explained her work is "not definitive and may not even be representative of what's out there." She did not investigate UFO sightings, analyze them in any way or deal with eyewitness accounts "in a scientific manner." Cameron simply decided to write a book about UFOs, so she placed ads in newspapers, asking readers to send her their accounts.

Instead of asking questions and seeking answers, she presented a parade of letters she had received from people who believed they had UFO experiences.

Some of these experiences were rather dull, such as simple observations of lights in the sky that could have been anything. Many, however (and this was certainly an artefact of the author's solicitation process), described wondrous encounters with aliens and spaceships. One parallel previous work on this subject is John Robert Colombo's *UFOs Over Canada* (Hounslow, 1991), a folkloric recounting of first-person accounts collected by the author. Cameron, however, admits she chose a UFO story contained in a letter and "wrote it as the person might have."

Since Cameron had no background in the subject (although she had written previously about mystery stories), the resulting book is a cross-hatch of curious tales, disturbing cases, and outright silliness. For example, in one remarkable account, Cameron related "Old Hank's Tale," told to her by a respondent who heard the story from Hank himself in the Sixties. Supposedly, Hank and his wife had been picnicking near Atikokan and saw a flying saucer siphon water from a lake through long hoses. Unfortunately, in another comprehensive work by Colombo, *Mysterious Canada* (Doubleday, 1998), this story was shown to have been a complete fabrication. However, Cameron's book remains a curious sociological study on the human condition.

The most revealing parts of the book make one stop to wonder about the veracity or sanity of the witnesses, or both. Throughout the book, people reporting UFO experiences and alien encounters are self-portrayed as near-paranoid and perhaps delusional (assuming the author did not deviate too far from their testimonies). Although Cameron's intent was clearly not to paint UFO witnesses in a negative manner and was attempting to present them in a compassionate vehicle, the result is somewhat different than what was conceived.

One abductee was quoted as saying: "I feel like they [the aliens] are watching me now. I often get the feeling at night that something's in here, in my closet." Another admitted that because of her encounter with aliens, "I have a phobia about cleanliness. I bathe constantly, up to three times a day. I gave myself eczema, and did the same to my kids ... I've been away from my kids twice in fourteen years. I am afraid to let my children go, afraid to let them out of my sight."

Even those who are not abducted weave disturbing images. After he related how he saw "a spaceship land in my backyard," a witness felt compelled to note: "My mother tried to stab me because she hated me from the day I was born."

Following his own sighting of a saucer, another noted: "I feel this ... [has] done something to my perspective on society. It has put a distance between myself and my community, and society in general."

Other writers on this subject — for example, psychiatrist John Mack

— insist they do not find such an abundance of dysfunctional individuals. It is possible that Cameron's solicitation process itself created a skewing of reports towards the bizarre and unusual elements. Certainly those "on a mission" (as one witness described her life after her UFO encounter) might have seen the author's invitation as a method of telling others about their experiences. Since Cameron noted that most people do not share their experiences because of a fear of ridicule, the sample of experiences in her book may not be truly representative, as she warned.

However, this would raise another issue: are such publications helping or hindering those people who are so seriously affected by their UFO encounters?

Psychological and sociological studies of abductees

Given the fact that at least *some* abductees experience distress of some kind following the memory of their encounters, it would seem that as a group, such individuals might show some signs of psychological ailments. Our society is more accepting of mood disorders, mental illness, and behavioural problems these days, and studies have shown that a significant proportion of the population has some need for clinical treatment by a psychologist or psychiatrist. It is considered common for many of us to experience depression at some stage in our lives or go through mood swings suggestive of mania.

As early in UFO history as 1970, sociologist Donald Warren came up with a theory as to why people see UFOs. Called status inconsistency theory, it postulated that status-inconsistent people — people with high educations and low incomes — were under stress because of their socio-economic situation. They tended to withdraw from society and cope with their frustrated lives by looking to an advanced race of being on other planets as a means of escaping from reality. (Not an entirely unreasonable desire, I suppose.) Other researchers, however, such as Fox (1979), pointed out that not all status-inconsistent people will likely cope in this particular manner. Some will certainly be more well-adjusted, and if stress is the main factor in people's desires to escape reality, then many non-status-inconsistent people will want to as well.

Certain people seem to have better imaginations than others, too. People with fantasy prone personalities (FPP) have vivid dreams, an openness to weird experiences, fantastic memories, sensory acuity, and strong responses to placebos, and are otherwise very suggestible. People who are very good hypnosis subjects tend to be FPP and often report psychic phenomena. Their imaginations are so intense that, according to one study, 75 percent of FPP people can experience orgasms from fantasy alone. (Stark, T. 1993. Hypnosis research overview. Published on the Internet in the *alt.hypnosis* newsgroup.)

Another attempt to deconstruct ufology was recently published by a political scientist. Her view was that the claim to have seen a UFO or been abducted by aliens is political in nature because it violates the *status quo.* As a reviewer noted,

> Alien narratives, in short, "challenge us to face head-on ... the dissolution of truth, rationality and credibility" in the information age.
>) *UFO Updates*, February 21, 1999
> www.ufomind.com/ufo/updates/1999/feb/m12-014.shtml.)

So, to social scientists, ufology is its own antithesis: the quest for "truth," so often claimed in ufology, is impossible because of the framework in which the quest is framed. Ufology itself is a reaction to mainstream society, and UFO witnesses and abductees are its "Million-Man March" on the fortress of reality.

The similarity of abduction accounts

There is also a debate among ufologists regarding similarities in abductees' stories. While certain aspects of the stories seem to be shared among abductees (such as floating, bedroom visitations, humanoid entities, and the observation of bright lights), the *details* of the encounters vary. Abductees do not have consensus on the specific physical characteristics of the aliens, nor their devices, clothing, instruments, or the interior of the ships. Aliens also give conflicting (or at the least, vague) information to the witnesses, though many assure abductees that they mean no harm by their painful medical examinations.

Nevertheless, MUFON investigator Dan Wright attempted to quantify the details of alien abductions, and reported that he found "myriad correlations" that could not possibly be due to "massive coincidence." His implication was that the abduction stories must be true because abductees in disparate locations could not possibly communicate certain details to each other for inclusion in their own stories.

Wright noted 2,174 details in 216 cases, and selected 68 details which were rarely, if ever, mentioned in the UFO literature and yet which were shared among several abductees. Of the more well-known details, levitation was reported in 104 cases, grey aliens in 76, and being examined on an operating table in 108. The rarer details included a "flashlight" or a rod with a light at one end. (These details and others are found on the website: www.debshome.com/abduction_stories.html.)

However, Stuart Appelle, another researcher, criticized Wright's conclusions. He argued that ordinary statistical sampling analyses might not apply in these cases because the details are subjectively obscure. It may not be reasonable to assume their uniqueness. In effect, Appelle said that Wright's evidence that some characteristics of abduction stories are found in several cases would *not* necessarily prove that abductions were real.

One reason why this could be so was suggested by psychologist Fred Malmstrom, who said that the archetypal "Streiber" alien face (made famous in William Streiber's *Communion,* 1987) is a genetic part of our psyche. He noted the alien-style face was

> a template ingrained into the brain back in the facial recognition area... Human beings are prewired to generate and recognize that particular UFO face with the large eyes and the triangular head. That is the template in the hypothesis that a baby is born with — and from which a baby learns, over a period of months, to recognize other faces.
> ("UFO faces are ingrained in human genes." *UFO Updates,* July 16, 1997.)

Another problem is that memory itself isn't permanent and unmalleable. Source amnesia is a characteristic of memory where the original event that created the memory cannot be recalled. If we forget the original source, we can confuse an imaginary event with a real one. Even though the memory seems real, it isn't. Stephen Ceci, a psychologist at Cornell University, conducted several studies on preschool children and found that memory could be influenced greatly. In one study, he repeatedly questioned the children about events that had never happened, and the kids eventually started believing the non-events were real:

> The false memories were so elaborate and detailed that psychologists who specialize in interviewing children about

abuse were unable to determine which memories were true.
(Golman, D. "Miscoding seen as root of false memories." *New York Times*, May 31, 1994.)

In a 1983 study, hypnotized subjects were told that, as they slept the night before, they had been awakened by the sound of a car backfiring. A week after the hypnosis session, many still believed they had actually heard the backfiring, and some insisted they heard it even after they were told they had been given the hypnotic suggestion. (Golman, *ibid.*)

False memories are a very contentious issue, especially with regard to cases of abuse. If memories of abuse can be so influenced by interviewers, it can make many abuse cases fall apart. The thorny issue of false memory syndrome has spawned lobby groups which rail against the acceptance of testimony uncovered though hypnosis and intense interrogation by interviewers with unconscious or hidden agendas. This has been particularly an issue in cases of alleged satanic cult abuse, in which victims and/or practitioners "remember" dismembering infants, offering sacrifices and engaging in bizarre sexual activity. In some celebrated cases, such memories have later been shown to have been completely fabricated.

Now imagine the influence of abduction experts upon confused and bewildered abductees seeking help in understanding their experiences. Is it any wonder that skeptics are concerned that abductees' memories of their alien examinations are altered or fabricated?

Given that abduction accounts share a similar basic structure but differ in details, how can we ever determine a unique explanation for them?

One possible answer is that we may not be able to do so.

According to popular abduction literature, aliens are said to be able to alter our perceptions of our environment, making us see things that are not there. They can control what we see and appear to us in many forms, depending on how they want us to react. They can even be invisible.

Abductees are said to display many varying kinds of marks on their bodies, ranging from the traditional scoop marks to odd linear scars and geometric bruises. Female abductees report miscarriages and are prone to cysts, tumours, and hysterectomies. Male abductees often have penile dysfunction, and have odd lesions around their groin. Abductees are given genital and anal probes, and have various bodily fluids withdrawn from them, and occasionally replaced with other fluids. Aliens force abductees to have intercourse with other aliens and other humans, often subjecting their victims to intergalactic voyeurism.

Abductees encounter aliens of every shape and size, and also see hybrid creatures in various stages of development. Some see other humans undergoing terrifying vivisection, and are warned that an uncooperative attitude will result in similar treatment.

Despite the apparent omnipotence of the aliens, their revelations and imparted knowledge to abductees leave a great deal to be desired. Their messages are a hodgepodge of New Age buzzwords and neo-mysticism. They talk of "kinship with the universe," encourage "transcendence of higher spiritual levels" and advise of humans being "on the verge of a new awareness of reality." There are no concrete guides to solving famine, curing cancer, or generating cheap energy.

The prophesies of early contactees have failed to come true. Today, abductees and contactees are again issuing warnings of "Earth changes" and disasters, but also promises of help from benevolent aliens. Alternatively, they warn of our enslavement by hostile aliens if we do not help the "good" aliens plan their (and our) defence. Some of this sounds disturbingly like Biblical warnings of false prophets and the Antichrist. As in the 1950s, predictions of our deliverance from extraterrestrial or terrestrial disasters may be false hopes in the minds of people disillusioned with our society.

It does not seem, after a review of many cases and studying what research has been done, that there is one simple explanation for abduction experiences. Because the abductions have at least some subjective elements, we also have to take into account the differences between the abductees themselves. And some of these differences, as we shall see, are remarkable as well.

CHAPTER TWO
Aliens We Have Known:

The Stories of Abductees

In order to understand more about the abduction phenomenon, we must look at some actual cases. During the past dozen years, I have been approached by many people with stories that seem part of the abduction milieu. Each one is different from the others. There may be a few characteristics that seem similar, but each case has enough unique elements that I find it impossible to group them into specific categories or paint them with a broad brush.

Perhaps the only true common characteristic is the abductees' sincerity. Nearly all the people who have come to me for assistance have presented themselves honestly. They all appear to be reaching out for help and hope that I can aid in understanding their predicaments.

The current wave of abductees seem to be classifiable into two basic kinds: abductees and contactees. In the 1950s, a significant part of the flying saucer literature was penned by those who claimed direct contact with the Space Brothers. These contactees were usually found at conventions where they would expound on the magnificence of the aliens' culture and tell great tales of trips to the Moon, Mars, and inside the Earth.

As noted earlier, I find little difference between the contactees of the 1950s and those of the present day who channel vague messages from Ashtar Command and claim they have been selected to be extraterrestrial emissaries. Another aspect of the historic contactees is that some claimed to be actual aliens themselves. Contactee Howard Menger was abducted by an alien princess whom he later married when she was incarnated on

Earth, and the two travelled the lecture circuit for many years. Today, there is a growing belief that some selected individuals on Earth are actually Star Children, born of alien genes but living here because of some master plan.

I make the distinction between abductees and contactees because they do seem to be different kinds of people in at least one respect. Abductees tend not to proselytize the way contactees do. In fact, most abductees I have met have insisted on anonymity. For the most part, abductees are baffled by their experiences and that is why they have appealed to researchers for help. In short, they don't appear to know what has happened to them and need some assistance in sorting out their lives, emotions, and world view.

Modern contactees, on the other hand, need no one to tell them what happened to them. They *know* that they have encountered space aliens and have been selected for some important purpose. They espouse great knowledge about how the universe "really is," and approach researchers not to get guidance, but for verification. What's more, many take it upon themselves to counsel other abductees and are sometimes regarded as experts themselves. Some feel they have been chosen by the aliens themselves to help others of like mind.

In order to protect the identities of abductees who have contacted me and shared their experiences with me, I have altered their identities in this book. In the cases of those who have used nicknames on the Internet, I will use different nicknames for them in order to give them added security.

Let's look at some actual cases.

Filip

This person sent me his accounts of UFO experiences via the Internet. At the time of his encounters, he was living in San Francisco. Although he did not claim any memories of abductions, his early childhood memories included some curious images.

> I'm twenty-six years old now but as a child I had two experiences with UFOs. I started having nightmares of demons capturing me and taking me off to a castle or a wooded area and trying to make me into one of them. I can also remember, as a small child, being scared of a ghost that would come through the wall to get me. I used to live outside the city, but now I live in the mountains.

My wife has recently had a dream of three men coming and telling her of war. I've also have been told of war in my dreams, but I've never told my wife of them even until this day. My son who can barely talk pointed to the sky and started saying "momma." It seemed strange to me. The dreams could be caused by who knows what, but I do know what I saw.

Filip had some sightings of unusual lights in the sky, but no close encounters with UFOs. Despite this, he believed his childhood nightmares were related to his observations of the nocturnal lights in the sky. The only characteristics which seem remotely like those of abductions were the images of a ghost or demon capturing him, which may or may not have been anything more than an active imagination. He was convinced he had been abducted, however, and that was why he contacted UFO investigators.

Veronica

Compare his case with that of Veronica, a soft-spoken and very modest woman in her twenties who lives near Toronto. To the best of her conscious recollection, she had a series of direct encounters with aliens beginning in 1985. During that year, Veronica was living on the ground floor of a three-level apartment building on the outskirts of Toronto in a populated area only a few hundred feet from a hydro substation.

She says a small craft of some sort landed in the back alley near her window two hours before sunrise one morning. She thinks mass autosuggestion was used on the drivers of vehicles in the area at the time, and other people were put into a deep "sleep holding pattern" so they would not wake up.

Veronica was taken by the occupants of the craft out of her window and told she was being placed in a black limousine. However, the "limousine" "took up two parking spaces and made a whooshing sound."

At the time of her abduction, Veronica had a kidney problem that was so bad her physician wanted to operate. On board the craft, the aliens removed "eggs" from Veronica, informing her they were merely examining them. They also operated on her kidney "cutting between the cells" and leaving no scars.

While doing so, they left behind an "implant" in her kidney to ease her pain. Veronica says that during a later ultrasound, the technician was surprised to see the implant in her kidney. However, Veronica says that the "implant" had since been flushed out through her urinary tract and lost.

Veronica says she had the impression that the aliens were human in appearance, but discovered they were actually the so-called greys, possessing large bald heads and large wrap-around eyes, projecting the telepathic illusion of human appearance. She says she was able to recall all the events consciously without the aid of hypnosis, because of a traumatic experience (a miscarriage) which affected her emotionally as well as physically.

While captive on the alien craft, Veronica says she was shown adult human bodies that had been "grown" from fetuses floating in liquid-filled tanks. The bodies took only four days to grow into complete adulthood, but contained no "spirit." When Veronica complained to the aliens about this process, she was told simply that we terrans do the same to animals, so their experiments were fully justifiable.

During her first abduction, Veronica was lectured by a female alien about the way we humans "spill or waste our seed, pollute our atmosphere, and treat others with disrespect." On subsequent visits, Veronica was shown other humans having their sperm and ova removed, alien/human half-breed children and another abductee named Ellen Robertson.

Robertson claimed she was a "missing person" from Rhode Island. However, before the two could speak with Veronica at length, Baxter was led away to what the aliens told Veronica was a "vivisection room." This caused Veronica to be fearful of her own life, and refrained from speaking publicly about her experiences for several weeks. However, she became more brave over time and began telling the media of her encounters. She is now a "part-time Christian minister" in Ontario and has become a vegetarian largely because of what she has seen on board the alien crafts.

Although Veronica has a number of abductee characteristics, her presentations to the media show that she believes she has been chosen to tell the world about her revelations and beliefs, putting her well into the realm of the contactee.

Seymour

Very similar to Veronica is Seymour. In 1976, he began hearing a series of beeping sounds in his right ear that he understood to be contact from an extraterrestrial being. The being encouraged him to study a variety of subjects such as science and spirituality, and he began writing about his life in poetry and prose. He was convinced that his body was now a "storage battery" and that his brain had been reprogrammed in order to translate the beeps into information about humans and their relation to the universe.

Seymour "realized" that the Earth had been visited by benevolent aliens in a convoy of spaceships in the year 5602 BC. They had come because a great villain named Lucifer threatened to destroy us. Unfortunately, a planetary alignment destroyed the "good" aliens' power stations in about 3500 BC, so we've been at the mercy of Lucifer since then. The good news is that another ship of "good" aliens is on its way and will be rescuing us before the year AD 2000. Seymour also believed humans to be the result of intergalactic interbreeding with extraterrestrials.

Seymour was largely uneducated and had a difficult life. In fact, he admits that he was physically abused as a child. Some researchers believe that abuse may give rise to delusions in later life. Could this be an explanation for Seymour's experiences?

British ufologist Peter Rogerson suggests that some abductees appear to be "psychologically disturbed people," often victims of satanic cults, and sexual abuse. His view that abductees are suffering from multiple personality disorder (MPD) or Munchhausen syndrome is interesting, since people with those afflictions have demanding, attention-seeking, and manipulative behaviour sometimes associated with abuse victims.

John Mack insists that abduction memories do not mask sexual abuse. However, Nigel Watson, writing in *Fortean Times* (No. 121, pp. 34-39), offered two cases which blatantly contradict this. One, an Australian abductee named Susan, was taken by aliens when she was prepubescent and subjected to a vaginal examination. She reported many abductions during which aliens had sex with her. It was later learned she had been sexually abused by members of her family. The case of Lucy, discussed in Jim Schnabel's book *Dark White*, involved another young girl who recalled aliens' sexual intrusion but who was later discovered to have been molested by a human.

Bruce Cornet

Some abductees are very well educated. The most prominent example of this is Dr. Bruce Cornet, who wrote a letter in support of Dr. John Mack when the latter was under attack from his Harvard peers for his continuing investigation of abductees. Cornet has a BA in biology, an MSc in botany, and a PhD in geology from Pennsylvania State University.

He has a string of scientific papers to his credit and worked in the oil industry for many years.

In the early 1990s, Cornet was witness to UFOs in upstate New York. This prompted him to get involved with other UFO buffs, many of whom were abductees. His scientific background allowed him to find "magnetic anomalies" in Orange County that proved to him that aliens were present. He became convinced that highly advanced aliens share the Earth with us and are involved in a long-term program to "educate" us.

Cornet's research led him to realize that he had been abducted many times in his life and that he has received telepathic communication from the aliens on numerous occasions. His strongest evidence includes dozens of photographs of alien ships generating "plasma bubbles" as they fly through the night sky, although to most people who examine the photographs, they appear to be fuzzy lights without any convincing details. Nevertheless, Cornet feels that his scientific background precludes the possibility that he is just imagining his experiences.

Dave Kowal

On March 13, 1988, my associate Roy Bauer and I met with Dave Kowal, an abductee who insisted on strict anonymity. Dave had come up to me after a public lecture at the University of Manitoba by ufologist Stanton Friedman at which Stan had introduced me to the audience. I called him later and we discussed his experiences briefly, but I wanted another researcher's opinion, so I invited Roy to help me assess Dave's case.

Dave was an aspiring musician and songwriter who was living with his brother and sister in a rural area just outside of Winnipeg. He was born in 1966 and was raised in a small farming community. The oldest of his siblings, he was from a Ukrainian Orthodox religious background and was sent to a parochial boarding school in the 1980s.

Dave originally contacted me in the hope of resolving a recurring problem. He feels that he was "under observation" and was "being watched." In fact, he was certain that this had been the case all his life. He had a real fear that something was occurring that was beyond his control. He felt like he was being "guided," but at the same time *prevented* from "knowing the reality" of what was taking place. He said he felt "like an animal," under the constant care of and observation by *them*.

When Roy and I met Dave, he appeared quite rational and sincere. He presented himself as a bit "straight" — churchgoing and conservative, yet open-minded and well-educated for a young adult. We thought it was possibly because of his otherwise normal background that his experiences were so disturbing to him. Throughout his life, he had refrained from mentioning his experiences to anyone, including his family, although he broached the subject occasionally with neutral results. Dave admitted that he read Whitley Streiber's *Communion* in 1987, and that this was what prompted him to seek the help of a ufologist in order to understand his experiences.*

In about 1970, when Dave was four or five years old, he had "vivid nightmares" of floating out of his bedroom through the window into a large field across from his home. He said the passage through the window felt "very strange," as if the window "moulded" around him as he passed through. However, he could not recall what happened once he was in the field, nor how long he was there. He did remember that when he returned to his bedroom, he floated above his bed and was surprised to see his bed was empty with the covers pulled down. (This differs from most accounts of out-of-body-experiences, in which percipients usually remember seeing their lifeless bodies down below.)

During these early childhood years, Dave would wake up at night and see fist-sized "globes of light" hovering at the foot of his bed. His normal reaction was to immediately hide under the covers (a prudent move, in my opinion) and he could not remember how they went away.

Another time, he was standing at a large picture window in his home when he saw a bright light pass close to the house. As it did, it emitted some kind of blinding flash of energy, striking him in the face. Dave felt that "something important" was imparted to him that day, and the word "bio-chip" stood out in his mind.

---

*Streiber's immensely popular and vivid accounts of his tormenting by aliens are benchmarks for abduction ufology, even though there is considerable criticism of his claims and interpretations. Skeptic Jerry Black points out that

> there is no evidence whatsoever to support Whitley Streiber's contention that he has had numerous encounters and abductions with and by beings he refers to as the Visitors. No objective and scientific investigator has ever investigated Mr. Streiber's claims. Thus, I can only conclude that there is no basis to believe any of the claims that Mr. Streiber has made. Until such time as Mr. Streiber allows a thorough investigation by objective investigators, there is no basis for anyone to believe that Whitley Streiber's accounts are true. ("Jerry Black's challenge to Whitley Streiber." *UFO Updates*, January 2, 1999. www.ufomind.com/ufo/updates/1999/jan/m03-015.shtml.)

Nevertheless, Streiber's series of books and the popular movie which was spawned from them are an integral part of the abduction milieu.

Dave says his experiences seem to occur in cycles of approximately five years. He says his medical records show that he was prone to violent headaches throughout his youth, although he has no recollection of them. He also has no recollection of certain injuries, such as one instance when he discovered three parallel, weltlike burns on his left wrist, without knowing how they got there.

During the summer of 1977, he was travelling with his family on vacation in Saskatchewan and was sleeping in the back seat. He awoke to see a light following the car. He couldn't tell how far away or how high it was at first, but it approached the car until it was above and just behind the car, out of view to his parents in the front seat. Suddenly, the light began to pulsate irregularly and Dave received the impression that it was "signalling" to him. He recalls being very afraid of the light and its "message," whatever it may have been. He says he informed his parents at the time, but his father was unsympathetic, telling him something like "Don't worry about it; it's just a light."

In the fall of 1983, while Dave was at boarding school, he had another strange dreamlike experience. He was asleep in his bed underneath a window, in a large room filled with other students sleeping in their own beds. He woke up with the sensation that he was unable to move, and he had the shocking impression that he was about fifty feet in the air over a vast, frozen lake. He felt a "power" flowing through his body and that "someone" was "testing" him by "throwing switches in my brain."

It was a moonlit night with many clouds, and Dave somehow knew he was facing east, with land behind him. He was facing into a strong, cold wind and could feel it blowing through his pajamas. Dave insisted he felt as if he "was really there," and that it was not a dream. He remembers looking at the ice on the lake, the Moon was behind him and that he was hovering above the treetops, near the shore, looking out across the lake into dark clouds. He had no memory of how he got there, and remembers that he was very scared and overcome by his situation.

Suddenly, the experience was over and he was in bed again. His legs and arms were slowly regaining some feeling, but he had no memory of how he returned from his voyage. He said he had the exact same experience on two other occasions during a two-month period that year.

Roy and I decided that it would be useful to obtain more details of some of Dave's experiences. We had read about how hypnosis had been used by abduction experts to regress abductees and uncover hidden memories, so we considered the possibility. Rather than just getting a storefront hypnotherapist or one with a predisposition towards the reality of UFOs, we opted to contact a clinical psychologist who used hypnosis as part of his therapeutic procedure when necessary. It took a bit of convincing, but he was slightly intrigued by Dave's story, so he agreed to see him on the condition that he could videotape the proceedings.

After an initial interview, Dave agreed to the arrangement, and an appointment was made for the hypnosis session. On April 25, 1988, Roy and I met Dave at the psychologist's office and we went into the regression area. Dave went into the interview room while Roy and I were allowed into the taping studio which was hidden from the interview room by a two-way mirror. After a few minutes to acclimatize Dave to the room, the clinician began the hypnosis procedure.

Once he was asleep and under the control of the hypnotist, Dave began to recall the events of a particularly remarkable experience. In November 1987, Dave had been watching TV late at night and had just turned the set off at about 1:00 a.m. He began getting ready for bed by saying his prayers and climbing under the covers. He listened to his clock radio for a short time, then turned it off and laid in the darkness, thinking about the day's events.

Suddenly, he realized that he could not move any part of his body. He consciously tried to will his arms and legs to move but could not budge them an inch. Simultaneously, he felt a tingling sensation through his body, "different than if they are asleep." At the same time, he sensed a "presence" in the room.

Although his body was paralyzed, Dave found he could still move his eyes slightly so that he could still see the digital clock radio face beside him on the bedside table. He was very frightened and worried because he could not cry for help from his family even though they were just down the hallway in their rooms.

He was shocked to see a shadowy face directly in front of him, only a foot or so away. It was a grotesque image, completely unfamiliar to him, with "folds of skin" around the eyes and cheeks, with small ears and a slitlike mouth. On top of the head was a "helmet" with two "knobs or stumps" protruding to the left and right. He was unsure if they were "devil horns."

Although his conscious recall did not include the rest of the figure, under hypnosis Dave was able to see the entire creature. It was wearing a black, tight-fitting garment, but he could not clearly observe its hands or legs.

At this point in the hypnosis session, Dave was calm and subdued during the retelling of his experience. However, as he described the creature, he became very agitated and anxious. He described how the entity was approaching his bed and appeared to be holding a short, cylindrical rod that had a light on its end. As the being extended the rod towards Dave's forehead, Dave became very upset. When light-tipped rod actually touched his forehead, Dave screamed in pain and reacted with such violence that the psychologist had some difficulty regaining control.

Dave said that "something was being put into [his] mind" and "collecting information." He described how "they were not interested in my personal life," but were "just pulling out things I've seen." He experienced flashes of images through his mind, such as television news reports, flashes of scenery, and faces of political figures. He said he "felt like a cow," being examined by forces beyond his control and held down for study. During this mental extraction, he was able to look beside him at the clock radio and was horrified to see the minutes changing rapidly: 23, 24, 25, 26 ..., flashing by as if they were seconds. He also seemed to be able to see a football-shaped light through the curtains of his window.

Without warning, the ordeal was over. The creature was gone and Dave was no longer paralyzed. Quite shaken, Dave sat up in bed and looked around the room. There was no sign of any disturbance. He stood up, shakily, and immediately walked over to his closet because "it seemed to be where everything had come from." But there was nothing unusual inside. He was too scared to open the door to the hallway "for fear of what I might have found." In the morning, he did not discuss his experience with anyone in his family, and he did not feel any after-effects from the night before.

Later, in our discussion with the psychologist, he told us that in his opinion, Dave's experiences were not physically *real* but represented very vivid dreams. He based this on many years of clinical observations of other patients and from certain cues and reactions of Dave under hypnosis. However, the psychologist also said that Dave's violent reaction as he remembered the rod touching his forehead was the most extreme he had ever seen in more than twenty years of clinical work, suggesting it may have been associated with a very traumatic event.

Dave is an intelligent man with no obvious signs of psychiatric illness and didn't seem to be making any of this up. He really seemed to have had a number of strange experiences during his life. He's a very good candidate for hypnosis and the psychologist noticed that he was very susceptible to suggestion. It's possible that his experiences might have been triggered or brought on during a subtle form of self-hypnosis that he often practices while preparing for sleep. He explained to us that he usually "meditates" with a candle burning beside him just before bed.

Dave had a fairly typical "classic" bedroom visitation from an entity

— a mainstay of the abduction genre. There's no physical evidence for his experience, but he is sure it really did happen and we are faced with the possibility that *something* happened to Dave to create such a memory of the event.

But some events in recent years are a cause for concern. Following the hypnosis session, Dave declined further appointments with the psychologist since he considered them "treatment," which he saw no need for in his life. Unfortunately, his continued observation by *them* and his perceived lack of control became a great strain on him. Dave attempted suicide and was placed in the care of a priest who was an intake counsellor at a hospital. When I discussed Dave's case with the priest, I found out he had no experience in treating abductees and viewed Dave only as a mildly paranoid schizophrenic. As a consequence, Dave left the care of the priest, too, and sought additional help on his own.

Dave contacted another UFO investigator who helped him set up a support group for abductees like himself. Dave claims he can now psychically detect "vibes" and impressions of people and objects. He has also seen a number of lights in the night sky that he interprets as alien spacecraft. He feels he has been selected by the aliens for a significant purpose, and that it is his job to help other abductees in need. Dave says he is no longer anxious about the aliens' intent and actions, although he still is convinced they are watching him constantly. A few years ago, he told me that he was awakened one night by the sudden appearance of a small, golden globe of light moving about his bedroom. He followed it down a hallway, where it vanished.

I wonder if an abductee support group was best for Dave. Knowing that he attempted suicide, I wonder also if a UFO expert is the best person for him to be associated with right now. Although I can imagine that Dave would be sympathetic towards other abductees, his contributions to a support group might not be ideal if he is suffering from delusions.

Again, we are left with the problem of deciding whether or not Dave's experiences were "real." Are Dave's contacts benevolent in nature? If aliens are behind it all, it could be they didn't intend to make him upset and suicidal. On the other hand, would they not know the damage they were doing? Maybe they don't care. Selective observation and sampling is a standard method anthropologists use in studying new peoples. Some UFO experts would see this case as more evidence that aliens are treating us like laboratory animals.

Dorothy Izatt

The experiences of Dorothy Izatt seem to parallel those of Dave Kowal rather substantially. She, too, began having unusual dreams when she was a child and observed several lights in the sky. She, too, is very religious and often meditates with a candle beside her bed.

One night in 1974, Dorothy had an urge to look out a window, where she saw a "mother ship." She began signalling to it by waving a flashlight up and down, sideways, and in zig-zag patterns. The craft responded with identical movements. She realized that whenever *they* appeared, a beam of light shone into her eyes. She said that she was able to communicate with the aliens through a form of telepathy and could later "command" a ship to appear for other observers.

At some point, Dorothy wondered if she was just imagining her contacts, so she got in touch with the host of a radio show who often had UFOs as a topic. The producer of the program visited Dorothy and advised her that people would only believe her if they could see what she saw. So, Dorothy took a Super 8 movie camera she had bought for her husband and began to film out her window. Dorothy took more than 8,000 feet of colour film, nearly all of it showing foreground lights as well as numerous bobbing and flashing lights in the night sky. As one viewer noted, the films are "hard to watch for an extended period." But occasionally, among the zig-zag images, an "overexposure" frame appears, showing domed, disc-shaped flying saucers close to the camera.

Once, when Dorothy was in bed, relaxing before falling asleep, she mentally asked the aliens, "What are you like?" The aliens answered in a series of faces which appeared to float through her door and across the ceiling. The parallel with Dave Kowal's experience is remarkable. Dorothy noted that the faces appeared to be so "real," she could see into their nostrils. The faces were in all shapes, colours, and sizes; some had pointed ears, domed heads, and sunken or bulging eyes. She even saw a number of animals float by. In fact, the images multiplied in such numbers that she had to mentally ask then to restrain themselves at one point. Today, Dorothy leaves the hall light on to reduce the "vividness" of the images that will appear to her at night.

But Dorothy's contacts do not stop there. She has also been able to *see* flying saucers *through* her bedroom ceiling. Not only that, she has used an ordinary flash camera to photograph the saucers through the ceiling and walls, producing a recognizable image. This ability has been suggested by some UFO investigators to be a form of interdimensional viewing.

Dorothy has also received written messages from the aliens through automatic writing floating in the air or projected upon solid objects.

Dorothy has been described by investigators as a "talented and composed lady." She has spent a considerable amount of her own money recording her experiences and presenting them to others, although she gets irritated by people who demand samples of her film or require additional proof. As one investigator noted:

> Her confidence in the experts' ability to extract a solution is quite obviously shaken. Her religion is her pillar of strength and her confidence in what is happening to her is strengthened by the continuing discovery that other people elsewhere have, and are undergoing wholly or in part, identical experiences. (Conway, 1996.)

Izatt believes she was selected because "there is a message to send out, and I guess myself and others with similar experiences act as a conduit." She claims she has had contact with the aliens "almost every day for the past twenty-four years." The aliens are here "to let us know that we should be more responsible in our ways where the Earth is concerned," while others are "collecting specimens for a modern-day 'Noah's Ark.'" Izatt has produced an astonishing 350 Super 8 movies of her observations, which show little more than lights moving about the frames.

Dr. Du-fay Der, a clinical psychologist at the University of British Columbia, is one of several experts quoted on a Website as supporting Izatt:

> She's a normal, average person, and we find no psychotic tendencies or depressive tendencies or any kind of mood disorders. If anything, the tests show us that she is a very modest person, honest with average [to] above-average intelligence.

Der seems to completely contradict Rogerson's notion, and suggests that Izatt does not appear to be psychologically disturbed at all. Other supporters on her Website insist that her photographs and films are confounding and that there is no explanation for them. Dorothy's experiences are detailed at www.manari.com, which includes many of her photographs for surfers to judge the veracity of her claims for themselves.

Nunzio

On the Sunday before Christmas, 1987, Nunzio was alone in his house in Regina during the evening because his roommate had travelled out of town that weekend. Because he was by himself, Nunzio decided to go to bed early.

He remembers waking up screaming after a particularly vivid "dream" that seemed very "real." In the dream, three small beings with slanted eyes were standing by his bed and another was waiting at his bedroom door. Nunzio recalled only that the beings were three or four feet in height. He could not remember any other details.

Nunzio had a friend who was a UFO investigator and an amateur hypnotist. He attempted to hypnotize Nunzio and regress him back to that night so he could remember more, but was unsuccessful.

In 1977, ten years previous to his dreamlike experience, Nunzio had injured his hand at work. An associate recommended that he go to a sports medicine clinic for an examination of his hand. The examining doctor had an x-ray taken of the affected area.

The doctor asked Nunzio if he knew he had a piece of metal embedded in his hand, behind his thumb. Nunzio could not recall how that object had gotten there, but decided not to bother with it because it did not seem to be a problem.

However, after Nunzio's unusual dream, and after reading books about alien abductions, he decided to have the metal object removed. In 1988, he underwent a minor operation to take the metal shard out of his hand. The piece was approximately 3/16" in diameter, very irregular, and appears as if it was a chip of bone. However, it was strongly attracted to a magnet, suggesting it was a metal fragment that had been calcified from being in the body for a long period of time. It appeared to have an "arrowhead" or "herringbone" pattern on its surface.

Nunzio admits readily that he read books on the subject of alien abductions and UFOs before he had his "dream." He did not wish any publicity though, and was hesitant about any further investigation. He is willing to submit the metallic fragment for tests by a scientific body and has been carrying the piece with him in his wallet ever since.

Roy Bauer and I have examined the piece and are in the process of getting it analyzed by an independent laboratory. When we inspected it, however, the implant was decidedly unimpressive, just looking like a calcified ort of some kind and without any special features that would suggest an otherworldly origin. Indeed, it bore no resemblance to the "microchip" that was removed from Scully's neck on the "X-Files" TV series.

Nunzio had other dreams as well; he once found himself wearing a toga-like garment and conversing with others in a Roman setting, complete with Doric temples and porticos. Again, we are forced to ask if his experiences are in any way real or just imaginary.

Eve

Internet Relay Chat (IRC) is an interactive, real-time discussion forum that allows users to "talk" with others around the world in a kind of party line by typing messages on their computers. Because the Internet is worldwide, users can share stories, exchange files, and send private notes to each other and receive immediate responses, even if they are on opposite sides of the globe.

IRC is divided into hundreds of "channels" with varying topics from favourite authors and TV shows to support groups for specific problems. (More than a few channels are all about sex, nearly all created and populated by randy teenagers.) There are several channels devoted to UFOs, and people on these channels discuss everything from the latest breaking news (mostly rumours) about UFO activity and rehashing old cases to reporting their own UFO sightings and abduction experiences.

Among the personal experiences shared with me on IRC are those of Eve, a quiet and shy Canadian woman. She detailed her experiences for me in several letters. The following were among her collections:

> I was in bed during the wee hours of the morning, and I felt like I couldn't move but I felt also that I was alive, if you know what I mean. It was in a different environment that was silent and dark, except for some light, but the background was dark. I looked to the left of me and saw a form of a body, but couldn't make out the face or gender. The body was not clothed and from the middle of both shins down the rest of the leg to the toes was missing. It appeared to me to be like a clean cylinder cut, and there weren't any body fluids or tissue coming from that missing area. The next morning I awoke really out of it and I knew something was wrong. That was the first time I was afraid of the beings.
>
> When they come, the presence and environment is still and quiet and they stay for weeks. I am awake when they come but they don't want to be seen. I can feel and sense their presence; they

usually come in the spring and fall. When they come, I feel a silent, still, greyish, hazy environment, but not dark, just a tint of haze, more like a mist, but not wet.

No matter where I live, they know where I am. About ten years ago, I was living in a city. During one afternoon, I heard this high sonic type of sound, and was wondering where it was coming from. I went and looked out the window down to the street and I couldn't believe that people were going about their normal activities and didn't seem to be looking for the sound, and then a few moments later, in my apartment dining room and two areas of the living room, I heard like a very quiet swoosh sound going upwards and after that the supersonic sound left.

That didn't scare me; my boyfriend was scared for a few weeks, though. I used to tell him about the beings following me no matter where I live, and he said, "Naw!" He didn't hear the sound, but some mornings when he was getting ready for work about 4:00 a.m., he heard things move. I had my bike hanging up and the windows were closed, and he said the wheel was turning. He woke me because he then realized what I meant.

Eve's bewilderment struck me as very sincere. She makes no attempts to proselytize, nor does she feel the need to convince others of her "truth," unlike some abductees.

Ibrahim

Another abductee who used to be in the UFO channel frequently was Ibrahim; he would often quarrel with non-believers about the reality of UFOs. He made his personal narrative available online as well:

04/05/95, 3:15 a.m.

I seem to be abducted every three months. Tonight's experience was unusual because I didn't wake up already scared ... it took a few minutes this time. I woke up and later went to the bathroom to find out that my underwear was on inside out. That's not like me. I'm very particular about that sort of thing.

I remember being taken to some kind of hospital or office

with five rooms. I walked in and was given some kind of injection that made everything seem like it was in slow motion. My mind was still thinking at very high speeds, but my body was moving much more slowly than a functional speed. I was terrified ... all the sounds seemed like they were played at ultra-low speeds. I couldn't make anything out. I yelled "HHHHHHHEEEEEEEEELLLLLLLLLLPPPPPPPP!" at the top of my lungs, but it came out all funny, or at least I perceived it that way.

I don't know exactly what happened during this abduction, but I don't think I was abducted by the aliens this time. I believe I was abducted by our government and was undergoing some kind of treatment/questioning under some drug to answer questions regarding my previous abduction experiences.

Four months later, Ibrahim had another vivid dreamlike experience.

08/17/95, 5:18 a.m.

I've just been abducted. As is becoming usual with my abduction experiences, upon waking I had a very clear recall of an earlier abduction in my life. This one was when I was, once again, with Kismet, my neighbour. We were in a car out in front of her house and this UFO came zooming by.

It moved at blinding speeds, and each time it made a pass overhead I could feel myself being pulled into an altered state. I jumped out of the car and ran towards it, at which time it came right to me and I blacked out. There was a much smaller sound accompanying this recalled abduction than I have heard in the past.

I was scared just like I always am when I wake up after an abduction. I just went to bed about 3.5 hours ago, so there's no reason for me to be waking up right now. I had all kinds of weird thoughts during my abduction. My body is warming back up ... it is always chilled a little after an abduction.

Fernando

Fernando had an uncomfortable feeling that he had had a UFO encounter but was unable to remember what had occurred. All that he knew was that there was more than a day in his life for which he could not account, and he was bothered by it.

Through his reading and interacting with the IRC group, he was able to come out of his shell and got brave enough to seek the help of a hypnotherapist. The following is his account in two versions; the first is what he could consciously remember and the second is what he learned through his hypnotherapy sessions.

It was a Sunday in September 1994. My parents are divorced and I was staying at my mom's house. The next morning, I had to drive about twenty kilometres to school. It was about 6:30 in the morning so it was a bit quiet on the road. I had just passed Wellington, a little village. I can remember that, but when I passed Wellington, I can't remember what happened after that. The next day about 6:00 in the evening I went home to my dad's house. I wasn't very hungry but I was a bit thirsty, so I grabbed a bottle of cola and went to bed. Once I was in bed I started to cry and didn't know why. After that I didn't speak much for a few months. My parents asked me what was wrong with me. I said nothing, because I didn't know.

When I went to the doctor a few weeks later, I told him that I was thirsty all the time, and I wondered if I had diabetes. I asked that because a friend has it, so I thought I could be thirsty because of diabetes. The doctor took some blood samples. The results of the tests were negative.

I haven't been under hypnosis yet but I think I will soon because I want to know what happened to me during the time between going to school and returning to my father's house. But I'm scared, so I keep saying to myself, "Soon."

I have searched myself for scars and things like that.... I have some little cuts on my hands, just little and straight. I also have a long one on my arm. I still have the scars but the one on my arm is fading. When I got to my dad's house my clothes weren't dirty so I think it has nothing to do with an accident because then my clothes would be very dirty.

After this I had many sightings of UFOs; maybe they are related or something. I sometimes feel like somebody is watching me when I see them [UFOs]. I think I've seen roughly twenty UFOs in the last one and a half years. Before this weird thing happened to me, I had seen just one, I think. So it is a tremendous increase in sightings that I have had since then.

I didn't tell this to many people, only to some very close friends, some of whom I've lost because of this. My parents don't know about it either; they thought I had stayed the night with a friend, because my brother told them that. My brother really thought that I had, because I was very depressed sometimes, so he guessed I'd stayed with a friend. I asked all the people I knew if they had seen me or anything but none of them had. So I had been away for one and a half days and I still don't know where.

The second part was written after Fernando had gone through regression therapy with a counsellor, including some hypnosis sessions.

I was on my moped, and after passing a village I saw a black thing in the sky moving towards me. I stopped and the thing came nearer. It came over and hovered above me. The UFO was a kind of oval shape and black. Then a light came out of it and I stood in the middle of it and it sort of pulled me up. I was then inside the UFO in a big white room. I remember that on my right side there was a sort of sail hanging there.

Then a little being about four feet tall, grey, and [with] big black eyes came towards me from the front. He gave me some sort of telepathic command that I had to follow him. He took me to a different room with six other "greys" and to a table which looked like a operating table or something. They all looked at me and then started to undress me. I tried to stop them but I couldn't resist them. After they undressed me they gave me the telepathic command to lie on the table, which I did. They pulled my left arm to the left and my right arm to the right and began to look at and touch them. Two of them who were standing behind me lifted my head from the table and began to touch it.

One of them came over with some sort of device and pulled my mouth open and put the thing inside. Then he took this thing out of my mouth and I saw it appeared to be some sort of lamp. The same being also put a similar device, only a bit smaller, into my nose. He stabbed me with it and pulled it out again.

After this they then took me [from the table] to the room with the sail and left me there. I was very tired and fell asleep. When I woke up, one "grey" was standing next to me and was putting some sort of needle in my left arm. There was also a box or something standing next to me on my left side. I think the needle was somehow connected to it. Then I was left alone for a long time.

After I slept for the second time, in came seven "greys" and they took me back to the room with the table. They were looking at me the whole time. Then another "grey" came in, only this one was bigger. He felt my body then he left again. After this I was able to leave.

Lorne Goldfader

One of the most remarkable abductees or contactees I have encountered was Lorne Goldfader. He believed so strongly that he was in direct contact with aliens that he assumed the role of an advisor on the subject of UFOs. He created the UFO Research Investigation Centre of Canada and installed a twenty-hour UFO sighting report telephone number so people could report their alien encounters directly to him.

Lorne often sent ten- or fifteen-page faxes to local news media, informing them of his latest observations and experiences, and also his elegant philosophy of the aliens' purpose here on Earth. He also believed that he was under surveillance by *them.*

The following are some typical pages from his extraordinary mission to inform the world of his contacts with UFOs. Because his faxes advertized that their contents could be freely reproduced, I feel comfortable sharing extensive sections of them here. I believe it was Goldfader's intent to let others know his particular insights into the UFO phenomenon.

During the month of April 1991, I would experience an unusual, tingly or prickly sensation undulating underneath my skin, followed by symbols or hieroglyphics appearing deeply etched into my skin. These completely disappeared from sight after one hour each time. On April 29, after the characters disappeared, I went outside to the grocery store. Just outside my residence, I was startled to see two individuals with the oddest appearance, walking very quickly on the street past my home. Both were male and appeared to be in their mid to late twenties, wearing identical pinstripe suits. The clothing looked as if it had just come from the factory and had never been worn. The shoes looked black, new, shiny, and unused. They both had Chicago-style hats on. As a matter of fact, they both could have been mistaken for Al

Capone's gangsters, except that they were both 6 1/2 to 7 feet tall and one had an extended and protruding forehead, which was unmistakable to me as being of alien construction. One of them, the individual with normal features, looked at me very surprised as if I had caught him off guard. In that instant, I became extremely drowsy and I actually heard two voices, very clear and simultaneously in my mind, saying: "Do not move; do not approach us. You are not supposed to see this. We are trying to stop activity you do not understand. Do not interfere. Let us pass. The activity you are experiencing is direct contact by others, which we do not want."

I could not bring myself to approach them. When I gazed into his eyes, I saw an absolute lack of all human feeling and emotion. I felt that he and the other one were biological constructs. They walked stiff-legged, without bending their knees. Their faces were very pale and they looked anorexic. I have never in my life seen such alien-looking people. Their walk was purposeful, deliberate, and robotic.

Goldfader encountered such individuals regularly, and it seemed to him that the aliens were definitely keeping a close eye on him. He attracted others of like mind:

On May 19, 1991, I received a call from a man who had said he had been experiencing unusual phenomena all his life. When I met him on May 21, he was wearing a golden pendant around his neck, in the shape of a harp. He told me he could heal the sick and that the pendant was "a golden harp" from which all wisdom, knowledge, light, and harmony originated. The pendant symbol was the same as my cornered triangle, except that the four lines or strings were inside instead of outside, meaning I was in disharmony. He told me that he felt he was not fully human and had been metamorphosized. He is in his sixties. He has agreed to contact me again. He told me that he was from Sweden and has baffled scientists at Stanford University, as well as hospital staff. He had permanent etchings on his forehead identical in nature to my phenomenon.

Goldfader theorized how the aliens were able to accomplish their tasks and control us:

The "Greys" have an interesting yet frightening device in their arsenal of behaviour-modification weapons, which they use against certain Earth humans. There exists an instrument which is organically grown to specifications, genetically engineered, brain-wave-sensitive, spheroid in shape, very lightweight and small enough to cup inside a child's hand. When positioned within 2 – 15 inches of a "controller's" forehead, thoughts can be electronically focused, magnified, and projected into the mind of any targeted Earth human. The usual and routinely anticipated outcome is to render the quarry ill along with induced headaches or severe stomach cramps and in some cases increased heart rates leading to artificially induced attacks and/or death. The illness is often concurrent timewise with an abductee's positive contact with the gentle and kind Federated species and is designed to implant into the subconscious mind the idea that the illness is alien-induced. Since most human Earth contacts are not able to discern the originating source, they assume that all of their extraterrestrial contact is bad and cease all UFO research activities.

In the mid-Nineties, researchers noticed that Goldfader's telephone was disconnected and that he had vanished. Perhaps he, too, succumbed to the aliens' influence. Earlier, he speculated on what was actually done to humans by the aliens in order to effect their changes:

Sometimes individuals, if they are viewed as a future potential threat, are brought directly into a craft lab, sometimes with their siblings, and vibrated violently on a table or against a wall, along with the use of sound waves and in conjunction with implanted ideas and memory block techniques are literally forced to avoid certain areas of growth, educational, and vocational pursuits in order to circumvent certain future potential events from occurring which could, if not checked, lead to further evolution of mankind and therefore become a danger to Grey objectives.

Previous to disappearing, Goldfader determined that an implant had been placed in him, because he was puzzled as to why the aliens seemed to be able to track his actions so well.

Some individuals have been given biological and microscopic detection and reflection systems in their bodies by the "others." The implant absorbs psionic energy sources in conjunction with the conscious will and intent of the abductee; it reflects the waveforms back to the thought control warrior. This is a risk that the Greys are willing to take, since the chances of originating source detection are almost nil at this stage of Earth human evolution and awareness.

In addition to his strange encounters with aliens and their consorts, Goldfader said he possessed some extraordinary powers which he used to sense things in his environment. He could, for example, sense when there would be a flurry of UFO reports in his area, simply by feeling a change in a tingling in his legs. Unfortunately, he was disappointed to learn that his abilities could not be tested in a laboratory, and he was frustrated as his power waxed and waned because "someone out there is switching my ability on and off."

One fascinating aspect of Goldfader's experiences was the way in which his personal and spiritual life was interwoven with the aliens' activities. He seemed to view aliens and spirits as one and the same entities. In one touching discourse, Goldfader struggled with the passing of his mother, with whom he was very close, and how the aliens are involved with the spirit world.

October 1992: The Heart

I had been flashing a symbol of a heart to represent my mother's heart in my window at night along with a note to heal her. She was in intensive care in the hospital, suffering from irregular heartbeats. I received a photograph of a UFO several days before her death on October 5, 1992. [Note: The light in the photo was somewhat heart-shaped.] At 5:00 a.m., I received a call at the time of my mother's death of a UFO sighting over a mountain near my home. When the lady witness called the telephone operator to see if there was a "UFO" listing, the operator said "Oh my God!" as his computer screen suddenly went dead, then started up again. These are clear messages to me that my mother's consciousness has survived. I am still not sure why all of these things happen to me except that my purpose and destiny have an important role to play in the affairs of mankind. In retrospect, now I understand the message in the photograph. Someone was acknowledging the sketch of my mother's heart which I put in the window as a request for them to heal her. The symbol of the heart in the air over land represented my mother on her journey away from this physical

Earth plane of existence. I do not know how my mother was able to do this. Perhaps she had assistance. The important lesson is that consciousness continues after death and, somehow, part of the UFO phenomenon can access this frequency of existence.

Goldfader's commentaries often contained astonishingly clear insights into the UFO phenomenon. He clearly was wrestling with his own beliefs, emotions, and world-view and how they fit within our society and prevailing reality. Unlike some contactees, he admitted he did not have all the answers and did not know how to assimilate all the disparate information that has been claimed by various UFO researchers and abductees over the years. His view on the true nature of UFOs is most revealing:

I believe that the UFO phenomenon communicates its messages through symbology and theatrics. Humans respond to a play or skit differently than to a direct vocalized conversation. For example, if I were to say to you, "The Native Indians are suffering," it might mean very little to you. However, if I gave you clothing to wear in the style of their culture, and subjected you to derision, ridicule, and deprivation, you may experience a deeper sense of empathy and understanding. It is quite possible that the abduction phenomenon is one aspect of this approach, directed at our species.

There are thousands of fetuses aborted every day on this planet. Many of the tissues are retrieved by the scientific community for the purpose of various medical experimentations. What if the intelligence behind the UFO phenomenon was concerned about our apparent lack of respect for the sanctity of life? How would they best relay this to me?

I submit that it is possible that some of the so-called abductees are participating in a theatrical production where the visitors are playing doctors by control manifesting in the form of fetuses. We are, in effect, the object of their experimentation. In other words, the whole scenario is reversed. In this way, we can truly sense, feel, and understand what we are doing to an unborn child.

All sorts of other things could be injected into this presentation. They may wish to portray to us various possible future repercussions of our own genetic tampering of the human species by doing a sample of it to us. If we are forced to look in a mirror to see our faults, then perhaps we will change. The transformation that many abductees undergo may be indicative of the visitors' wish for our whole species to metamorphosize. Perhaps only through these modifications of attitude, behaviour, and actions can we really hope to evolve.

Goldfader took synchronistic events, meetings with strangers, and some personal tragedy and combined them into an extraordinary world view in which aliens and MIBs (Men in Black) play an important role in manipulating our lives. But even more extraordinary is the fact that he functioned quite normally in spite of all the attacks and games he was forced to play because of outside elements.

Several years ago, Goldfader became convinced that he was being regularly abducted from his bedroom and set up a low-light video camera to record his sleeping. He claimed that he once "caught" an alien in his bedroom, taking his lifeless body away to parts unknown. I never saw the video, but I can only wonder that if it really contained images of someone coming into his bedroom, could any of his stories have had some basis in reality?

I regret that I was unable to locate Goldfader for additional comments and for an update on his experiences.

Leroy

Sometimes abductees have an obsession with reading books about space and UFOs. We can wonder whether it is the obsession that brings about the experience or a real experience that creates the obsession.

Several years ago, a professor at the University of Manitoba met me for lunch to talk "business," as he described it. He informed me that for no apparent reason, he seemed to have been suddenly overcome with an obsession to read and talk about UFOs. His profession was not even remotely related to UFOs or space travel, yet he found himself speaking with other faculty members and even students *during* his classes about news reports about UFOs, crop circles, and other strange phenomena.

His addiction became so bad that his marriage began suffering. His wife even declared the subject off-limits in their house, although he still managed to sneak some books home. Once, when he went to hear ufologist Stanton Friedman lecture on campus one day, it increased his interest in the subject exponentially and it took him many weeks to "come down from the high."

Some abduction researchers might read into his behaviour that he had been contacted by aliens and his subconscious was dealing with the experiences. However, this was not quite the case. After some time, he realized his interest was carried a bit to the extreme and decided to consciously bring it under control. He "rehabilitated" himself to the point where he still had an interest in the phenomenon, but was no longer obsessed.

I and others found him to be quite rational and there was no reason to suspect anything was "wrong" with him, yet it remains curious that the obsession appeared so rapidly, without precedent, and persisted for so many months. What is most interesting is that he was able to check his own behaviour pattern and steer away from such obsessive behaviour. In effect, his early stages of AAS were "cured." To me, this suggests one of two things: either his contact experiences really had ceased, or there never were any such experiences and his obsession was the result of a some psychological need.

Nila

On November 1, 1992, Nila, a nurse living in southern Winnipeg, was awakened at about 2:00 a.m. by a loud thump on her door. She thought it was her noisy neighbours, who were often very loud and disturbing. She decided to get out of bed and see who was in the hallway outside.

When she entered her living room, however, she was startled to see two "little people" standing in the middle of the room. At first, she thought they were children and ordered them to get out of her apartment. She asked them: "How did you get in here?"

She then realized that they were not children, but unusual beings with large round eyes and wearing long white gowns or robes. They were very small, only 3 1/2 feet in height.

She asked them to leave, but they just stood, facing her. They did not seem to have any other facial features, but they somehow began communicating with her by what she assumed was telepathy.

She asked them: "What do you want?"

They turned their heads to look at each other, then turned back to her. They told her that they wanted to take her for a ride into space.

Suddenly, Nila found herself in a very large room, like a "hangar," in which a cigar-shaped craft of some sort was parked. She did not remember how she had gotten there. There were no other craft in the hangar, which was very modern in appearance and looked "brand new."

Nila was led across the floor of the hangar by the two beings, who walked or floated, one ahead of her and one behind her in a single file. They approached the cigar-shaped craft, which had a small door in its side. They entered and walked down an aisle in the interior of the craft, towards its bow. There, the aisle opened up into a "control room."

The control room had three chairs, in front of a table that had three rectangular screens and two sets of coloured buttons or control mechanisms. In front of the table were large windows which seemed to show a very dark blue "sky."

Nila was told they were "going to the stars," and watched as the beings on either side of her manipulated the controls. As they took turns pressing the buttons, the buttons would light up. The blue sky in the forward windows deepened in colour to black, and she soon could see many stars.

Watching the beings in action, she noticed that their hands were more like "mitts," with no fingers, and that they used their entire hands when depressing the buttons.

An undetermined length of time later, Nila found herself back in her room.

Nila was convinced that the experience had been real. She insisted that she did not normally have vivid dreams and that she did not read science fiction novels, go to SF movies, or watch TV shows with such themes. Her religious background was such that she felt she could not tell any of her friends about her experience, else they would chastise her.

Nila called me and came to my office later that week. She wanted to relate her story to me, but insisted that she did not need to undergo any counselling for any reason. She explained that she had her life well in order and only wished to contact me because she had heard that I was a UFO researcher and interested in such accounts.

She says she was "bothered" by her experience at first, but as she recalled more and more of it over time, she became calmer and was not frightened in any way. She did not want to have her name made public and did not feel she needed to be part of a support group.

Nila did not fit my expectations of a typical abductee. She was not interested in UFOs, and did not seem motivated to get interested after her experience. Her reason for talking with me was as logical as her professional training: to provide me with data. She was not convinced her experience meant that she was under observation by Reticulians, nor did she feel like telling the world about some great revelations. She merely reported her alien encounter as someone would report seeing a light in the sky. To her, it happened, and that was that.

One of the most significant elements of Nila's story is that her aliens were not "standard-issue" greys. Their round heads and round eyes set them apart from most other abductees' accounts. This may suggest to some diehard abduction buffs that her experience was only a dream and not related to "real" abductions by aliens. Alternatively, it may reinforce the view that differing species of aliens are at work.

However, it is interesting that Nila was relatively uncontaminated with popular UFO imagery. She hadn't read UFO literature at the time and did not have preconceived notions about the appearance of aliens as they "should be." We could speculate that her experience may have better reflected the "real" aliens, as not only did she seem to have no reason to fabricate the memory, it also came to her without any hypnosis or counselling.

I was greatly impressed with Nila. She was not seeking notoriety, she was puzzled by the memory (but not obsessed by it), and she was in a professional occupation where she had the resources to understand psychological phenomena better than most people. Because it occurred early in the development of abduction ufology and came to my attention while I was just starting to form my own views on the phenomenon, her case was one which made me stop to wonder. While it seemed to me that most abductees visibly displayed at least some degree of emotional or psychological problems, Nila was representative of a group of abductees who seemed to be in a category of their own. I could not concretely define this group's characteristics, but I sensed that they were not contactees or abductees in the common sense.

I'm still not sure if I can define these characteristics yet, but my view is that the "90 percent rule" of ufology applies within abductions, too. The rule states that only about one in ten UFO reports are "interesting." This is because most UFO sightings are explainable, have insufficient information for proper analysis, or have enough information that they seem to have possible explanations. Only a small fraction of reported cases actually are well-witnessed, well-investigated, and also unexplained. Even these few don't mean we are being visited by aliens — only that there are some interesting cases that don't have any satisfying explanations. So, in abductions, I would argue that only a small percentage of them (not necessarily a full 10 percent) are "real" abduction cases. As for what constitutes a "real" case ... I think we need much more research and study in the field.

Gabe

In the mid-1980s, I received a plaintive letter from a man living in Northern Quebec. In no uncertain terms, he was appealing for help for his problems. He, too, was in direct contact with "something," but wished to confirm that he had indeed been changed by his experiences. He wrote:

> Well, I don't know how to begin, because I don't know who is holding this letter, but I guess I can trust you. In fact, I do not think there is anyone I can trust more than you. You are concerned about strange things or phenomena, and I guess that it's about time for me to do something. Maybe this letter will help you in your research for the truth. It will help me, that's for sure, because I think you can help me to understand.
>
> First of all, I must tell you that I am really scared; scared by the fact that I tried many, many times to get help and understanding. All I have got are smiles and doubts about my health.
>
> It was in 1971; since that year, I have kept the strange secret to myself. I am 31, married, with four kids. Believe me, I didn't expect something like this in all my life. Before it happened, I wasn't one to think of things like UFOs, solar systems, galaxies, stars, the universe, and the meaning of life.
>
> In 1971, I changed completely. I began to buy books about UFOs, strange phenomena, the universe, and so on. One night in June, like every other night, I was looking at the stars over Montreal and I had a thousand questions in my head, and no answers. Suddenly, I was freezing and couldn't move. I cried because I wanted to go back there among the stars and because my place was in the stars, not on the Earth. Then, it was warm again, I stopped crying and smiled, thanking the stars for giving me an answer. It was only the beginning; I was certain that something else was going to happen.
>
> I went to bed that night, happy like a man who won a million dollars. I closed my eyes and calmed down, thinking only of the stars. After a few minutes, the unknown was in touch with

me. Something made me jump out of bed; it was there in my head: a sound like an electric razor. It became stronger, stronger, then changed into a much more bearable tone. I was frightened and out of breath. Then, with another change in the sound, little by little, I took control of myself. I got back into bed, closed my eyes again and noted that the sound was still there.

What could I do? I thought that if someone or something is in touch with me, it must be able to communicate. So, in my mind, I asked him if he was hearing me. The answer was very clear; it was a "yes," but not the word "yes." We were communicating by sounds — acute sounds — and for him it was maybe the only way. When I asked questions, if the answer was "yes," that was a long, acute sound. If it was "no," that was two acute sounds. Numbers and letters were also short sounds. Yes, I know it is hard for you to believe, but how do you think it was for me? Since that first night and for the next nine years, it's been there in my head, all the time, twenty-four hours a day.

Gabe began communicating regularly with this unseen entity. It started to control more of his life. Although his obsession started out similar to that of Leroy, his experiences took on a much more tangible element.

What happened after the first night is almost unbelievable. My memory wasn't the same; it was changing inside me, like cleaning a house of all the garbage. At the same time, UFOs started to appear to me over Montreal. Most of the time, I was alone when I saw them and it was strange that nobody ever reported seeing one of them. It was always the same thing, every night: a star among other stars, standing there without a movement at 9:45 p.m. every evening. Then, after I was outside, I could see them, moving slowly and disappearing after a few seconds.

His confusion was evident when he noted: "I am not sure about anything. In the beginning, I tried a few times to get rid of him, but there is no way, I am sure."

Gabe's aliens, too, controlled his married life.

When I met my wife, the unknown thing didn't take it very well. I ran into all kinds of trouble. The first two or three months were a nightmare for us. When we started living together, we got a disease, a very unusual disease. We tried everything the doctor told us, but there was nothing we could do. In fact, we got that disease for almost a month, enough to make both of us crazy. It was an itch problem, and what an itch! We will remember that for all our lives. We were fighting with each other, and most of the time for nothing. So, my wife left home for a few weeks and the itch disappeared. I knew who was responsible, so I had a long talk with my unknown friend and everything went just fine after that.

He added: "That's rather incredible, isn't it?"

His was an urgent appeal for help, and he sincerely wanted someone to help him "find the meaning" of this phenomenon. He said he was willing to undergo hypnosis if necessary, and also to have an "IQ test" done on himself, because he was convinced his entity had increased his intelligence and overall awareness.

Gabe's signals were very similar to those received by the woman whose implant was removed by Canadian researchers. Ufologist Larry Fenwick noted that in that case,

the abductee reported hearing what she called "signals," like in Morse Code, for years after her third abduction on July 12, 1961, in Don Mills, Ontario.... From 1961 until a few years before the implant was removed surgically, these "signals" gradually bothered her less and less as their strength receded. She also said she heard words at times, but could not understand the language.
(Fenwick, *op. cit.*)

Gabe's letter to me had been forwarded and bounced around the post office several times because his address for me was incorrect. It took several months to reach me, and by the time I tried to contact him, my letter was returned as well. I don't know what became of him, but I hope he is doing well and his marriage has recovered from its unwanted visitors.

Edgar

A few years ago, I received an e-mail message from someone in Thunder Bay, Ontario. My correspondent had a remarkable history of experiences. He sent me some details of the encounters, which may or may not have involved several other members of his family.

As a young boy, in July 1979, he was with a group of children one afternoon when he heard one of them yelling: "Look! Look!"

> Just seconds before, I heard my nephews and nieces running around outside, playing tag and hide-and-go-seek, but suddenly it was quiet, a signal to me that something was wrong. I walked out the kitchen door, expecting to find one of my nephews hurt. Instead, they were all looking westward, towards the road or the field beyond the road. I looked and immediately saw four objects in the sky, all in a row from south to north.

Each of the four objects consisted of several balls of light. Some of these balls were small, whereas some appeared much larger and the smaller objects seemed to be "orbiting" around the larger ones. The largest was described as "menacing" and caused Edgar great fear.

> I yelled, "Run!" I jumped off the steps and ran and grabbed Bessy. The others were already running north on a trail that leads into the bushes. I remember that Cindy was crying. Bill was yelling at his younger brothers to run faster. I ran behind them all. Josephine suddenly turned and ran back, out of the bushes. I practically threw my niece at Jerry and turned back, running to get Josephine. When I got out of the bushes she was standing in the driveway looking at the objects. I was yelling, I was so furious at her, then we ran back into the bushes. When we were inside the bushes, I looked at all of them. They all looked scared. At this point, my memory feels foggy.

Edgar's memory is very indistinct. He says he asked the other children if they remembered the incident, but some did and some didn't. However, one of the children didn't recall the lights but remembered that about the same date, a bat tried to fly into their bedroom window, scaring them all. But Edgar didn't remember a bat at all!

Most interesting, Edgar's blurry memory and vague images of things in the sky have made him very anxious. He noted:

> I am beginning to feel uncomfortable of writing about this information. Not from fear of ridicule; more because when I read what I have written, it is very suggestive of abductions. I do not remember ever being abducted. I have seen the machines they use, but I don't remember having a chance of seeing the inside.

So, while he appears unable to remember any memories specific to abductions, he does display some fears and worries about some events in his early childhood. He does remember some definite UFO sightings with his family, and many observations of objects while he was by himself.

The monk in the bedroom

One thing I have noticed is that some elements of abductee/contactee cases are virtually indistinguishable from those of hauntings and poltergeist cases. The witnesses are disoriented; they feel the presence of an entity of some sort; they feel they are being watched.

I would ask the question: "What is the difference, if any?"

For example, one haunting, investigated by paranormal researcher Roy Bauer, shows great similarities between UFO entities and spirits.

Mrs. C, her husband, and son live in a seventy-five-year-old, two-storey house in Winnipeg. They moved into the house in 1978, but within a month began noticing unusual things.

Mrs. C began to get feelings that she was being watched, and occasionally felt "cool breezes." Their dog would sometimes act "strangely" and hide under the bed for no reason. The dog also seemed to be afraid of going near a particular area in the basement. On other occasions, Mrs. C heard a birdlike fluttering sound, dishes rattled, and lights went on and off by themselves.

But the most dramatic events occurred one night when Mrs. C observed a ball of light hovering in the back hallway. Although frightened, she did not tell anyone of the experience. Later that evening, she and her husband were talking together in bed when an "apparition" appeared.

Mrs. C said she was suddenly aware of a "monklike" hooded figure about six feet tall and only three feet from the bed. The white form had no visible face, and simply stood by the bedside with its arms at its sides. It stood motionless for three or four minutes, during which time Mrs. C did not say a word to her husband.

The next day, when she mentioned it to him, he grudgingly admitted he had seen it too, but was uncomfortable in mentioning it.

Given the wide variety of images and incidents in this chapter so far, I would ask the reader if there was really any fundamental reason why Mrs. C's case could not be considered an alien contact case instead of a haunting. There is the ball of light floating in the house. An entity beside the bed. Birdlike sounds. Why could these not be viewed as alien contact effects?

One reason, I suppose, is that the witnesses themselves did not interpret it as an abduction or alien contact. They considered the effects more like those described by others as ghost-related. It seems logical, therefore, to wonder if the personal interest of the observer has some control over what is perceived. That is, if a person is interested or obsessed with UFOs, he or she will see aliens. If it's ghosts, it will be ghosts. If it is someone who is highly religious, it will be a religious figure.

Several years ago, a woman drowned near a town in northern Manitoba. Her grieving relatives travelled by boat to the spot where she drowned and some were shocked to see the figure of the Virgin Mary standing on the water among the reeds. If this was not a miracle as claimed, it would be tempting to suggest that the vision was a product of intense mental anguish and stress, combined with suggestible states of the witnesses. Is it possible that one's own mental state and belief system can determine the kind of paranormal event experienced? Would religious persons tend to see angels or other spiritual entities whereas the mind of someone with a more pragmatic approach to life would have to create a more secular image such as a flying saucer or aliens?

Tupper

Another abductee with an apparently documented implant is Tupper. He posted his story to the Net, too.

> In 1954, I turned six years old. I regard the experience as a dream. I was asleep and came to full awareness and my body seemed to be doing things on its own. I got up out of bed and went out the back door of the farmhouse. I walked around the back of the house and crossed a barbed wire fence and out into the freshly plowed field. As I walked I noticed the sky was alive with lights moving around. One in particular, a sphere of about eighteen inches in diameter, came down and landed in the furrow I was standing in. As I looked at it, it began to spin and make a hissing sound. I was so frightened that I overcame the force that was holding me and turned to run. As I turned I heard an explosion and felt pain in my left arm. I blacked out. I remember nothing after that point, but woke up some time later and was disoriented.

Tupper had some UFO sightings from time to time as he grew up, and was convinced that the UFOs were spacecraft from other planets. In 1971, he was in a car accident and injured his arm. On an x-ray, he saw a spot within his hand.

> I touched the spot and felt a small lump. I pointed it out to the doctor and he examined it and told me that it was just a small cyst and nothing to worry about. However, it brought back a memory of a long-forgotten "dream," namely that night I blacked out in the field. Then, in 1984, I was doing a little construction work and bought a stud finder that had a LED that would light up when you came across a nail. Basically it was a miniature metal detector. I remembered the "cyst" and ran the stud finder over it. The LED lit up. So much for the "cyst," as I know of none that have the property of metal.

Tupper didn't even consider the possibility that the metal object in his hand was simply a metal shaving from a long-forgotten accident. He was sure that the aliens had him under observation.

> In 1974 my fiancée and I were leaving my parents home when we saw another UFO. I signalled with my headlights and it started to descend towards us. My fiancée went into hysterics and that alone scared me and I got down on the horn in hopes that neighbourhood would come out and see the object. It seemed to detect the stress it was causing and ascended and left.

Tupper became obsessed with UFOs and aliens as a result of his experiences, and was convinced that he had been somehow selected or chosen to help others understand the aliens' plan. He found himself reading about advanced physics and became convinced he was able to construct a device that could alter the force of gravity. He became more and more certain of his important role in unravelling the alien agenda.

> From that time to now I have been in a state of wondering what my life has been all about. I feel as though I am in some small part just a key player in the unfolding of a new era for man. Some of you will take this lightly as entertaining, others will find it laughable. Those of you who I am to reach, I will, and those of you who seek flaws to exploit, will find them.

In other words, those who don't believe in Tupper's advanced mental ability and the reality of his experiences are "lost," but those who listen to him will be "saved."

Liam

One of the most fascinating persons I have met on the Internet is Liam. He was one of the "regulars" in an Internet chat group at one time, although he's not online as often anymore. He is very knowledgeable about the UFO scene and also well-read on a number of other subjects. We've been corresponding for some time, and I regard him as a friend.

Early in our correspondence, Liam described to me the experience which had changed his life. He's honest about it, straightforward, and seems as puzzled about it as anyone else.

Musicians are notorious for getting into mischief and my contemporary rock trio of the Sixties was no exception. We had been travelling from night club to night club for four years, but it seemed like forever. In keeping up front with you, we all drank, used a little grass, and I took LSD twice over a period of four years. By today's standards, we used very little. I was a draught beer and rum man myself.

My particular incident began at an Ontario night club on Saturday, January 10, 1970. The venue was a very old hotel with four floors and a solid roof canopy over the main entrance. The front desk was just inside on the left next to the staircase. Matt, our bass player, received a room on the second floor directly overlooking the canopy. My room was above his on the third floor. The drummer's room was down the hall from me. It reminded me of those old mansions you see in vampire movies, especially the second and third floors.

Shortly before show time I received word some friends would be in the crowd. That meant a party afterwards. We gathered in the bass player's room after one a.m. as planned, and began having a few drinks. The others elected to light up some hash but I had this feeling of foreboding and passed.

Our percussionist had an album he wanted us to hear and handed me the cover as he placed the record on the turntable. At the time, Black Panthers were in the news, and it became clear this album was a recording of their propaganda. As the album played, I had a sudden feeling that someone was in my room on the third floor. I jumped up and made a dash for the hotel entrance, nearly terrified.

When I passed the front desk, the night clerk yelled, "Where do you think you're going?" His voice sounded vicious and clearly said I may not leave the hotel. My next choice was getting to my room as fast as I could run. I remember the door exploding off its hinges from my impact as I slammed into it. Inside my room by the bathroom door stood a dark human figure about six feet tall. The momentum of my entrance carried me toward the intruder.

My next recollection was sitting on the bass player's bed one floor down and surrounded by police approximately forty-five minutes later. Band members informed me I went through my bedroom window and landed among chunks of glass on the canopy over the hotel entrance. I remember regaining consciousness and feeling extremely happy to see the police. I felt glad they came to rescue me. One officer returned to my room with me. Another police officer was in my room looking around when we got there and I noticed the door was on its hinges as if nothing had happened.

A detective informed me I was under arrest for possession of narcotics and attempted suicide. Police said the charges would never stick but he had to come up with something because of the commotion earlier. I spent from early Sunday morning till Thursday afternoon in the county jail. The nice way they treated me by comparison to the others was more disconcerting than stern treatment. The hotel owner picked me up in his black Cadillac and talked with me as though nothing had happened. We returned to the New Grand and the band members did not say a word about it. They seemed very nervous if not frightened. Thursday night's audience seemed very quiet and non-responsive to our music. They said nothing about the incident either.

Liam was completely baffled as to what had really happened. If he had simply caused a scene while blasted, the band would have been fired and their gig would have been cancelled. Why didn't he have any injuries after a fall through a window? What prompted him to dash to his room, and who was the intruder?

Curiously, shortly after the incident, his band was booked to perform at a nearby USAF ICBM base. Liam noted: "That gig went without a problem although some personnel acted very weird when I was around." As for the figure in his room: "I can say now that the human form in my room that January morning in 1970 could best be described as a man in black — a MIB."

Liam's accident is listed by the local police department as an attempted suicide. But he notes: "I can sincerely tell you suicide is not an option I have considered at any time during my life."

The imagery of Liam's experience stayed with him. He thought about UFOs enough that he actually recorded and released a song based on a UFO encounter.

While Liam admits that he had been using some drugs around that time, his conscious memory clearly is in conflict with others' versions of the events. He has always wondered if he had simply hallucinated the entire event, and recently told me that he now believes he did in fact have a bad trip of some kind brought on by his drug use.

Yasmine

Yasmine's story had been mentioned to me by some of my associates, and I had not had a chance to talk with her until this book was in production. Her experience has all the earmarks of alien abduction, but some elements shed some light on the line between reality and surreality.

Yasmine's alien encounter literally occurred immediately following a severe emotional shock. She had been at the bedside of her sister, who passed away after a long battle with cancer. After comforting her brother-in-law and her nieces and nephews, she started the long drive home.

> I had approximately eighty miles to drive home, and it was 9:30 p.m. I was extremely tired and emotionally drained, and I am aware of the implications of this to my story. I was *so* tired …
>
> I stopped at a rest stop on the interstate about twenty miles from my home. I had only just shut my eyes … and I was not in my body any longer … but out of it and observing it with another "being." I was watching myself sitting at the wheel of my car, with my head back, eyes closed, mouth wide open … and some other beings were shining a very white light down my

throat. The beings were in a craft that was ahead and above my car. The being that I was with was telling me about the lessons that I had to learn .... and that I would get cancer, too. They told me over and over about "the lessons that I had to learn." The being that I was standing by had very soft, dark brown skin, almost velvet feeling.... I don't remember touching it/him/her but remember the very soft feeling of, well, suede. Suddenly, I was back inside myself and I was starting the car. I seemed almost numb. I don't think my hands left the steering wheel all of that time.

Yasmine didn't actually see a UFO, she only visualized one in her dreamlike state. Was it, therefore, "real?" What makes the case more curious is that the alien's prediction came true. Yasmine was, in fact, diagnosed with cancer, and while she is in remission, she knows the emotional strain it has placed on her.

Further, Yasmine discovered an "implant" in her ear, again suggestive of alien abduction and tending to support the possibility that there was more to her "dream" than might be thought.

Recently [early 1999], I found something in my left ear-lobe. I can tell when an object is foreign to my body ... this was!!! It was charcoal-coloured, very dark, glossy, had a tiny yellow stripe at each end. I only wear very small gold hoops in my ears and leave them in all of the time, through swimming, sleeping, bathing, everything. I never wear earrings with backs on them. This thing was not from an earring. My reaction was one of shock when I saw this thing — and I am a very non-emotional, critical-thinking person. I looked at it, and started to examine it. I applied pressure on it with a fingernail. I even thought that it looked like a seed ... or an insect egg ... Yuck! It broke, and looked to me like it was hollow. I started to cry, but I don't know the reason for the emotional feeling. Every time I talk about it I get very emotional.

Yasmine sent the pieces of the "implant" to a UFO expert who specializes in such things. However, she was less than impressed with his attitude.

At first, he was very pleasant. But then he stopped answering my e-mails, and then seemed to become impatient when I prodded for answers. Did the samples contain cells, what kind of material was the object made from? glass? plastic? metal? What? I was very insistent that I be informed often about what he found out about the pieces. Initially, he said that they looked very weird. "Very weird," those were his words.

But then the situation took a more bizarre turn. As Yasmine fretted because of this expert's unresponsiveness, she mentioned her earlobe implant to another person, who happened to be in a position to test it himself. When she wrote to the implant expert and told him she wanted hers back so she could let someone else examine it, his reaction was less than enthusiastic.

This expert sent me an e-mail, telling me not to communicate with this other person. Of all the nerve! Not in this lifetime will someone tell me who to talk with!

After a series of bitter exchanges, her "implant" was finally made available to a researcher who easily identified it as an insect egg.

What this case shows me is that the lack of professionalism within ufology is greatly hindering the advance of knowledge in the field. What's worse, witnesses and abductees who are turning to ufologists for help are being met with misguided enthusiastic efforts to bolster belief in aliens but at the same time are failing to get adequate support and help in dealing with their experiences.

Yasmine now is certain that her dreamlike imagery of her abduction encounter was a dream after all. This is supported by the memory of standing outside her body, one indication psychologists view as indicative of dreaming. She admits having read some UFO books and seeing some UFO-related TV programs, so it's possible her dream memories originated within her subconscious. I would ask, though, why these particular images surfaced during her stressful state. Why did she see aliens, and not, for example, her sister's spirit?

Bob

Given that how we perceive our world may influence our perception, we can also wonder how outside influences can affect our actions. If a person were paranoid, for example, then every simple element of his or her life could be interpreted as further proof that *they* were watching or controlling.

Some UFO literature is based on the view that a major government or military conspiracy is in place to cover-up whatever evidence is around. In some cases, this is carried to the extreme, such as the belief that clandestine lease agreements exist between the US government and alien races wishing to use underground military bases. Others insist that NASA knows all about the Face on Mars and deliberately destroyed their own space probe to prevent it from relaying the truth back to Earth.

Such stories aren't always new or original. Conspiracy theories go back much further than JFK. Some conspiracy buffs have argued that Hitler created a new world order and still rules the Earth today from a secret base in South America (with full knowledge and co-operation from the American government, of course). Others insist that cures for cancer have already been discovered and that the oil companies are suppressing information about cars that run on a water-based fuel. And AIDS was created by government researchers in a germ warfare plot.

Since conspiracies are largely unprovable, there is usually no way to convince a conspiracy buff that his or her belief is unjustified. If someone is convinced the CIA is monitoring his phone calls, there is no way to reassure that person that they are not. (It is, of course, possible that the CIA *is* monitoring the phone for some other national security reason, but that's another issue. For example, it has been alleged that a Canadian UFO contactee group had some members under RCMP investigation because of their association with a terrorist organization in the 1970s.)

In terms of UFOs, the major conspiracy perpetrators are the infamous Men in Black (MIB). In the 1950s, a flying saucer buff claimed that he had been visited several times by ominous persons who dressed completely in black and drove black Cadillacs with dark tinted windows. These MIBs threatened the saucerologist and suggested that he had gotten too close to the "truth" about the saucers. They pressured him to abandon his saucer hobby or face dire consequences.

In recent years, diligent UFO researchers have found convincing evidence that the original MIB story was likely just a fabrication. Despite this, since the 1950s, there have been dozens more reports of MIBs stalking and terrorizing UFO investigators around the world. The general theory is that MIBs are agents for a clandestine worldwide organization that is somehow involved in propagating UFO flights. In recent years, the MIB legend has been given new life in the TV series "The X-Files," including one hilarious episode where game show host Alex Trebek was revealed to be a MIB operative.

The MIB concept is accepted at face value by many ufologists. Very few actually have claimed encounters with such archetypal figures, yet the stories live on.

Several years ago, I was greeted after one of my lectures by Bob, a student who was very keen on UFOs. Like so many buffs I have met, he asked me question after question about popular UFO stories ranging from secret underground bases to cover-ups to captured aliens. He was well-read on many of the issues, and could recite many of the cases verbatim. He continued to contact me occasionally and present me with his own theories as to the nature of UFOs.

But I was more than surprised one day when he presented me with a notebook full of his writings on the subject, including many accounts of his own UFO contact experiences. He had even documented his conversations with others interested in UFOs (including his meetings with me) and some correspondence with a social scientist at another Canadian university who told Bob in confidence that he had worked at NASA on a secret project that was studying the remains of aliens who had crashed on Earth.

Crashed saucer stories have been with us for fifty years, and the focus of this book is not about this very involved and complex topic. What was most interesting in this context was how Bob's own belief in a conspiracy was enhanced or perhaps verified by his conversations with others. So, it was not surprising that his own UFO experiences were interpreted by him as part of a much larger contact scenario. The question is whether or not there is any truth behind the conspiracy allegations.

Here is a sample of Bob's experiences and thoughts:

On August 16, 1981, I was alone in my basement bedroom at the home of my parents. At about 10:30 p.m., I was listening to heavy metal rock music on my stereo. Suddenly, violent banging began on my bedroom door. My mother and brother confronted me, demanding that I turn down the volume on the stereo. We all got into an argument during which their eyes "changed" and took on cold, glassy stares. Their temperaments also altered and they became violently hostile towards me. It appeared to me that someone else seemed to be in control of their actions, and I became confused and somewhat frightened. At that point, I shut and locked my bedroom door against these "strangers" who were threatening to have me physically removed from the premises.

It did not occur to Bob that perhaps his music was simply annoying. However, he got the message and decided to leave the house and drive to the family cottage where he could be undisturbed.

As I drove, I listened to the radio. Suddenly, I heard a song unlike any I had ever heard before. To put it mildly, it induced in me a semi-religious mystical state, brought on, I believe, by the consciousness-altering quality of the music being performed. I continued to listen to the program, overwhelmed by what I just heard.

After midnight, another disc jockey started her own program. As I drove, I noticed that I was the only car on the road as far as the eye could see in either direction. The disc jockey opened the microphone on a telephone caller who excitedly reported that she had just seen a UFO over north Winnipeg. Since I was about twenty-five miles north of Winnipeg, I thought nothing of the news. However, several moments later, casually glancing out my driver's side window to check the mirror, I first glimpsed the UFO.

My immediate impression was that it was huge. It was about 150 feet from top to bottom and was comprised mainly of what appeared to be a mass of long, slender, glowing cables, bunched together in the middle and hovering suspended in midair. On closer inspection, what I actually saw was a central core from which were emanating long and slender filament-like projections that gave off an extremely bright, neon-like glow of a luminous orange-red colour. The filaments had to be at least fifty feet in length each and numbered about two dozen, twelve pointing up and twelve pointing down, giving the object a "fibre optic" aspect or, better yet, a jellyfish with spikes. The "tentacles" were arrayed equidistant from another and formed a conical shape beneath the central mass, and an inverted conical shape above it.

The UFO was about a quarter mile away at the time and was hovering about 100 to 150 feet above the ground. It was situated over a flat, wide open farmer's field and there were no trees for miles around. It was not connected to the ground in any way, nor was it being transported by any other means. A series of hydroelectric towers were nearby and I hypothesized that the UFO must be drawing power off them in an attempt to regenerate its own power supply that I reasoned must be electromagnetically based.

So that I could watch it more clearly, I pulled the car onto the shoulder after I negotiated a curve. I got out, but left the car engine running in case I had to make a fast getaway. I had lost sight of the UFO, but regained sight of it as it moved majestically across a point directly in line with the nearly full Moon and swept across my field of vision as if in some type of surreal dream. At this point, it began to draw nearer to the highway and was maintaining its height at about 100 to 150 feet above the ground.

As he watched, the UFO drew closer, and Bob made "contact" with its occupants:

Dimly outlined from the glow inside the portals of the central mass were two or three figures whose features were not discernible but whose heads and shoulders indicated that they were clearly humanoid in shape. I raised my hand with an open palm, in the manner of the inscriptions on the plates on Pioneer 10 as a sign of peace, friendship, and goodwill. The UFO responded first with a flash of red light and then a green one from outside the hull. I had a strong sense that the UFO intended me to follow it, but I wasn't exactly sure how to go about this. Furthermore, a possible abduction of myself was the farthest thing from my mind, although had the thought entered my mind, I would have welcomed it.

Bob also has had several encounters with the infamous Men in Black during his life. These are said to be alien or government operatives secretly working to annoy or otherwise disrupt UFO witnesses' lives, obfuscating the "truth." Once, Bob believed he was abducted into a black automobile and remembered only regaining consciousness after being "rolled out" as it sped away. Another MIB chased him in his car at high speed down an isolated highway.

What could possibly have happened to Bob that night? Could he really have been the victim of a rural chase by a MIB because of his close encounter with the chandelier-style UFO? Why didn't anyone else see such a spectacle that night?

As for the "changes" in the personalities of his mother and brother, could it have been something as simple as his playing his heavy metal rock music too loud? (Not being a heavy metal fan, I'd have to be sympathetic to this possibility.) There may be something to this viewpoint.

Vladimir Simosko, a musicologist at the University of Manitoba, specializes in the study of how music affects us and our environment. When I asked him for assistance in interpreting Bob's case, he immediately pointed to the heavy metal music as a problem.

"People can be greatly influenced by music," Simosko says. "In the case of heavy metal rock music, it is not the content which is necessarily the issue, but the beat and volume. Our brains can only take so much of it before we are adversely affected. I'd have to say that Bob was likely in a very suggestible mental state at the time and he came under the detrimental influence of the music, which was driving, overpowering and very controlling."

In other words, apart from any need for spiritual development or confusion in his life, Bob's UFO experience and the bizarre behaviour of his family might have had something to do with the music, too.

However, I'm not sure the recording industry would agree.

Richmond, BC

With the proliferation of UFO-related Internet sites, it is becoming much easier for people to report their UFO sightings. At the click of a mouse, you can upload your UFO encounter story to a variety of UFO organizations. Unfortunately, most of these are simply run by teenagers or inexperienced buffs who have a talent for Web design. In reality, witnesses who report their UFO experiences to such groups do not contribute to the true worldwide co-ordinated effort to collect and study the UFO phenomenon. On the other hand, the simple reporting of a UFO experience is undoubtedly therapeutic and beneficial to the witness, so there *is* a certain value to doing so.

While scanning a few such UFO Web pages, I found the following case report. Although no UFO was seen and there is nothing in the story itself that might indicate that UFOs were involved, the witnesses believed their experience was an alien abduction of some kind. This alone indicates how strongly ingrained the alien abduction story is within our culture.

Of course, since the story was posted anonymously, there is no way to follow it up.

I'd rather not say my name for obvious reasons, but here's what happened. I live in a fishing village called Steveston, which is in Richmond, British Columbia. At the shore, you can see an island which is about 100 – 200 feet across and acts as a wave barrier. It's only about 200 feet across at the most. One side is covered in trees and the other is covered in sand and brush.

On May 22, 1996, a friend and I went over there in a rowboat we had borrowed. When we got there, we hiked around for a bit, then sat down to eat some crackers.

The next thing we knew, it was nighttime and it was raining. We had gotten to the island at about noon, so obviously there was something wrong. We immediately got up and ran for the boat — about a five-minute run. But when we got there, the boat was gone, leaving only the oars.

We knew that at the other side of the island was a rock bridge that was only crossable at low tide. We were too tired to run, so it was a good half-hour walk. We managed to cross the bridge just before it became covered and impassable.

At first, we thought that we had just fainted or something, but after reading that one of the common elements of an abduction is missing time, we concluded that that was what had happened to us. We feel that we can write this here because there is no way of tracing us and we don't want to have this let out. We feel that we would have many hassles and be called liars if we did. Thank you for listening.

Angie

One of the most disturbing aspects of the alien abduction milieu is the reaction of medical professionals. With only a few exceptions, UFO abductions are treated by such professionals very lightly and considered little more than mental aberrations. The trouble with this is that since abductions are being reported in greater numbers each year, ignoring them is doing little good.

The situation becomes more complicated when we look at how those few physicians and psychologists actually are treating abductees. One case that was brought to my attention brings this point home and creates a sense of uneasiness when one considers its broader implications. It involves a woman who says it was her *psychiatrist*, not her, who was convinced she had an alien encounter. This, to me, was a completely unexpected turn of events.

In the fall of 1986, Angie began to experience fatigue and stress that appeared to be related to her working two jobs and attending university concurrently. She quit her jobs and decided to apply for Unemployment Insurance, which required her to obtain a medical certificate attesting to her illness. In October, she went to a psychologist for treatment of the stress and to obtain a signature on the medical document.

The intake psychologist advised Angie that she needed a psychiatrist, not a psychologist, to sign the form. She asked Angie about her stress and what she did to cope with it. Angie truthfully told her that during periods of high stress, she would "switch to auto-pilot and keep going." Angie claimed that the psychologist interpreted this to mean that she "had another personality" and urged her to see psychiatrist for treatment of multiple personality disorder.

Angie said that when she met this psychiatrist, she "obtained a diagnosis from [him] that I was suffering from a condition known as multiple personality disorder" and began to receive treatment from him for this condition.

She noted:

> During the course of my treatment ... I became convinced by [him] that my parents had sexually abused me, which caused my multiple personality disorder. I initially denied having been sexually abused by my parents, but as a result of [his] influence and my failure to maintain my convictions in the face of [his] insistence, I began to confess untrue allegations that my parents had sexually abused me as a child.
>
> During weekly psychotherapy sessions ... he would constantly question me about having any memories or dreams about incest or sexual abuse by my father or any other people when I was a child. [He] also convinced me that all of the bad habits such as smoking and consuming alcohol that I developed after the commencement of therapy were the result of a different personality that had been dormant in my mind, waiting to take over my body.
>
> After taking therapy with [him], I began experiencing depression, weakness, headaches, and physical responses attributed to the effects of hypnotic therapy.

Angie became intoxicated one night and says she was sexually assaulted by a man. She was admitted to a psychiatric ward by her psychiatrist, who "dismissed my sexual assault as a form of memory transference." She later said:

> Throughout the course of my admission [to the hospital], [the psychiatrist] conducted hypnotic psychotherapy on me. I subsequently became convinced that all my dreams were flashbacks of real events. This form of therapy caused me such psychological and emotional damage that I became completely dependent on [the psychiatrist].

Angie was prescribed Halcyon by the psychiatrist, and began experiencing violent episodes, again interpreted as another personality, not as side effects of the drug itself. At one point, she lost consciousness and was told by her psychiatrist that she had experienced a "MPD trance."

More serious was Angie's charge that:

> While I remained in [the psychiatrist's] care, [he] refused to allow me contact with my family because [he] took the position that exposure to unrepentant abusers would put me further into danger of being abused by them. I had never experienced sexual abuse at the hands of my family prior to this point in time, but I was so influenced by [him] that I did not question [his] advice in this regard.

Then, this psychiatrist terminated his involvement with her. Angie's dependence reached a crisis point, and she "was completely addicted" to her medication. During the next two years, Angie sought additional help and was "able to beat my drug addiction and overcome my emotional instability on my own" without the aid of any medication.

Through further therapy, Angie said that:

> I discovered that I did not, at any time, have multiple personality disorder. I discovered that my emotional and physical problems prior to the treatment I suffered at the hands of the [psychiatrist] was caused by stress and nothing more. I also discovered that I had never been sexually abused by my parents or anyone else and that my belief that I had been abused was caused by the effects of

the hypnotic psychotherapy, suggestions implanted in my mind by the [psychiatrist].

I had been following the literature regarding MPD (or as it is known today, Dissociative Identity Disorder) and its relation to UFOs. I did not expect to be drawn into the debate until Angie called me to tell me her story. She said that among her "false memories" of events in her past life revealed through hypnosis with the psychiatrist were indications that she had been violated by alien beings on board their spacecraft. She said (and alleged in a later court appearance) that her psychiatrist helped her "remember" being abducted aboard alien spacecraft where she was, among other things, impregnated and made pregnant with an alien hybrid baby.

Angie said that on a later visit to the ship she could recall being shown her "child" and wondered what was going to happen to it. She said that after her psychiatrist returned from a conference in the United States, he told her that he had been educated regarding such creatures. According to what he told Angie, the alien children are placed on Earth and grow up to become clandestine citizens, even to the point of blending in with the community, holding regular jobs.

Indeed, some MPD experts refer to alien abductions and suggest there may, in fact, be a connection between alien abductions and satanic abuse. One expert noted he himself was unsure of how to treat patients who thought they had been abducted. He noted that:

> Expressing doubt damages the treatment alliance; whether failing to express doubt reinforces a delusional disorder, I don't know. (Ross, C. 1994. *The Osiris Complex*, p. 149.)

In other words, the psychiatrist himself didn't know what to say to an alien abductee in his care. If this is an example of the lack of understanding of alien abductees' stories held by the top medical professions with specialties in this field, is it any wonder that there is so much confusion and incomplete information offered to therapists for their treatment or counselling of abductees?

Angie is suing her former psychiatrist for negligence in his treatment of her and, ultimately, for his deviation from medical practice in order to further his own gains in developing theories and treatment for MPD.

Who do we believe? The medical professional with an outstanding reputation for research — or his patient, who may or may not have multiple personalities?

Soon-Yi

As word got around on the Internet that I was preparing a book on abductions, I received more and more personal testimonies from sincere individuals. Another whose story I trust is Soon-Yi, a woman who earnestly wants to understand what happened to her. She was very kind to offer her story to me in the hope of both aiding my research and helping others understand their own experiences.

Soon-Yi said that she had no interest in UFOs before 1982. At that time, she and her significant other were driving and saw

a horseshoe-shaped group of lights that flew very low over the car at the same time that we passed underneath some power cables, scaring the pair of us. The thing matched our speed and ran parallel with us for some time along the road. From the side it was a big, bright, egg-shaped light with a faint set of smaller coloured lights rotating around inside. I guess it was between fifty and one hundred feet away and the whole thing was at least the size of the length of our car.

The car suddenly acted as if it had run out of gas and died along with the lights. We had an argument as to who would look under the hood and then got out together. I decided to keep my eyes on this thing as it hovered silently over the field.

The next thing I knew was that we were both back in the car, with the engine running, lights on, and the craft was still hovering. I did not notice this gap in my memory until later. We basically felt very quiet and subdued, for want of a better explanation, and just drove off as fast as possible. We never spoke the rest of the way, or I do not think we did. We arrived home not at 10 p.m. as expected, but 1:30 – 1:45 a.m.!

The following day, I had a severe nose bleed. I've never had one before or since. From that night on, I have been generally in ill health. I have been doing drawings, writing, and typing. I had a very bad burn mark on my chest which has scarred, and a "V" shaped incision on my back. The rest of my medical problems are too much to catalogue here, but I was fine before. My lifestyle, eating habits, and personality have completely changed. For three years, I was afraid to go outside.

In 1988, Soon-Yi was hypnotized by a therapist specializing in UFO abductions. She recalled that:

> As the hypnotist started to put me under, a beam of light appeared in the room, the video and audio equipment malfunctioned and spun around, the skeptic who came to observe was pinned to the chair with such force as to leave claw marks on his arms, and all the clocks in the house stopped.
>
> I never got hypnotized, but they did bring in a psychic investigator.
>
> A UFO researcher tried showing me a TV movie titled *The Betty and Barney Hill Story*, but I became completely hysterical, and he had to call the hypnotist on the phone to try to calm me down. I felt a flood of memories come back and a lot of disjointed memories slid into place. I have never seen the film or any other UFO film like it to this date. I can't.
>
> All I can remember is being in a room with a large perspex-type pedestal in the centre. I remember being led to it. I didn't struggle (I don't know why not) and I was laid down on the thing. I remember sensing the whole procedure was clinical, like the tagging, weighing, and measuring of a wild animal. The "greys" never spoke out loud, just telepathically, and there was a taller, blond-haired person. I don't know what happened, only that I get very upset if I try to remember. I won't undergo hypnosis as I feel that will spoil or taint the result. When I am ready to face it, I will remember.

When asked if her experience was just in her imagination, Soon-Yi replied:

> There were two of us. Also, I have written things I have no knowledge of. I want to know how come what happened to me is almost identical to what has happened all around the world. That is too common to be a coincidence, if you ask me. Life was fine before. If the experience was because of a trauma or something that happened twenty years ago, why did it occur just then? And then, there's my real medical problems. How would that fit in with a psychological disorder?

Soon-Yi's lucid and rational analysis of her experience is very impressive. She raises some very good points in her question and answer section. For example, if it really was a mental blackout, why did it affect both of them?

A better question would be to ask why Soon-Yi is so upset at the thought of remembering what happened that night. Why should she be so anxious over a simple thing such as the car engine cutting out? Why would she "imagine" (if that's what it was) the abduction scenario, if she hadn't been that interested in UFOs before the experience? It would make sense in the case of a UFO buff, but why a disinterested person?

Ida

A few weeks after hearing me on the radio in June 1993, a woman called me and said she wanted to share her experiences with a sympathetic ear. At her insistence, I met her at a park in south Winnipeg. She did not want her husband to know she had contacted me because "he doesn't believe in this stuff."

Ida claimed to have had a wide variety of paranormal experiences. The most vivid and puzzling of these was an encounter with a red ball of light in 1985 or 1986. She had been sleeping in her bedroom in south Winnipeg (her house has since been demolished) and was awakened in the middle of the night by what she thought was a fire in the living room.

She walked out of her bedroom and saw a glowing ball of red light, motionless and about two feet off the floor. It was approximately two feet in diameter and not more than fifteen feet away from her. To Ida, the most puzzling aspect of the experience was that immediately after discovering the ball of light, she turned around and went back to bed. She was astounded that a person who witnessed something so incredible, especially if at first it was thought to have been a fire, would ignore it and go back to sleep. Ida insisted that she had not been dreaming and that the experience had been real.

Ida also recalled on several other occasions, when she saw a beam of white light "shooting out of the bedroom window" towards a star-like point of light in the night sky:

May 24: I woke up with a brilliant light on my face, only to see a beam of white light going through my closed bedroom window to what looked like a far-off, low-set star. I was terrified. But I do remember falling asleep within minutes, which seems strange. This bothered me for quite a few days afterwards.

Ida said she also has had numerous occasions on which she "felt" or "sensed" a presence nearby or behind her. On at least one occasion, she felt a presence near her bed. When she was young, Ida said, her bed sometimes "lifted right off the floor." On another occasion, she felt that she was somehow being "sucked out" of her body by an unseen force.

Summer 1991: I would awake from a brilliant white light, terrified. Something unseen to the naked eye was pulling me (like a vacuum) but it didn't seem physical. It seemed more spiritual. I was aware of everything in the room. It was clear to see [things in the room]. This [unseen] force was trying to draw me out past the bedroom door. I was panic-stricken and fighting for my life. This force almost won and I think the only thing that stopped it was that I thought of Christ and at that moment, it was over. The second time is the same but with a much greater force which I could barely fight off. If it were to happen a third time I would probably win. It takes every bit of strength you have, and then some, to overcome it.

Other experiences seem to relate more directly to aliens and UFOs. Again, we see that religious belief has been grafted onto more modern ufology. Once Christ has been invoked as a saviour from persecution, there is a greater sense of safety.

Ida's memories and images show a marked interweaving of concepts and ideas. One night, she dreamed about "aliens and babies," but noted that she had been reading Budd Hopkins' book *Intruders* that evening. Clearly, Ida's attraction to such popular reading material caused her some anxiety and may have influenced her memories as well.

May 13: I dreamt I was in a library and went to go home but couldn't find home. I ended up on a road outside of town in sight of buildings. I looked up and saw a UFO diving for me. I thought, "Oh, no, not again!" and said to myself, "I've got to get out of here!" The next thing I knew, my body couldn't move. I went down on the road, and that was it. Then I woke up out of my dream, knowing that they took a skin sample. I was slightly aware of being given a message.

Here we see her having a fairly common "getting lost" dream, but her imagery injects the now-familiar abduction motifs and procedures. Are her dreams simply "contaminated" by popular ufology, or is there more here, somewhere?

Ida has sought some counselling to try to understand her experiences. She has had a practising hypnotist try to uncover more details and memories of her experiences, particularly the incident involving the red ball of light, which still troubles her for some reason.

Penelope

Penelope came to me shortly after her move to Winnipeg from California. She said she was in contact with spiritual beings called Reticulites, with whom she was co-operating in their work on Earth. Penelope was hesitant to speak with me and show me her diary, mostly because she claimed she had been "abused" by members of a UFO group in California and did not know if I was "any different." After a few positive meetings and building of trust, she shared certain sections of her diary with me.

Penelope, like many other abductees, felt she had been selected by the aliens for a very important mission. Hers was a bit more curious than most, as she seemed to be an *ex-officio* Terran bureaucrat invited to participate in alien board meetings. Not only that, but her religious UFO connection went one step further than that of Ida.

June 25, 1994   3:45 a.m.
A long time ago, I volunteered. As the leader to my world, I volunteered to help the Earth make a transition. Now that I am ready, and the people around me are ready, I feel like I need a holiday. If I can complete this job, I can go home.

I have to begin by remembering why I came here — not necessarily to remember the exact job but to remember the feelings and the ambition of the quest. I know my people are proud and I can't take any longer than I've had to. This is my job.

It's very important for me to keep a record of these experiences in order to bring them to a new level — a new consciousness. About forty-five minutes ago, I chaired a meeting with the Reticulites, a group of very active travellers.

They are somewhat enlightened, in a different way than we are. They have a language of their own — untranslatable, as all languages are. The meeting was not the first one I've attended, although it was definitely the first meeting that I was aware of, in a semi-conscious, meditative state. (I knew I was not dreaming; I knew I was not completely in my body.) I've been told a "light body" takes over. My full understanding of a "light body" is that indeed I feel heavier than [when] I am fully in or when I am consciously on all (most) levels working/living/experiencing most here on Earth in my physical body.

Contents of the meeting included the "jar incident," the 1967 (?) crash of some sort, raising Earth's consciousness in order to increase visitation, and places to visit/land. I'm still having certain difficulties with the concept, but I believe I did a fine job.

I went to the eleventh floor to negotiate. I protected all who were there. There were quite a lot of them. At first they all seemed to be talking at once. Then I understood; I mean, they became clear. Their patterns of talking all at once perhaps did not change, but I did.

Before the meeting, I went to Sossanda, whom some believe to be Jesus. I believe this, too. I think I had words with him. I feel uncomfortable about this.

Penelope's uneasiness with her alien hosts in some ways parallelled her relationship with humans on Earth. She seemed not to "fit in" with terrestrial societal norms, and enjoyed her visits with the aliens.

I feel like an alien in my own environment. It is a very separate-type feeling. It just occurred to me when I was upstairs. I was in the kitchen and the house was dark. I opened the cupboard and took out the ice tea mix. I went back downstairs. Sometimes my parents come downstairs. It is like they are visiting me. I'm lonely, but I don't want them to visit me.

Penelope joined a UFO group and went with them on some "field trips." They would travel to an area where there had been some reported UFOs and then try to psychically communicate with the aliens in an attempt to invite them to land. Or, they would simply go to observe the saucers' aerial displays.

However, Penelope encountered something which jaded her towards UFO investigators. She was completely unprepared for their unprofessional behaviour.

Last night, there were a few good moments in the field work. The group shows promise in our ability to work together. There were some moments where I felt, as the only woman in the group, excluded. This, I feel, is potentially harmful to the group and the work we do, and also to our credibility.

The first time during the evening where I felt this was with a man named Bill. I was standing with my knapsack on my back and from behind, he took the waist strap in his hands and brought it around front. I took it out of his hands and told him what it was for. The second time I was sitting again with my back turned and he poked my back several times with his finger. I turned around and he smiled.

I am not something to play with!

My therapist, who was with us, also contributed to this by making comments such as "who's going to hold the girl's hand?" and using the phrase "being in mixed company" as an excuse for his inability to tell a joke. I want to be treated as an equal. I want to be treated like everyone else. As for the joke: if I could not tell a joke in mixed company, mixed being male/female, black/white or whatever, I would question if that joke was even worth telling.

I am upset that this is work I have prepared myself for and I'm still preparing myself for. If this group does not work out, I know I will be involved again in the future. This group not working out will be a disappointment. I will be very upset, as I am now.

I am really angry.

I could not apologize to Penelope for her treatment by the UFO investigators. I have met several UFO "experts" whose demeanour was less than professional. Of course, with no code of practice or formal educating body for UFO research, is it any wonder that anyone can claim to be a "ufologist," whatever that means?

Within her abduction memories, Penelope was experiencing an intimate relationship with Sossanda and the other aliens. Her sensitivity to her experiences had been completely ignored or overlooked by the others in the UFO group, including her therapist.

Daphne

One of the nicest persons I have met online is Daphne. A former church secretary, she readily admits that her experiences were rather unusual. On one level, the reader can view her story with a skeptical view and find it too bizarre for serious consideration. But from a humanistic standpoint, her descriptive narrative carries with it a great deal of emotion and pathos making it all the more credible. Because her story is very personal, I have altered it to be as discreet as possible.

Daphne had a good relationship with her boyfriend. They shared a keen interest in UFOs and sometimes went on sky watches together. One night, they travelled to a farm and camped out under the stars in an effort to invoke a UFO encounter. They were rewarded with a number of objects "playing" with them, darting from one side of the sky to the other. Both Daphne and her boyfriend believed that the aliens were somehow communicating with them.

Several days later, they had an argument which resulted in Daphne walking out of their house and trying to clear her thoughts. She was very upset and hoped that the fresh air would help her calm down.

As I walked I looked into and across the skies thinking that they were out there somewhere. I was wishing they would show up, and somewhat insulted that they didn't. When I got back to the house Ned and I talked. I decided I would leave anyway around 4:00 a.m., as I didn't like driving late at night.

I decided to take a shower so I would be ready for work when I arrived in town. About halfway through my shower I suddenly felt a presence and sensed I was being observed. The feeling was quite strong and upset me. I can remember thinking, "they are here," but paid no attention to the thought. I looked out the windows as I felt it so strong. I thought maybe a person was around Ned's house. At first I said nothing to Ned as I didn't want him to think I was flipping out, even though I had learned to trust my intuition.

After we went to bed, I remember seeing a bright white light. I wondered what it was but then decided it was the neighbours pulling into their driveway which was maybe five hundred feet away from our house.

We started to make love. After a short while, I suddenly felt a presence in the corner of the room. Then I felt someone else in my mind. I also at that time got a mental image of some beings.

It was of the greys. It seemed like a whole group of them, but two stood out in particular. One who was taller and behind the other. He was familiar to me, but at the time I didn't know he was familiar to me. He was very stern and serious, like he had to get a job done and his juniors better do it and he was going to ensure it happened.

I experienced that for a few seconds. I then adjusted to it and thought that it was a really cool way to communicate. Pure communication. No worry as to if I would understand. Words were not really important.

Then I became angry. I was angry that the being who was in my mind was using my mind to perceive emotions and sensations. It was then I started to communicate back and was totally aware of what I was communicating. I told them I was getting mental pictures of more than one observing me (it was a whole group). I felt like a guinea pig and got even more pissed off as now I was on display while trying to have sex with my boyfriend and they were doing this. I communicated to them that I really was angry and if they wanted to watch they could, but I was still ahead of the game as they couldn't do this or experience it for themselves. So, to hell with them! I then continued on with what I was doing. I had pictures in my mind of them just watching and the one in my head was sensing my emotions and sensations.

Apparently, the aliens do not or cannot experience emotions as we know them, and were using Daphne as a conduit to channel these feelings to them as an experiment. She continued to regularly sense their presence, and often expressed her anger at them for using her in such a violatory manner.

I awoke one night and they were there. I finally had it and got very angry with them and told them if they could not arrive in front of me with their bodies that it was very unethical and they should leave as it wasn't okay to do this to me. I told them that was the only way I would continue communicating. Of course, I would have died of shock if they would have done that!

Daphne was also very concerned that the aliens would abduct their child. She brought her to bed with her and spent many sleepless nights in an effort to protect the baby from them.

Finally, Daphne entered into counselling to help cope with stresses and emotionally upsetting incidents in her life. In doing so, however, she uncovered even more troubling images.

> Through counselling, I learned that as a baby, I had been abducted. They would come in the dark and take me for awhile and bring me back. One time in particular they took me somewhere in the night. We were outside. They laid me down and they all went off to the side and were in a heavy discussion and I knew it was about me and what to do with me. I remembered one of the greys telling me I was chosen to help them and I didn't object.

The most important point, however, is that Daphne is certain that the aliens' intentions are benevolent, even if their methods leave something to be desired. She noted: "As far as I recall at this time, I have never been hurt."

Over time, Daphne has learned to adapt to the presence of her haranguers. They have been troubling, but not completely so.

> I have changed some of my opinions and don't feel so threatened anymore by these beings, whoever they are. They may not communicate much anymore due to not wanting to upset me. I haven't figured that out yet. Or maybe it isn't time yet.
>
> I want to get back into communication with them. They came to me last night, which they haven't done for a long time. I think they came to request some sort of help.

Gary Stollman

A discussion of the varying characteristics of UFO abductees would be incomplete without a note about Gary Stollman. His belief in a far-reaching conspiracy led him to invade the set of an American TV show and issue on-air demands. What's most interesting is his post to a UFO news group, detailing his ideas about how aliens were involved in the conspiracy. Gary is still active in ufology, and is still of the opinion that alien forces are in control of not only his life, but yours as well.

I asked Gary if I could quote him at length, and he gave me his blanket permission to do so.

"What does it matter?" he shrugged.

My name is Gary Stollman, and I am the person who in 1987 jumped onto the live set of KNBC in Los Angeles, California, and held a toy gun to the head of TV Consumer Advocate David Horowitz and forced him to read a statement about how the CIA and aliens had replaced my family and friends with clones, and forced me illegally into many mental hospitals.

In that statement I had Horowitz read were examples of information I had garnered about UFOs, which have been verified to me since then by independent sources. One of these concerned the status of so-called "Hangar 18," the now-infamous place in ufology where bodies of the alien crash at Roswell were taken.

The first time I knew something was wrong in my family was when I started receiving crazy phone calls from my dad asking me if I remembered some hotel with crystal staircases and such — as if we had ever been there, which we hadn't! I knew then that my father was being forced to say that against his will. It did not occur to me that if he was being held prisoner somewhere somehow, who was running the store? My mom's calls also got bizarre to the point where I did not know what the hell was going on, but knew that something was fucked up big time! I didn't know what to do. I knew the phones had to be tapped, but visits to the local phone company office just produced more of the same kind of bullshit. It came to a head when I called up my "mom" in a frenzy and demanded my passport out of their safe-deposit box. It didn't sound like my mom somehow; the voice was several octaves deeper. I have perfect pitch. Suddenly, my dad jumped on an extension phone and screamed, "No, Gary!! Passports can be forged!!" Then his line went dead, but my clone mom said I was too confused and was coming down here. I suspected it wasn't my real mom, but had to be sure.

I made sure the following day. When my "mom" came in the door the voice was totally different, and the personality was totally different. I wanted to be absolutely positive, so when she went to sleep that night, I tied tons of heavy string around the doorknob to my bedroom that even I couldn't pull open. The next morning, my "mom," without even calling to me, almost took the door off the hinges with one tug! That was a complete giveaway, cause my real mom is the most gentle person in the world, and at the very least would have called to me to ask me why the door wouldn't open. I wound up driving away from here into the night in terror!

Gary's concern for the changes in his parents is very reminiscent of Bob's comments. He was placed in and out of psychiatric institutions for many years, and has written about his persecution at the hands of evil clones. One major difference between Gary and Bob is that Gary also found some solace in religion.

> Fortunately, there is a good side to all this. I have discovered that my enemies were into witchcraft, and that God and Jesus and all the angels in heaven have just about solved the problem for me now. So there is a spiritual side to all this, and not just alien in nature. But a good deal of it has been.

Since Gary's view of reality is so markedly different from most of us, we have to ask if it is the perceived reality of the abductees or contactees that has changed, or if it is the percipients who are altered. Indeed, is it more likely that the experiencers' view of reality has changed? Why?

(Stollman's story is on several websites, including: www. fringeware.com/anathema/AR/mail/stollman.htm.)

Absinthe

Absinthe called me from a town in Northern Manitoba after reading an article about my UFO research. She said that she thought a frightening experience that occurred to herself and her three-year-old daughter might be related to aliens and UFOs.

Absinthe woke up in the middle of the night, terrified. She found her daughter in bed with her as well, also very frightened. For several days and nights, her daughter acted traumatized and spoke about "monsters" doing things to her and to her mother.

Absinthe was very concerned about her daughter, and even spoke to a psychologist about this incident. To further her understanding, she decided to contact a UFO researcher who could address the alien abduction issue, which she had heard might be a possible explanation.

She shared her account with me, and I would like to present it in detail because I feel it is so important. I respect her for her openness.

Evening of May 4, 1995
I was struggling so hard with all my energy. I felt like I was suffocating. I could hardly breathe. I was screaming, or at least

I was trying to, but couldn't. I tried so hard to move and scream. I was terrified. I can't remember seeing anything. It was just kind of like lines swirling around me, almost like I was coming out of a drug or I was dizzy. Next thing I knew, I was sitting on my bed, on my knees, facing the pillow.

Zoe was at the edge of the bed at the top. She's never lain there. She was crying softly, like a whimpering, and shaking, all curled up. She was real scared.

Right away, I said, "Zoe, are you okay? What happened? What happened, Zoe?" She wouldn't answer. She just kept shaking and whimpering. I'd never seen her like this before.

I lifted her over to the middle between Fred and me where she usually sleeps. She was stiff and shaking. She grabbed the covers and pulled them over her head. I kept trying to pull them down a bit so she could breathe, but she had a real good grip and wouldn't let go and kept pulling them over her. I was scared; I didn't know what had happened. I thought maybe I hurt her when I was struggling in my dream. It took awhile before I could get to sleep [again]. I was so worried about Zoe, and [wondered] what the hell happened.

May 5th

I lay in bed this morning, trying so hard to think about what could have happened to Zoe and trying to make sense out of my dream. There had been no people in it, just lines swirling around [and] feeling [like I was] suffocating, struggling to move, and most of all I was terrified.

She seemed okay during the day — nothing unusual.

When I put Zoe to sleep this night, she was real tired. I lay down in her bed with her and nursed her to sleep. When Fred and I went to bed, I carried Zoe into our bed. I put her in the middle. She started to grab the covers again and was pulling them up over her head.

She was curled up and shaking a bit and her eyes kept opening up. She would drift off to sleep and then pop her eyes open again. I said to Fred, "This is so strange; she's never been like this." He agreed and we talked about it. I started to think that something must have happened to her and maybe to me. I'd never seen Zoe so scared. I started thinking about the dream. It was so strange because I couldn't see anyone [in it]. I can't remember waking up; I was just there on my knees in bed.

I was worried about Zoe. Then, she sat up and said, "I'm sorry I'm so scared of the creepy monsters. I won't be scared no more." I think she sensed I was so worried.

I said, "It's okay, Zoe, it's okay!" I asked her, "What colour was the creepy monster?" She said "green" right away. I asked if it was big or little. She said "little." I asked if it had little or big eyes. She was quiet and like she was in a daze (it was like she was picturing it in her mind) for about fifteen seconds. She said "big."

Fred and I looked at each other. Zoe kept asking if the creepy monsters were coming back. I just told her, "no." She wanted to search the house, so I took her hand and we looked under the bed and in the closets. She went to her room to check it out.

She wanted breakfast. I told her it was nighttime, but she wanted breakfast, so I said, "Okay, let's go have some cereal." She was eating some Rice Krispies and she said, "There were this many creepy monsters, mom," and held out her hand with five fingers up.

I asked, "What did they do?" She said the monster had a long stick and I touched it on my hand and then he went like this (and she was poking other parts of her body). She put her head in my hand and cried a little; she looked so deeply depressed. I put my arms around her and held her so tight. She didn't want her cereal anymore.

Zoe has never seen any such shows on TV! I would like to know how a little girl who just turned three could tell me what hundreds of other people have experienced. The way she was laying on the bed so scared, in a way I've never seen her before, I know damn well something must have happened, no matter how crazy this sounds.

May 6th
She said she had an "owie" in her nose. I went to look. She said, "It's okay, mom."

I noticed a little mark, like a needle mark, on my forehead by my hairline. My right leg was in pain since yesterday. Zoe has some marks like a needle mark and some faint marks around her hairline.

When we came home from my mom's, we were outside the door and she looked around and looked up and asked me if any monster was going to get her. I said, "No, dear, they've gone home."

She woke up with a jolt in the middle of the night and the covers were over her. She was scared.

May 8th

[In the] evening, Zoe was in my arms on the couch. She said, "I have 'owies' inside me. The bad guys put it in me." She said that I have it, too. I asked how they put it in me. She pointed to her eyes and above and around her forehead, by her hairline. I gave her a hug and put her to bed.

Although Absinthe and Zoe seemed to have many characteristics of alien abductees, I wanted to understand more about what they had experienced. I needed to be sure there was no other possible explanation for Zoe's trauma. I asked Absinthe if she was sure there was no other event that occurred about the same time as Zoe's trauma.

Finally, Absinthe hesitantly told me about something else which had occurred the day that she and Zoe had their night terror. She said she didn't want to think about that other incident, but now, grudgingly, agreed that it perhaps was relevant. She wrote a slightly different version of her diary entry for May 5, which mentioned it:

May 5th

[In the] morning, I started thinking about what happened. I thought that maybe since I'd seen [my psychologist] Wendell that day and talked about things that maybe I dreamed about it. So, I started to think back about that day.

I think he had his hand over my mouth, the other holding my hands, maybe above my head. I just know I couldn't move. I could hardly breathe. I was trying so hard to get air. I'm sure I thought I was going to die from suffocation and pain. I don't remember seeing his face. I just know he was on top of me.

Absinthe had been raped.

The same day she had finally taken the crucial step to talk about it with a therapist, she had the night terror. One can only imagine the flood of emotions and anguish she experienced when that event was relived, over and over again. It seems very possible that because her memories of the trauma had been forced to resurface, she had experienced very vivid nightmares that night, reliving the terror.

Absinthe admitted that Zoe sometimes would wake up and come into her parents' bedroom. Zoe may have come in and found Mommy struggling, gasping, saying, "Stay away! Let go of me, you monster!" What would a small child have thought?

The "owies?" Well, children have a hard time thinking in terms of emotional or mental pain. Pain usually comes from an actual physical injury. We put Band-Aids on their boo-boo's, kiss them, and things are fine again. But Mommy didn't look like she had a scraped knee or a bleeding nose. It must have been something else.

Yes, this is only speculation. We don't know what transpired that night. It's possible that aliens chose that particular night to abduct Zoe and her mother, forcing them to undergo traumatic physical examinations. But it's more probable that Zoe watched in horror as her mother wrestled with demons of a very human kind.

Absinthe's case makes me wonder, however, about how many other abductees have hidden or suppressed memories of traumatic events. John Mack has stated that none of his abductees displayed any indication of sexual abuse, yet I know from my own investigations that some abductees have such a history. Are these a minority? If so, shouldn't they be given more compassionate and clinical care, beyond standard abductee support networking? Absinthe's trauma didn't surface until after several meetings with her. When I hear about abductees visiting an abduction "hypnotherapist" once and getting hypnotized that same session, I get very uneasy.

Xeno

A former American military officer has been discussing UFO research with me for several years. A crack Internet surfer, his ability to browse the net for useful information is admirable and a great resource. Over the course of our acquaintance, he has provided me with many useful files and has helped make available for public consumption some of the most accurate and intelligent posts about UFOs at various Web sites.

I naturally asked him why he had such an ardent interest, and not surprisingly he related to me his own account of a strange series of experiences which seem to have been centred around a UFO sighting.

He, too, appears to have experienced some "missing time," and to this day has wondered about it. A rational and critically thinking man, he is baffled by the events which occurred to him forty years ago in the midwestern United States.

I spent the summer of 1958 working on a farm that consisted of many square miles of farmland in numerous fields scattered about the area.

Early one afternoon while plowing, I saw an unusual object in the sky. Right there in front of me, less than a thousand feet away, an airplane was coming down. It was going to land. No! It was going to crash! As I watched in near disbelief, the craft descended, from right to left, at an angle of about thirty degrees, until it went behind the low ridge-line in the next field to the north.

I fully expected to see a big cloud of smoke as it crashed into the gully that was just beyond the ridge-line, but there was none

The craft was only visible for a few seconds, but I could clearly see a row of five or six (certainly fewer than eight) "windows" on the side. The colour was white or light metallic, with the area between the "windows" being dark blue and forming sort of wide stripe along the side. I had an almost perfect horizontal side view, so no wings were visible. Also, I have no recollection of seeing any kind of tail structure or stabilizer assembly. The tractor engine was unmuffled and loud, so I was unable to hear any sound from the craft.

Needless to say, I was rather excited and determined to go and investigate. What healthy fifteen-year-old boy would pass up a chance to investigate something like this? I decided I would drive the tractor to the fence and then go to the crash site on foot. Then, my memory comes to a grinding halt.

Xeno seems to have a memory gap at this point. Try as he might, he cannot think of what happened after he reached the fence.

I woke up sitting in the passenger seat of my boss's truck. I use the term "woke up" rather loosely here, for I hadn't been asleep. I had been sitting upright with my eyes already open, but I had been totally oblivious of my surroundings.

It was rather disconcerting, as I realized that I hadn't the foggiest idea of how I got there or where we were going. After a sideward glance to confirm that the driver of the truck was indeed my boss, I pondered the situation in silence. Amnesia? Insanity? Was I losing my mind?

We were now off the road and driving through the field, heading north toward the tractor and plow. At a certain point near where I had observed the craft, the memory came flooding back along with the excitement. "I saw a plane go down there, just beyond the ridge." I blurted out. "It crashed into the gully!"

"Yes, and damn it all, you drove the tractor right up against the fence!" my boss shot back. "How many times have I warned you about that?"

He was in a foul mood from all the hard work we'd been doing, so I let it go at that. To my disappointment, he had completely ignored my comment about the plane. A little while later, he said something I thought was totally offbeat.

"When I picked you up, you were just standing there along side the road shaking like you were having some kind of fit or something."

I hadn't a clue as to what he was talking about.

"You know exactly what I mean," he replied. "Just let me tell you this, I can't let you drive the tractor any more — if that happened while you were pulling a plow, you'd fall off and be cut into a million pieces."

I fully understood the implications of his words, but found it totally inexplicable that he should say such a thing. I'd never had any kind of fit or anything. I certainly wasn't an epileptic or anything like that, so why on earth would he be telling me this?

Curiously, *petit mal* epilepsy also fits some of the symptoms of AAS. Before the onset of a seizure, many epileptics experience a sensation called an "aura." Some people feel a change in body temperature, others experience a feeling of tension or anxiety. In some cases, the epileptic aura will be as apparent to the person as a musical sound, a strange taste, or even a particular curious odour. What's more interesting is that the latest calculations show that at least one percent of the population has some form of epilepsy, a figure very close to the number of people reporting abductions, according to the Roper Poll.

During partial seizures, the patient has strange or unusual sensations including sudden movements of one body part, distortions in hearing or seeing, stomach discomfort, or a sudden sense of fear. However, consciousness is not impaired. In complex-partial seizures (also known as temporal lobe epilepsy), the patient appears dazed and confused and exhibits behaviour such as random walking, mumbling, and head-turning. Interestingly, these so-called "automatisms" cannot be recalled by the patient. And, in generalized absence seizures (formerly *petit mal*), patients have five- to fifteen-second lapses in consciousness. During this time the patient appears to be staring into space and the eyes may roll upwards, but then can return to "normal" as if nothing had happened. For many kinds of seizures, all that you might experience would be some strange feelings or sensations, and a "loss" of some amount of time.

In fact, after I had given a public lecture about UFOs and related subjects, I found myself talking with a fascinating person who regularly experienced epileptic seizures. Having been through many episodes, it was her opinion that some of the experiences reported by abductees could easily be due to seizures. She suggested that the disorientation and distorted view of reality which occurs during a seizure can transform the voices and appearance of nearby people into distorted aliens peering with large black eyes.

According to an informational page on the Internet,

Common feelings associated with seizures include uncertainty, fear, physical and mental exhaustion, confusion, and memory loss. Some types of seizures can produce visual and auditory phenomena, while others can involve a "blank" feeling. If a person is unconscious during a seizure there may be no feeling at all... Depending on the type of seizure, they can last anywhere from a few seconds to several minutes. In rare cases, seizures can last many hours.
(*Frequently Asked Questions About Epilepsy*, Version 4.3 — 96/07/15, http://debra.dgbt.doc.ca/~andrew/epilepsy/FAQ.html.)

It was many, many years later that Xeno recalled the incident. He had been involved in UFO discussions by this time, and something triggered his memory. He realized his actions and his conscious recall of the event were unusual, and it began gnawing at him.

Perhaps it was a mental block of some kind, but for whatever reason, it was not until summer of 1995, when I was thinking yet again of the incident, that the following two questions took form in my mind. "Why hadn't I gone to investigate?" After all, the gully was only several hundred feet away. And, "If I hadn't gone to investigate, then what had I done?"

Imagine my amazement when I realized that I couldn't answer either of those questions. An interesting development. Only then did it occur to me how "out of character" it would be for a healthy fifteen-year-old boy to observe what he believed to be an airplane crash in the next field, yet not walk over to check it out.

I remembered that I kept watching the western end of the ridge as I continued to drive toward the fence. I stopped the tractor at the fence, got off it, and ... And what? Logically, I should have slipped through the three-strand barbed-wire fence and started walking (or running) toward the gully, but I had no memory of having done so. In fact, I had no memory of doing anything after getting off the tractor.

I went over the whole scene again from the beginning, but with the same result. I still couldn't remember much of anything beyond getting off the tractor. But by now, I wasn't just remembering, I was trying to visualize. That's when it happened! I had been holding a mental image of the tractor stopped at the fence, when the memory suddenly came to mind.

As Xeno remembers it, the events of that day were as follows:

(a) Saw a craft descending toward the gully
(b) Got off the tractor at the fence line with the intention of going to (c).
(c) ? Missing time
(d) My boss came upon me standing beside the road shaking.
(e) Came to in the truck as we were on the way to the tractor.
(f) Remembered seeing the craft because we were at that spot again.
(g) Got scolded and fired for driving the tractor close to the fence.

I have no memory of anything that happened between the time I got off the tractor and when I came to in the truck. The amount of missing time could be anything between twenty minutes and an hour.

I do have a vague memory of suddenly being blind and not in control of my body, yet conscious, and alarmed and confused over what was happening to me. Also, there were what seemed to be loud noises inside my head accompanied by a feeling of extreme physical discomfort. Unfortunately, I am unable to place this memory in any spatial or temporal context, so it could be entirely unrelated to this particular incident.

Now ... the question arises, do I think I was abducted? Well, I certainly don't feel that I was in any way targeted for abduction that day. At most, something similar to the following might have happened.

Zwrx1: Oh darn! Now we'll never get all these soil samples aboard on schedule. That imbecile of an earthling farmhand actually turned around to watch where he was going long enough to get a good look at us as we made our final descent, and now he's heading this way.

Zwrx2: No problem, Zwrx1. I'll just scramble his brain a bit and have him go stand beside the road shaking till his boss comes along.

Zwrx1: Good thinking, Zwrx2. Get right on it, will you? He's already climbing through the fence.

Not being the least bit suspicious that something out of the ordinary might have happened to me that day, I did not check for marks on my body afterward. I certainly didn't notice anything unusual, though.

As far as I know, the incident has not affected my life in any way. I now regard it as an oddity and have pretty much accepted the idea that I'll never know for sure what happened that day.

Xeno remains puzzled by the gap in his memory, but he is not obsessed or troubled by it as others have been by their own vague recollections of events. He doesn't want to get hypnotized, he doesn't need therapy, he just continues on with his life.

Xeno seems relatively well adjusted to his post-encounter life. We still don't know if he was abducted or not. All he recalls — or doesn't recall — is a "hole" in his memory. He has had plenty of time to "fill in" the hole with any number of images taken from popular ufology, but has not done so. Is he simply much more capable of coping with his experience? Since he has not ventured down the road of hypnotherapy and regression, one can suggest his is a much less contaminated story than others. Perhaps his experience was no more no less real than other abductees, but his level of functioning is certainly different than most. Again, we are rightly bound to ask, "Why?"

Val Johnson: "Encounter of the Decade"

I first heard about Val Johnson's UFO experience on the late news one night, several days after it occurred. I called the station and was told that as far as they knew, it had already been investigated by the Center for UFO Studies (CUFOS). Since it was just within UFOROM's investigation range, I would have otherwise left to check out the site. However, I thought it would have been adequately investigated by American ufologists by then. By chance, my associate Guy Westcott was vacationing in Minnesota around that time, and he took time out to visit the area on his own. Not only did he come back to Canada with a rather detailed investigation report, he reported that CUFOS had not been there by the time he had left.

On September 16, 1979, Westcott obtained a taped report from Deputy Johnson. It is interesting to hear what transpired, in his own words:

> This is Deputy Sheriff Val Johnson.... I report in connection with an incident that happened August 27th, 1979, at approximately 1:40 a.m., western section of Marshall County, approximately ten miles west of Stephen, Minnesota. This officer was on routine patrol, westbound down Marshall County Road #5. I got to the intersection of #5 and Minnesota State #220. When I looked down south #220 to check for traffic, I noticed a very bright, brilliant light, eight to twelve inches in diameter, three to four feet off the ground. The edges were very defined. I thought perhaps at first that it could be an aircraft in trouble, as it appeared to be a landing light from an aircraft. I proceeded south on #220. I proceeded about a mile and three tenths or a mile and four tenths when the light intercepted my vehicle causing damage to a headlight, putting a dent in the hood, breaking the windshield and bending antennas on top of the vehicle. At this point, at the interception of the light, I was rendered either unconscious, neutralized, or unknowing for a period of approximately thirty-nine minutes. From the point of intersection, my police vehicle

proceeded south in a straight line 854 feet, at which point the brakes were engaged by forces unknown to myself, as I do not remember doing this, and I left about approximately ninety-nine feet of black marks on the highway before coming to rest sideways in the road with the grille of my hood facing in an easterly direction. At 2:19 a.m., I radioed a 10–88 (Officer Needs Assistance) to my dispatcher in Warren. He dispatched an officer from Stephen who came out, ascertained the situation as best he could, called for the Stephen Ambulance to transport me to Warren Hospital for further tests, x-rays, and observation. At the time the officer arrived, I complained about having very sore eyes. At Warren Hospital, it was diagnosed that I had a mild case of welder's burns to my eyes. My eyes were treated with some salve and adhesive bandages were put over and I was instructed to keep them on for the remainder of the day, or approximately twenty-four hours. At 11:00 a.m., Sheriff Dennis Breckie, my employer, picked me up at my residence in Oslo, and transported me to an ophthalmologist in Grand Forks, North Dakota. He examined my eyes and said I had some irritation to the inner portions of the eye which could have been caused by seeing a bright light after dark. That is all I have to add except to say that my timepiece in the police vehicle and my mechanical wristwatch were both lacking fourteen minutes of time to the minute.

A fascinating account of a *very* close encounter! What's more, the UFO incident was thoroughly investigated by police immediately after it occurred. Westcott's interpretation was that the ball of light was ball lightning. He makes an interesting case in that the previous evening had been hot and humid and could possibly have created a charge in the atmosphere during that day. Another supporting point is that Johnson estimated the object to have been only five kilometres away near some trees, which just happened to be along a power line.

If we can assume that the plasma carried a large charge of some sort, upon contact with the leading edge of the car (the grille and headlights) it could have discharged some or all of its energy through the electrical system. Ball lightning is a natural phenomenon that is poorly understood, but is thought to be capable of such releases of energy.

The bending of the antennas, in Westcott's opinion, was *not* due to an object travelling at high speed and striking the two aerials. CUFOS investigator Allen Hendry was widely quoted as saying that the bends occurred from an impact with an object. Westcott suggested that the aerials bent after whipping forward when the brakes were applied and struck the red outside dome light on the roof. In support of this, Westcott noted two melted indentations in the rear of the dome light that could have been caused in that manner, and the bends are at what were appropriate heights in the antennas, each with "discolouration" of the metal. The aerials were taken to the Honeywell Labs in Minneapolis, which concluded that they were bent "by force" and "not heat." The magnetic pattern scan done on the car showed it had not been subjected to a strong magnetic field.

UFOROM's investigation continued, and reached a major stage when Johnson and the investigating officers were invited to Winnipeg to address the first Manitoba Conference on Ufology on March 16, 1980. Johnson's experience was the main focus of the meeting.

Frankly, it is one of the more puzzling incidents in the history of ufology, partly because the case involves a man who has been described as "the perfect witness." At the time, Johnson was a Deputy Sheriff in Marshall County, Minnesota, and a trained observer as well as an experienced police officer. The physical evidence suggests that something very strange happened to him in the early morning on a lonely stretch of road near the Red River. The time sequence of events is very firmly established by both tape-recorded and written logs of his actions that morning. The physical traces were examined and measurements were made immediately after the encounter by trained police investigators, and Johnson was taken to a hospital by ambulance directly from the site.

At MCU, the case was discussed and reviewed in detail by all participants, as presented by guests Val Johnson, Deputy Sheriff Everett Doolittle, and Officer Greg Winskowski. Doolittle was the first individual to reach the site after Johnson radioed for help, and Winskowski conducted the initial police investigation. Many fascinating points were noted, including physiological effects.

When Val Johnson was found by Everett Doolittle, he was slumped forward over the steering wheel and in mild shock. A bruise later appeared on Johnson's forehead, presumably caused by impact with the steering wheel. He was dazed, and said that "everything was in slow motion." He had an intense pain ("excruciating") in his eyes, and, having done some welding in his career, knew what welders' burn was like, comparing his pain to this.

"It was as if someone had hit me in the face with a four hundred pound pillow," he said of the sensation of his head. However, he stated repeatedly that the only pain he experienced was from his eyes. This is extremely interesting in the light of dental examinations he had one week previous and one week after his experience. At the first, he had an extensive series of x-rays taken, in preparation for major dental work. His bridgework, including the caps on his front teeth, was intact. At the second examination, the dentist found that Johnson's bridgework was broken at the gums. Yet, no swelling or pain was felt.

When Doolittle arrived on the scene, Johnson's police car was front-end-first in the left-hand ditch, with the other end sticking out into the left-hand lane of the road. The "impact point" was determined by the location of the broken glass of the headlight on the road, 953 feet from where the car was found. From that point, "yaw marks" (described as faint skid marks caused by putting a car out of gear without applying the brakes) travelled in a straight line for 854 feet down the road. These became dark skid marks from there to where the car stopped moving, going in a straight line for most of the remaining length, turning abruptly at the end toward the ditch.

The right member of the left pair of headlights was broken. There was a round dent, approximately one inch in diameter, directly over the master brake cylinder, on the hood. This dent appeared as if a hammer had struck the hood at an angle between forty-five and seventy-five degrees from the horizontal. A photograph taken with a UV filter showed that there was a deposit left on the flat bottom surface of the dent.

Val Johnson's police car, showing the damaged windshield. Protruding just above the rotating light is the antenna, bent at a forty-five degree angle.

The windshield of the car had an interesting pattern of breakage, in the shape of a teardrop (point up). This was located on the driver's side. There were three main impact points visible, though the lowest of the three was the largest and most complex. Testing of the glass by the Ford Motor Company suggested that there were signs of both inward and outward motion of the windshield. They were apparently unfamiliar with the breakage pattern. It is fairly obvious, though, that even a small stone could have been driven through the windshield, even at relatively low speed, so it is hard to interpret the shattering as an actual impact. However, it was noted at the conference that the analytical findings bare some resemblance to those of a shock-wave-induced breakage.

The roof light that was affected had its glass knocked out. The police radio antenna on the centre of the roof was bent about five inches up from the roof, at about a forty-five degree angle. The CB antenna on the trunk was bent near its tip, at an angle near ninety degrees, three inches from the top.

An interesting observation made by the police investigators was that all the damage on the vehicle occurred in a straight path no wider than twelve inches in diameter. Because of this "linear" formation, it was suggested that an object had struck a glancing blow to the car, initially impacting the headlight, rolling over the hood, up the window and over the roof. However, at the conference, it was realized that this scenario could not account for all the damage in the form it was observed. An object hitting the car at the front would not have the capability to redirect its force downward further up the hood, graze the window and still have enough force to bend the antennas.

The antennas are spring loaded, so anything bending them would have to have been travelling extremely fast to create the shape they are now in. It was also proposed that the antennas were bent by a strong deceleration, causing them to whip forward. But the design of the antennas is such that they can withstand a strong deceleration without acute bending. Any deceleration of sufficient strength to bend them backwards as they moved forward might have killed the occupant. Most curiously, the insects adhered to the antennas were not wiped off from the impact, as might be expected.

The battery of the car can no longer hold a charge. It has been proposed that the headlight and roof light were imploded by a high-energy electrical source. Ball lightning was suggested as a cause, but it could not have created the dent in the hood, nor the impacts on the window, let alone the bending of the antennas. The electric clock in the car was found to be missing fourteen minutes. Strangely, Val Johnson's mechanical wristwatch was also lacking fourteen minutes. This is indeed odd, because both were synchronized with the clocks in the police station earlier in the night, and all time checks after that agreed, as late as 01:00, only a short while before the incident.

Finally, the CB radio in the car, although not in the best working order before the incident, was described as being "even worse" after it.

Allan Hendry, of the Center for UFO Studies, sent a gaussmetre to the police investigator in order for them to test for changes in the car's magnetic pattern. These results were, apparently, negative.

There was evidence of dust particles in the shattered glass, and it was suggested that this dust was the residue found in the round dent in the hood.

The psychological effects

When Val Johnson called for help, his voice was described as being "weak," and like "someone coming out of a daze." He had been, apparently, unconscious for thirty-nine minutes, from the time he heard glass breaking and felt the light "hit" him, to the time he woke up, opening one eye to see the red ENGINE light on his dashboard. During that period, the car had travelled in a straight line for 953 feet before veering into the left lane and on into the ditch. He does not remember applying the brakes, yet the skid marks show that they were definitely applied.

At MCU, Johnson was asked what he thought had happened to him that morning. He said that he believed he "had seen something (he) wasn't supposed to see." Questioned on this, he could only speculate that he had stumbled upon somebody doing something that wasn't meant to be observed, and that his powers of observation had been effectively neutralized.

He also was asked if the procedure of regressive hypnosis had ever been suggested to him. He replied that the *National Enquirer* had asked him to submit to a regression, and offered to pay him for the exclusive rights of the results. He rejected their offer. He was then asked if he would agree to a hypnotic regression with a clinical hypnotist, for research purposes, and not for publication. He said no, and added that he was "not curious" about what happened to him that morning.

Doolittle said after this that their file on the case was now closed and their investigation was terminated, after reaching no conclusions. They stated that their investigation was over, and that the matter was now in the hands of the ufologists. They would not subject Johnson to either a polygraph or a regressive hypnosis, as they felt it was not necessary for their investigation. All three were asked if the Air Force, CIA, or FBI had approached them, and they all answered to the negative.

Johnson was asked if he had since experienced any other unusual incidents such as extremely vivid dreams, MIB, or psi phenomena. In response, he revealed a highly interesting thing; from time to time, he said, he will find himself thinking three words, which somehow stick in his mind. The words stay with him "like a McDonald's commercial," and he can find no reason for thinking them. The three words are: " I am committed." He concluded by noting that if he ever saw that light again, he'd stop the car and "yell for help!"

This case was reviewed in detail at the conference, and photographs of the car were examined closely. Additional evidence was brought forth and theories were presented to try to account for all the evidence. Westcott stated that he had found a "burn mark" in the field beside the road, while he was examining the site. This mark, about six to seven feet in diameter, had no vegetation on its surface and bore some resemblance to a fertilizer burn. Johnson said that a representative from the USDA (Agriculture Rep) had expressed a personal interest in the case and had taken infrared aerial photographs of the site. These showed that the ditches on either side of the site had a "different" chlorophyll absorption than the surrounding fields.

After much debate, it eventually was concluded by the MCU participants that the incident was inconsistent with the theory of the car having been struck by an object of some sort, including ball lightning. The idea of hits by multiple objects was considered and found marginally tenable. However, there are thirty-nine minutes to account for, a complex sequence of impacts by several objects and, some effects caused at a short distance that still need satisfactory explanations. Actions by unknown individuals can be included in the list of possibilities. It is easily demonstrable that something very unusual happened that morning.

At the present time, there is no adequate explanation for the effects noted in the case, based on the proposed theories. While Johnson doesn't display many of the indications of alien abduction, he does have a period of missing time which can be absolutely verified, unlike most abductees' cases. Further, he has some kind of "message" replaying in his conscious memory, again similar to abductees, but without any drive to proclaim himself as a leader or healer for others. Many questions still remain unanswered, and

153

they may remain unanswered for some time to come. The Stephen, Minnesota, incident is listed in UFOROM files as "unknown."

Twenty years later, the case is also labelled as "unexplained" on the books of the Marshall County Sheriff's Office. Recently, I spoke to Everett Doolittle, now in Minneapolis with a different law enforcement agency. He admits he is still baffled by the case.

"We had no idea what happened to him," Doolittle told me. "Val was a good police officer and never made anything up before that. We tried to figure it all out but couldn't come up with anything."

"But it's too bad what they did to him," he added.

Doolittle explained that after his encounter and after the investigation, Johnson was subjected to endless ridicule and derision.

"It got so bad that he couldn't live anywhere in the state anymore," he said. "People were always bugging him about his 'little green guys' and he practically had a nervous breakdown."

What didn't help, apparently, was that the sheriff at the time decided to keep the incident in the public's mind by impounding Johnson's police car. Instead of locking it up, the car was placed on display in a local museum, where it stands today as part of a UFO exhibit.

For Johnson, the memory of that night in 1979 simply wouldn't go away. He moved far away from the area and is still recovering from the alien abduction he never had.

"UFO Car" on display at the Marshall County Fairground in Marshall County, Minnesota.

Never mess with the Space Brothers

Although relatively few abductees or contactees have claimed their mentors had obvious malevolent intentions, some aliens clearly come from the pulp fiction moulds of the 1950s. A case in point is that of Olive.

One night in 1977, I had been interviewed on a local television show about a series of UFO reports in southern Manitoba that I had investigated. That evening, I got a phone call from a woman in a northern Manitoba community. This person, Olive, explained that she had intimate knowledge of aliens and their spacecraft, and that she spoke to the Space Brothers at least twice a week. She felt she needed to tell the world about her experiences and believed she had been chosen by the aliens to act as their messenger. She wanted to know if I was interested in having her present an illustrated lecture about her experiences to me and my colleagues.

Although there was no formal group in existence at that time, there were enough independent investigators and researchers in contact with each other that an emergency meeting was arranged in my small downtown apartment. Regardless of what she might have to say, a lecture by a full-fledged contactee was rare at the time, so it seemed a perfect opportunity to have a group meeting. In fact, Olive was so anxious to speak with us, she stated that she would leave the next morning on the long journey south to Winnipeg and lecture to us that evening.

About twenty interested and a few slightly disinterested people gathered in my home. Olive arrived with her husband in tow, and they brought in pamphlets, books, photographs, and a small movie projector. Her husband elected to sit on the steps of the apartment block rather than go inside. (Because he had "heard it all before," he explained.) And Olive began her soliloquy.

"I died when I was six years old," she began, "but I rose up again on the third day. I soon found that I could talk to the insects and animals...."

Olive went on to describe how she felt she was psychically gifted, and she began her contact with benevolent space beings at an early age. The Space Brothers took her to other planets, and even inside the Earth through holes in the north and south poles. Her station wagon was "teleported" while she was on a long road trip, and she proudly showed off the "burn marks" on her car (although to the untrained eye they looked remarkably like rust).

She lived part of the year in maritime Canada, where she had a large following in the form of a church-like congregation. She would often hold religious ceremonies in fields where "scout ships" had landed, encouraging others to tune in to the spiritual guidance of the "Space Brothers." Her group built a pyramid in the middle of a field, and would sit inside so that spiritual energy could be better focused upon themselves in meditation.

Olive told us that one day, she had been given a vision by these entities that she should strike the ground with a wooden rod at a certain location (slightly reminiscent of a Biblical story), and a well would be created. According to her testimony, she did so, and water did spring forth. This water was used by her to heal the sick, cause the blind to see, and the lame to walk.

At this point, it appeared that the Space Brothers (for it would be unkind to call them aliens) were benevolent and were interested only in helping Olive bring humans to galactic salvation. Alas, there was one incident which raised some doubts in this regard.

It was easy to see the undercurrents of strong emotionality towards her "teachings." Olive told the gathered listeners that she and some others had watched a "scout ship" land on a hilltop, and the next morning, a cross-shaped patch of burned grass was visible. She declared the site "holy," and it was immediately roped off. Soon, pilgrimages were made to the venerated landing pad.

However, a few unenlightened local residents thought the whole thing was rather silly, and procured a bulldozer to erase any sign of the shrine and drive the worshipers out of the area. Perhaps expectedly, Olive's faithful peacefully protested by laying in front of the bulldozer, and the attempt was halted. A few days later, however, Olive gravely explained that the bodies of those trying to demolish the sacred site were found in a lake with their bones broken, as evidence that we must not tamper with the will of the Space Brothers.

Even in the realm of contactees, apparently there is inherent danger in the contact.

"Yoda"

Until the middle of 1995, the National Research Council (NRC) in Ottawa would receive reports of UFOs from ordinary citizens as well as police and military personnel. A staff member would take reports by phone, fax, teletype, or mail and sift through them for possible observations of meteors. This was because several decades ago, the NRC had several staff who were interested in the observation of meteoric fireballs and the recovery of meteorites on the ground.

In order to accomplish this, the government entered into a co-operative arrangement with the RCMP whereby the police would investigate observations of lights in the sky (read: UFOs) and send their investigation reports to Ottawa. In effect, this unprecedented situation meant that UFO reports were being collected and investigated by a respectable, nationwide force of people who then sent them to a central repository for analyses. Plus, this was all paid for by the taxpayers of Canada.

In short, it was an ideal way to study UFOs. Of course, that meant there was something wrong with it.

What went awry were two things. First, the scientists at the NRC made it clear that they were *not* studying UFOs. In fact, one NRC researcher, astronomer Peter Millman, was an archskeptic rivalling Philip Klass in stature and publications. Once, when the noted Langenburg UFO "landing" case of 1974 was being discussed at a public forum, Millman explained to a scientific audience and the media that the impressions left in the grain (this was long before the advent of modern-day, British-style crop circles) were nothing more than the effects of fairy-ring mushrooms. Of course, he had neglected to note that he had not investigated the case himself and that fairy-rings never form in grain.

What the NRC actually did with the reports they received now seems rather trivial. Because they were only interested in meteors, they scanned the reports for probable sightings of bright, fast-moving, and short-duration UFOs. Everything else was ignored.

This meant that close encounters of stationary or landed, seemingly solid objects like flying saucers could be discarded under the NRC's specific mandate. These "other" reports were collected and filed in the top drawer of a filing cabinet in the office of an overworked civil servant on the main NRC building. No one looked at the reports, compiled statistics, or gleaned the interesting, unexplained cases for later study. It wasn't part of their job.

At the beginning of each calendar year, the previous year's reports were taken out of the file drawer and sent to the National Archives. Archives staff would examine them and then "sanitize" them, removing all identifying phrases such as names, addresses, and telephone numbers of witnesses. This was done in order to protect witnesses' anonymity, because these were, after all, public records.

The reports were then sent to the Archives for deposit, where they sat in coded boxes awaiting their discovery by researchers. And researchers did trickle into the Archives to look at the cases. I visited the National Library in Ottawa every few years or so, as did Stanton Friedman, Scott Foster, and several others.

What we found was often amazing. Close encounters reported by police or military personnel; manoeuvring lights witnessed by airline pilots; cases witnessed by as many as two hundred people at the same time. An average of about 175 to 200 cases each year, with records dating back until the 1950s. The NRC files are probably the least-known but best public records of UFO sightings in the world.

The second problem was that because the files were getting "sanitized," there could be no follow-up of the cases. A really interesting close encounter could not be verified because the witness was no longer identified in the file. This greatly decreased the value of the report, and we were left only with the police notes as to the veracity of the witness. (In many cases, there were comments such as "Did not appear to be under the influence of alcohol.")

If cases other than simple lights in the sky were ignored by the NRC, you can imagine what was done with the more bizarre reports. Within the files are a number of abduction/contacts that were reported to the NRC or RCMP directly. Sometimes, the witnesses were directed to other agencies; more often than not, their letters were simply viewed with amusement.

On March 19, 1995, at 4:35 p.m., Master Corporal Caprice Brunelle of the Canadian National Defence Operations Centre in Ottawa (NDOC) received a telephone call from a woman who believed that her eight-year-old son had been abducted by aliens at about 1:30 a.m. on March 16, 1996.

On March 18, the boy told his mother that in the middle of the night, he woke up to see an alien enter his room through his second-storey townhouse window. The alien was between 2 1/2 and 4 1/2 feet tall, with pointed ears, slanted almond eyes, and three fingers on each hand. The boy drew a picture of the aliens in which they each resembled Yoda from the *Star Wars* movies.

The alien somehow took him out of his bedroom, through the window, and out to a flying saucer that was waiting outside. The ship was a "dovetail shape" and was grey in colour. Upon entering the ship, the boy noticed "pinky, orange cushioned walls that smelled similar to paint."

Five other aliens were waiting inside the ship. They communicated to the boy without moving their lips. They assured the boy that he would be all right, although the boy was convinced the aliens had five-fingered, rubber medical gloves. They all wore necklaces with star-shaped pendants.

The boy said he was placed on a table located at the front of the ship. Some sort of instrument was placed on his chest while "medical tests" were performed on him. He believes his chest and brain were examined.

One alien placed a hand over his eyes and he fell asleep. However, the boy says he woke with a start when the aliens were moving his body and accidentally bumped him into something. He was then returned to his room through his window and he went back to sleep.

When his mother asked him how long he had been gone, the boy at first said "two seconds" and then estimated it as long as five minutes.

When asked why he didn't tell her earlier, he replied that he had thought he had been dreaming.

The boy made numerous drawings of his experience for his mother. She says that on his chest, he has several scabs in the shape of a "square horseshoe" over his breastbone.

The woman explained to the officer that she was unable to take photographs of the scabs because she has no film and no money to purchase film. The officer suggested that the mother take her son to a medical facility for an examination and also file a report at a police station where photos would be taken.

The names of the woman and her son were deleted from the official National Research Council file on the case. If this was just a case of an overactive child's imagination, why did his mother take it seriously enough to report it to the Air Force? Perhaps she was convinced of alien intervention, too.

CHAPTER THREE
In the Best Interests

Louis

Louis first contacted me in March 1999, to talk about some of his experiences. He is a young man in his twenties, and is very articulate, thoughtful and sensitive about the unusual nature of his memories. His parents are from China, but he was raised in Canada and only returned with them to their native country a few years ago. He left China after high school and eventually returned to Canada.

Louis remembers being in his bedroom in about 1987, asleep in a top bunk while his brother was in the bottom bunk. He recalls waking up and sensing there was something wrong. He felt paralyzed and unable to move or open his eyes, although he sensed that the room had been somehow engulfed in yellow light. Suddenly, he felt cold, clammy hands grab his calves and his arms, pinning him to the bed. He squirmed and tried to scream, but he was unable to resist whatever was attacking him.

"The more I struggled, the more I was caught," he explained. "My eyes weren't open, but this didn't feel like a dream and I knew I was awake."

After what seemed an eternity, whatever it was that was holding him let go, and Louis was able to open his eyes and he fell back into bed, hitting his head on his headboard. There was no sign of anyone in his room, and no indication that there was anything out of order.

Ever since then, Louis has had a morbid fear of the dark. He can only go to sleep with the light on, no matter where he is and who he is with.

His fear of the dark subsided somewhat when he was a teenager, but it began again when he moved with his parents back to China. Then, when he moved back to North America, his feelings intensified.

"I just know something will happen if I leave the light off at night," he said. "I just feel that something is wrong, and I don't want to allow them to get me."

Louis is unsure of who or what "they" are, but admits reading some UFO books and senses that aliens might be involved.

One of his earliest UFO sightings occurred in Winnipeg when he was a young boy. One night during a warm summer, he and two friends were in a camper trailer in his family's backyard. Unable to sleep, they were watching the stars, and pointing out the various constellations. Suddenly, they all observed a bright point of light that moved across the sky and stopped near the horizon, then seemed to dart towards them.

"I don't remember it ever reaching us, but I remember we all were very frightened and we ran inside the house," he said.

He has other memories which seem to suggest alien visitation. In 1997, in China, he recalls that he was sleeping in his bed, facing the wall, when he woke up to the sound of rustling in his room. He opened his eyes, turned around, and saw the silhouette of a small figure in the doorway. It was very small, barely up to the level of the doorknob, with a disproportionately large head and long arms. As he watched, the visitor stepped back and walked away down the hallway.

Louis remembers feeling very calm, despite this intrusion, and he slowly collected his senses, got out of bed, scratched his head, and looked around. He went down the hallway and found that the rest of his family were sound asleep, and there was no sign of anyone else.

Over the years, Louis says he has awakened many times with a feeling of paralysis while in bed, and a pressure on his chest, making breathing difficult. He's found himself wheezing, choking, and unable to yell for help.

Another bizarre incident took place around the same time, also in China. He and his friend Norman stayed up late one night, talking. About 3:00 a.m., he and Norman decided to step outside for a cigarette. While outside, Norman complained that his back was sore and didn't know why he was in such pain. Without any apparent reason, Louis had a panic attack and made a dash to go back inside. They both lay down when they were finally calm enough to try to sleep, but Louis left the patio door open, something he religiously did not do because of his fear of intruders. He did, however, turn on the television to give off some light and background noise so he could be soothed to sleep.

"Suddenly," Louis recalled, "I was standing in the room with Norman beside me. I was very queasy, and felt like throwing up."

Then, Louis felt as though he was being "taken" by someone or something. He closed his eyes in fear and he brought his clenched fists up to his chest to try to protect himself. Internally, he was yelling "Leave me alone!" but he could not make a sound. Again, he was paralyzed. He felt his feet suddenly pulled out from under him and he was floating horizontally in the air, heading for the patio doors, feet first.

Through a tremendous effort, Louis forced his eyes open because he wanted to see who his aggressors were. However, as soon as he did, he found himself back in bed, drenched in sweat. Everything appeared normal.

In the valley

For many years, Louis has been keeping a diary of his experiences. He was willing to share some of his entries with me so that I could get a better sense of what he was going through. One particular entry had to do with an experience he and his friend Norman had while camping in China a few years ago.

Not long ago, Norman and I were on a hiking trip in China. About two and a half hours into a three-hour hike, I had the feeling that we should just walk right into the mountains instead of going through the main pass. We came upon a dry river bed which led directly into one part of a valley. There was nothing but dried mud and sand, and there was no sign of anyone. I told Norman, jokingly, that this would be a perfect place for a UFO abduction. He just smiled and said, "I know."

Soon, we decided to call it a night and found a spot to lay out our sleeping bags, sheltered from the night wind because we had not brought any sleeping bags. After eating a quick meal, by about 9:00 p.m., Norman suggested we should hike up a hill and get some dry shrubs to make a campfire. We had just started walking when I noticed a light up in the sky. It appeared to be only a few miles away from where we were standing. It was oval in shape and very bright. I pointed it out to Norman, and he just thought it was a plane or something.

I looked at the light for about ten minutes before it surprised me by winking out then turning on again. Then, far to my right, I saw a twinkling star. As I watched, this "star" flew quickly to where the first light was hovering and seemed to unite with it.

I started freaking out because I couldn't believe what I was seeing. To my amazement, another twinkle appeared off to my right, and another "star" flew over to the united lights. Again and again this happened, at least seven or eight times, all the same shape and size and colour.

I ran down the hill to get Norman's camera. We had just put a new set of batteries in it and a new roll of film and had taken some shots earlier in the day. As I ran up the hill to take a picture, I turned on the camera. But instead of turning on, a blue spark shot out of it and the camera died! That's when Norman started freaking out, too. By this time, all the lights had joined together and they descended behind the mountains. Norman and I returned to our camp and sat down to talk about what had happened. The camera still wouldn't work.

As I sat there, I began to get images in my head of a doorway with many "aliens" walking out of it. They seemed to have human faces, but had big eyes and no hair, yet they seemed to be very friendly. Some were grey and some were white. The white ones seemed to be looking at me, but the greys were turned away.

I don't know if these mental images have any relevance, but they were very intense. Norman said he got a powerful image of a yellow triangle. Later, we noticed blue sparks of some kind near us. After about an hour back at camp, the camera began working normally. We both went to sleep after that, but I kept waking up to have a drink of water from our reserve.

To this day, Louis sleeps with a light on at night.

"I think they would come if it was off," he says. "It's like something is staring at me, waiting for its chance."

Case investigations

Many abductees approach UFO investigators and "abduction experts" for assistance in understanding or coping with their experiences. Yet few researchers have officially adopted any code of ethics for the treatment and therapy of abductees, although such a code was formulated by Dr. David Gotlib several years ago and presented at a major UFO conference.

Essentially, anyone can claim to be an abduction researcher, citing years of experience in UFO report investigation or perhaps a Master of Arts degree from a university. Some such experts have no formal training at all, but feel they are compelled by conscience or personal experience to help abductees deal with their memories. Although hypnosis is the least-preferred method of clinical treatment for abductees, it is not uncommon for abduction experts to possess a certificate in "hypnotherapy" from some accredited (or supposedly accredited) institution.

My approach is much different. I recognize that abductees have had traumatic experiences and that they should be given compassionate care. They need to talk with someone about their experiences, without fear of repercussion, ridicule, or personal condemnation.

Louis illustrated this well when he explained, "I wanted to tell someone about this who wouldn't automatically tell me I'm crazy. I need to confide in someone in order to understand what happened to me, without worrying that I will be laughed at. My family doesn't believe me, and I have to have someone in whom I can trust."

Louis came to me for help. His sincerity was obvious, and his desire to learn more about his bedroom encounters was strong — strong enough to risk further embarrassment. What right do I have, as a scientist, to simply give him the brush off and tell him it's all in his head? No clinical psychologist would do that, yet many skeptics would take such an approach.

More to the point, what kind of training do most UFO researchers have that enables them to be qualified therapists for abductees? Nothing, of course. Abductees are seeking counselling, and yet the people to whom most of them turn for help are little more than avid readers of popular UFO literature, which we know is largely sensational and misrepresentative of serious UFO research.

I firmly believe that abductees should be helped primarily by qualified clinical or medical personnel. This is not to say that all abductees are in need of medical attention. What this does mean is that abductees who are bothered or upset by their experiences and who are highly anxious should be seen by clinical psychologists or psychiatrists who have the experience and training to deal with emotional problems and mental health issues.

The reason for this is that, as revealed in the literature, many abductees display symptoms of severe trauma, possibly as a result of their experiences, and also possibly from earlier times in their lives. As compassionate and caring researchers, we owe it to those who seek our help to provide them with the best assistance possible, regardless of our own biases and beliefs.

Naturally, there are a few problems with this idealistic approach. For one thing, few psychologists or psychiatrists have any real interest in ufology. While this is good in the sense that it means they can be more objective in their approach, it also means they do not have the background necessary to understand the true scope of the phenomenon. An expert in autism, for example, needs years of training and an understanding of case studies and related literature regarding that condition before he or she can be truly effective in treating a patient. Similarly, a psychologist or psychiatrist should be well-informed of the abduction phenomenon before proceeding to help any abductee. Unfortunately, few clinicians have the time or the motivation to wade through the largely anecdotal abduction literature for background in serious case studies. Furthermore, those case studies that are available may not always be the most reliable or objective, either. For example, criticisms have been levelled at psychiatrist and abduction expert Dr. John Mack regarding his apparent willingness to believe abductees' stories at face value. If even a learned individual's views on abductees are questioned, how is the average clinical psychologist supposed to help an abductee cope with his or her anxiety without a proper perspective?

Looking for support

In 1994, I faced an interesting dilemma when asked by one abductee about the availability of a local support group. He had read about abductee support groups in some of the popular abduction literature, and expressed a keen interest in talking with other abductees, discussing their similar problems, and sharing coping strategies.

On the one hand, support groups are a valuable tool in helping individuals come to terms with their shared life experiences. This is true whether the group is one devoted to abductees or a more traditional service such as Alcoholics Anonymous. The theory behind their use by counsellors in abductee recovery is that abductees will find solace and support from other abductees, and feel safe talking about the intimate details of their encounters.

The downside of this is that because abductees' memories are often vague and distorted, and may be influenced by popular media, a detail found in one abductee's story may be incorporated consciously or subconsciously into another abductee's memory through contagion. This argument is at the heart of the noted case of Betty and Barney Hill, for example, where Betty's describing of her dreams to Barney are thought by some to have influenced his own recall of events.

Furthermore, if an abductee does have a morbid fear of aliens harming him or her, listening to others tell of their own suffering in alien hands may cause deeper fears to form.

Among abductees, there is a great sense of camaraderie and sympathy. While each has his or her own subtle differences in their experiences, all abductees appear to share a sense of "not belonging." They often are ostracized by their co-workers, their friends, and their families.

Abductee support groups act as surrogate families for these who are in such distress and need some love and compassion. Some abductee support groups were founded by abductee therapists; others by abductees themselves who were wishing not only to help fellow experiencers but also sought therapy for their own emotional crises.

The ultimate benefit of abductee support groups is debatable. On the one hand, abductees need some kind of support or assistance from people who have an understanding of their experiences and who are going to be non-judgmental. But there are some caveats that must be addressed, too. From a research point of view, once one abductee speaks with another, there is always the possibility that the stories of their own experiences will begin to blend together. This form of data "contamination" is a problem for abduction ufologists wanting to sort out the phenomenon.

But another problem is related to the health and well-being of the abductees themselves. At least some abductees and contactees show signs or symptoms of psychological disorders. If these individuals are "counselling" or "helping" other abductees who are not ill, but are confused or are in some form of psychological distress, then are they helping or hindering the recovery of the new experiencers? In other words, when it comes to abductees, can the blind really lead the blind?

Helping each other

After I had been called by many abductees seeking help, I finally decided to seriously consider creating some kind of discussion group that might be of some use to them. I turned to the professional care community for advice, and was warned by clinical psychologists to refrain from designing it as a support group because of concerns over both the benefits for the abductees and the legal ramifications. This was because a theoretical situation could arise in which an abductee might commit suicide after learning from another abductee of the hopelessness of breaking free of alien control. In that case, whose responsibility would it be?

After careful consideration and consultation with colleagues at my university, I decided to facilitate an initial abductee support group meeting for several interested individuals. But in order to be fair to the participants and also to ensure that I was not advocating the use of the group as primary therapy, I presented a working document that outlined my concerns. It read as follows:

Information Sheet for Participants in the Discussion/Support Group

Thank you for coming to the first meeting of the Discussion/Support Group. Many of you are here tonight as a result of conversations with me regarding your experiences. For that reason, I would like to make you aware of some details.

First, the intent of this group is as a forum where you are completely free to share your thoughts and feelings, without feeling anxious, embarrassed, or afraid of ridicule. The intent here is for therapeutic discourse and support.

In terms of therapy, I am not in any way recommending this group as your sole form of therapy and/or support. I would suggest that a more formal appointment with a clinical psychologist or physician would be more medically correct in helping you deal with feelings of anxiety, depression, and other emotions you may have as a result of your unusual personal experiences. Indeed, I know that some of you have already been seen by such clinicians.

The reason this group was initiated was because of repeated requests of me to offer a private forum for people who have had unusual personal experiences. There is a great deal of debate now in ufology and related fields on whether or not group therapy or support groups are beneficial to experiencers. My own view is that while I do not advocate such groups, I suspect they are probably useful in some cases.

You should be aware that not everyone else in this group will have identical stories or feelings to relate. From my research and studies in ufology, there appear to be two distinct types of experiencers: abductees and contactees. In this setting, these are defined as follows:

Abductees generally believe they may have had physical contact with alien entities as a direct result of some physical encounter with a UFO. This physical contact may have involved some form of unwilling participation in medical examinations on board a physical craft at the hands of these entities. The majority of abductees describe their experiences as unpleasant.

Contactees, on the other hand, generally believe they may have had physical contact with alien entities, but are now interacting with the entities on a physical or spiritual level and are trying to spread the entities' message or assisting them in some way. The majority of contactees describe their experiences as pleasant.

Naturally, there is also a third category of people whose experiences fall somewhere between the two types, and may share some of the characteristics of both abductees and contactees.

This is a very simplistic classification, and you may feel that you do not belong in any of the categories. If so, that is perfectly acceptable, because this is a very subjective area of study at the present time and everyone is entitled to his or her own opinion on what is "really" going on. Indeed, I do not claim to know what is "really" going on, and I suspect that no one knows what is "really" going on. I can only tell you what appears to be the trend and thought in ufology at this moment.

Some of you have expressed an interest in having yourselves hypnotized for the purpose of uncovering blocked or hidden memories. In the formal scientific community, the use of hypnosis in this manner is considered very controversial and is not employed without some careful consideration of the well-being of the person seeking help.

Some therapists view hypnosis as a useful tool in unlocking the mind's secrets. The group's facilitator does use hypnosis in her counselling and if you wish to set up an appointment with her to explore your "lost," "hidden," or "blocked" memories, you are free to do so.

If you do not feel comfortable in this group, please do not hesitate to say so.

Please be patient and responsible in your participation in this group. Please allow each other time to express a thought or share an experience. However, please do not use your given opportunity to speak as a time for proselytizing or otherwise monopolize the group's attention.

Please show respect for one another.

All discussions of a personal nature within this group are considered confidential. Your anonymity, if you wish, will be respected by me; your name will not be released to any media representative without your consent. I am a writer and educator and may feel that some details of your experiences would be useful to others in the community for understanding what is "really" going on. If so, I will ensure that your privacy will still be respected. I will not publish your name or identify you in any way without your permission.

In the same way, I would ask that you respect each other's confidentiality and not cause each other undue embarrassment by arranging undesired publicity. Please be "up front" with each other.

In order to be "up front" with you, let me say that while I believe each of you has had a unique experience, I do not necessarily believe that aliens or other entities were directly involved. Call me an "agnostic." I am well-read in matters relating to both sides of the debate over the "reality" of your experiences: spirituality, psychology, ufology, hypnosis, psychical research, false memories, multiple personality disorders, post-traumatic stress syndrome, and religion. I do not know what has caused you to have such experiences. However, I am open-minded and am willing to at least consider all possibilities. I do not believe that your experiences can be easily dismissed as "all in your heads." But neither do I believe that your experiences are perfectly attributable to alien intervention.

If you have any comments or wish to express yourself outside of this group, please feel free to speak with either the co-facilitator or myself.

Having thus set out the basic guidelines, I started the group in motion and carefully monitored its progress. Not surprisingly, it fell apart after only a few sessions. One reason for this was because of the inherent nature of the group. Every abductee had his or her own views on what happened to them; they had experiences with what appeared to be different aliens; they had markedly different experiences; and they had different understandings of the aliens' intentions. Some abductees had fairly standard abduction experiences such as bedroom encounters. Some had bizarre experiences, such as one woman who had sex with an alien and had her ova "harvested" during a later abduction. Some had dream fragments of being at a different time and place on Earth, such as Greco-Roman periods, and conversing with "the masters." Still others believed they were chosen by the aliens for spiritual renewal and proselytizing the "truth" about the aliens' concerns for humans.

As a result of the disparate nature of each others' abduction accounts, members dropped out of the group and sought other support (although, to be fair, some continued to meet with each other privately and socially). Admittedly, the ideal situation would have a clinical expert at the helm of such a support group, and perhaps this might make a significant difference. Yet, if that facilitator had his or her own agenda, the support group would be of little true value in helping abductees cope with their experiences and might only serve to drive them deeper into possible psychoses. My own experience with this particular abductee support group makes me have grave concerns for abductees seeking help from counsellors and therapists.

Caring for Louis

In my initial stage of working with Louis, I met with him twice to talk about his experiences and to learn more about his views on UFOs, religion, and about his background and his family. I then contacted Cliff Noble, a clinical psychologist with whom I have been working for several years. He has acted as counsellor and therapist for or has otherwise overseen others' working with many abductees since I first approached him a decade ago. Initially wary and reluctant to take on abductees as clients, he became more curious through the course of his therapies with them, and is now more than a bit fascinated by the abduction phenomenon, although still retaining a solidly objective stance. Noble agreed to have Louis visit his office for an initial intake interview the following week, and I was invited, with Louis's permission, to sit in on the session.

Louis showed up at my office almost a half hour before he was scheduled. We were to walk over to Noble's office together because he was unfamiliar with the location. I asked him if he was nervous about meeting Noble, but he quickly reassured me he was not.

"I'm feeling all right about this," he told me. "This is what I want to do."

Nevertheless, in order to dispel any anxiety, I talked with him about a variety of issues and made sure that he was calm enough to discuss his experiences with a clinical psychologist. In my opinion, he was one of the most confident and self-assured abductees I had ever met. He was prepared to take that next, often-fearful step: to tell an "outsider" about his experiences.

When we arrived at Noble's office, we were led into a private room where we were joined by one of his associates, who would be sitting in to learn more about the abductee phenomenon first hand. The professionalism with which Louis and I were treated only added to the respect I have for a clinician open to seeing abductees.

Unlike some hypnotherapists' offices I had been in with abductees, the room we were in had no crystals on display, no New Age Muzak playing in the background, no distant surf white noise to induce lowered mental states, no incense burning, and no portable bells or drums to play while invoking a higher spiritual level. This was a clinical setting, and as such, a session with an abductee was exactly like a session with a person going through therapy to overcome grief due to a loss of a family member, or a person trying to overcome a crippling fear of flying.

Louis sat on a couch by himself, while the two psychologists sat across from him. I sat off to one side, clearly an observer.

Noble began by talking in general about his work with people and reassured Louis that his sessions were completely confidential. (I should note that I have changed some details in Louis's story to protect his anonymity.) He then asked Louis to explain why he was seeking help in coping with his fear of the dark, which was the clinical reason Noble was willing to see him.

Louis talked about some of his experiences; I didn't detect any major variances in his stories. Whenever there was a pause, Noble would ask a question to get more details and to clarify some issues. When Louis had finished his narration, Noble asked some more questions that seemed rather odd but made perfect sense from a psychological point of view.

"Have you ever had people come up to you as if they knew you, and you had no idea who they were?" he asked Louis. "Have people insisted they had seen you somewhere and you didn't remember ever being there?"

These were quite important, because Noble was trying to determine if Louis had any signs of Dissociative Identity Disorder (DID), a condition similar to the often-invoked Multiple Personality Disorder (MPD), whereby a person "becomes" someone else for a short period of time, without his "other" self knowing anything about it. The question was employed not to diagnose Louis, but because people with DID sometimes have problems while hypnotized, and its use is not recommended in such cases. As it turned out, Louis did not seem to have any symptoms of the condition.

Noble then went into great detail about the limitations and clinical use of hypnosis. He explained that hypnosis does not make you do anything against your will, but only loosens your inhibitions slightly, as if you "had a few beers."

"I want to know the truth," Louis stated.

"Hypnosis will not tell you the truth," cautioned Noble, surprising Louis a bit. "It can allow you to recall some details with greater clarity, but it can't ensure that only events that really happened will be remembered. It's not at all like it is portrayed on TV and in the movies."

Noble explained that hypnosis is a tool that has been practised for thousands of years. Not everyone can be hypnotized, but about one in five people make good subjects. Of those, about ten percent can be placed in such extreme hypnotic states that such things as surgery can be performed without any other anaesthetic.

However, hypnosis cannot make someone do anything that he or she wouldn't do while awake.

"If you don't normally disrobe in public, you won't under hypnosis," Noble advised. "And we won't make you forget everything you remembered under hypnosis. The idea is to allow you to remember."

Noble told us that once, while he himself was hypnotized by another colleague, a fire alarm went off. He heard the fire bell very clearly, but he remembers thinking, "What a nice fire alarm that is, and so nice to listen to!"

Before the intake session ended, Noble gave Louis a copy of the Minnesota Multiphasic Inventory (MMPI), a diagnostic test designed to check for signs of certain mental conditions and illnesses. Studies of abductees using the MMPI have indicated that abductees do not show any signs of "overt psychopathology" — that is, they are not mentally ill.

Not too surprisingly, Louis's MMPI was normal. The test revealed he had some minor elevated levels of distrust of authority and "wild ideas," so he seemed to be a typical young adult male. This was good news, because it meant that there was little danger from hypnotizing him.

When we met the next week, we went into the same comfortable room, except this time, the video camera was rolling. This was described by Noble as a very positive thing for Louis, since it meant that there was no reason to be fearful; we were all here to give him reassurance and support and would have a record of the session for his own comfort.

Noble and his assistant Cory sat directly in front of Louis, who was seated on the couch. I sat on another couch, off to one side and well out of camera range where I wouldn't disturb the proceedings.

Noble started by once again explaining the procedure and limitations of hypnosis. His goal was to give comfort to Louis as much as possible, without getting him anxious about the session. We all talked a bit about which consciously recalled incidents would be most interesting to explore, and decided on three: the camping trip, the levitation, and the figure in the doorway. Then, Noble began the relaxation techniques he uses to initiate a trance.

He told Louis to sit straight, with his hands on his legs, then to close his eyes. He began telling him to imagine the parts of his body were slowly getting relaxed and at ease. He directed him to remember a time and place where he felt very relaxed, and then encouraged him to imagine himself there again. He counted to ten slowly, instructing Louis that he would feel more and more relaxed at each number. It took about ten minutes before he got to a point where Louis was under.

"Hold your right arm straight out in front of you," Noble said, and Louis obliged. "Most people can hold their arm like that for a very long time, but you will suddenly notice your arm is getting very heavy, as if it were made of some dense material. The more you try to hold it up, the heavier it will feel, and you will be unable to resist its pull down to your leg. You can't fight it, even though you are struggling ..."

I watched as Louis visibly tried to keep his arm aloft, but failed. This was one of several tests for a hypnotic state which Noble employed. Finally, he was satisfied that Louis was in a sufficiently relaxed and suggestible state that he could be given instructions to go back in his memory to some incidents.

The first target was the night he saw the figure in the doorway. Noble told him to go back two years to that night, and asked him what he remembered.

"I am pinching myself," Louis said, deep in a trance. "I'm pinching myself to make sure I am awake."

"What do you see?" Noble asked.

"My wallpaper," was the reply. "The animals on my wallpaper."

"Anything else?"

"No, there isn't anything else."

This was a bit confusing, because he had said consciously that there had been a figure in the doorway.

"What happened just before you pinched yourself?" Noble asked, patiently. "What were you doing?"

Louis's brow furrowed over his closed eyes. "I'm looking in my brother's room. He's asleep."

Curiously, he had gone past the event to the end of his experience. He was remembering it backwards.

"My mother is asleep in her bed, too," Louis went on. "It wasn't her. Everyone else is asleep. But who was it?"

"Go back to just before this," directed Noble. "What happened before this? What did you see?"

Louis searched his memory for a moment. "I thought I heard some rustling or a noise like that in my room. I woke up facing the wall and listened."

"It's all right to turn your head to look," Noble said. "Go ahead."

Louis paused. "There's someone there ... a small person."

"Describe that person," Noble said. "Don't be afraid."

"I'm not afraid," Louis responded. "I feel calm. Tranquil."

Louis showed no sign of his fear of the dark or other anxiety. He was very relaxed and at ease, and his breathing was regular.

He went on. "It's very small. Just standing there, looking at me. It has big teardrop eyes, looking at me. Then it turns and walks away. Just like that."

"Can you see any other details?" Noble asked.

"No, just the head ... a big head, like a light bulb," Louis intoned. "It has long arms, very thin ... but I don't remember its legs." He shook his head slightly. "I don't see its legs."

"Can you remember anything else about it?"

"It's wearing kind of straps across its chest, like an X," Louis recalled.

Noble shifted his position in the chair.

"You're doing very good, Louis," he reassured. "Very good, indeed. Don't be afraid."

Louis shook his head again. "I'm not afraid. Peaceful."

"Okay, Louis," Noble directed. "Now, think back to a different time. The time you had gone through the patio doors. You remember that night clearly. What do you remember at the start?"

Louis concentrated. "Norman woke me up. It was about three o'clock in the morning. He woke me up and said he had a sore back. He wanted to have a cigarette, so I went with him outside and sat on the steps."

He paused. "He went back in right away. He must have smoked it fast because I'm all alone outside, and I'm still smoking mine ... I'm scared ..."

At this point, for the first time, Louis became visibly agitated. His forehead furrowed and his breathing started to become irregular.

"Why are you scared?" Noble asked him.

Louis started shaking. "I know they're out there. They want to do something. My stomach hurts. I feel sick to my stomach."

Seeing that Louis had started to sweat, Noble acted quickly to avoid an unpleasant mess.

"You're okay," he said to Louis. "There's nothing to be afraid of here. Your stomach is fine now. What is happening?"

"Norman is standing beside me and I'm bent over, holding my stomach. Now — my legs!" He got more agitated. "My legs are in the air! I can't stop them!"

"It's all right," Noble persisted. "You're safe. What is happening?"

"My legs are in front of me and I'm floating in the air ... I'm clenching my fists and I'm telling them to stop. I'm fighting them!"

Louis was indeed clenching his fists, and he continued: "I'm going outside through the patio doors ... I feel the curtains around me as I go through them."

"Where are you going?" asked Noble.

"There's a table outside ... I'm laying down on it ... I don't know where my undershirt is ... I sleep with my undershirt ... and my shorts ... are pulled down to my ankles..."

Louis by this time was almost gasping. He was very upset. His nose was running, tears were on his face and he was getting highly emotional. Noble tried to get Louis to describe what was occurring, but he simply couldn't — or wouldn't.

"Is there anyone with you? Can you see anyone beside you?"

"No," Louis shook his head, sobbing. "I don't see anyone."

Noble then told Louis to stop remembering that experience. Almost immediately, he became calmer and his breathing began to return to normal. Noble decided to end the session there. He started the waking-up procedure, which finished by getting Louis to count forwards to ten, getting more awake with each number. Finally, Louis opened his eyes and was awake.

We talked for a bit about what he had recalled, and I asked him if he could draw the figure in the doorway, which he did immediately. I then asked him if he remembered anything more about the incident where he was laying on the table.

"I get the impression there were some people there," he said, "a few in front and a few in back," although he said he couldn't be sure.

When Louis had recovered enough and we had talked through some of the remembered images, we left and the session was over for that day.

The third session

I had expected that the third session with Noble and Louis would involve hypnotic regression to probe beyond the boundary of his memory of being on the table outside. But Noble elected to go in a different direction.

When all of us were sitting in the room, Noble began to talk with Louis about his experience again. He pointed out that Louis seemed to have a lot of anxiety about the table scene, and talked with him frankly about his family life, friends, and sexual experiences. Then they talked about memory in general, how it operates, and how images can be locked up until they are triggered by other events.

Noble tried repeatedly to search for ways to independently verify some of Louis's memories. While Louis said that Norman did remember some events from that night, he did not share some of the same memories. Also, Norman was not available for any sessions or regression.

"Since you were outside, do you have any memory of hearing some ambient noise?" Noble asked.

"None," Louis replied.

"Were there any streetlights shining into your room?"

Louis thought for a moment then said, "Yes, there was a streetlight shining in my window. That's why I usually closed the curtains. But I don't remember it that night."

Noble talked with Louis for nearly an hour, comforting him and gently probing his conscious memory. Finally, Noble explained why he was not going to do further regression at this time.

"You seem to have a relatively consistent recall of events up until that point," he said. "I'm afraid that since you have read a considerable number of UFO books, your memory of what happened next may be affected by what you have read."

Noble pointed out that Louis did display some rather significant anxiety and fear. He suggested that the next logical step would be to work with Louis on some relaxation techniques designed to reduce these fears and anxiety. Then, when Louis had gained more confidence and was more calm in preparing to deal with his fear of whatever happened that night, another hypnosis regression session could be scheduled.

He told me later: "There is no use in trying to force the memory.

When I work with abuse victims or victims of crime, any good lawyer can tear apart a testimony based on images brought out only through hypnosis. What we need to do is to help Louis relax to the point he can consciously recall further details and then refine his memory from there."

Noble's concerns do seem to be justified when one thinks of the tenuous nature of memory. Researcher Elizabeth Loftus has suggested corroboration is one of the best bets for dealing with recovered memories. In a major article in *Scientific American*, she noted that

> ... simply because we can implant false childhood memories in some individuals in no way implies that all memories that arise after suggestion are necessarily false. Put another way, although experimental work on false memory creation may raise doubt about the validity of long-buried memories, such as repressed trauma, it in no way disproves them. Without corroboration, there is little that can be done by even the most experienced evaluator to differentiate true memories from ones that are suggestively planted.
> (Loftus, Elizabeth. 1997. "Creating false memories." *Scientific American*, September 1997.)

In fact, this issue is so contentious, a ban on using any method to recover memories was imposed on members of the British Royal College of Psychiatrists. This was because of concerns that false memories could be produced, giving rise to false allegations.

> The Royal College guidelines say there is no evidence that recovered memory techniques can reveal memory of real events or accurately elaborate factual information about past experiences.
> (Hall, Celia. 1997. "Recovering memory banned by psychiatrists." *London Daily Telegraph*, October 1, 1997, p.6.)

A spokesman for the College said: "We clearly came to the conclusion that it is possible in the intense relationship that can develop between a therapist and a patient to produce entirely false memory."

Louis was scheduled for several additional appointments for the relaxation training. Since this part of the case was not related to UFOs, I deferred to Noble's expertise and his private therapy with Louis. Noble assured me that if any further details of that fateful night surfaced during relaxation exercises, I would be called in immediately. And, when Louis is finally comfortable and better prepared to deal with his own memories, we can then explore beyond the curtains.

Louis's dilemma is best illustrated by his own thoughts, written in his diary. They give a sense of why he is troubled by his experiences, and why we should show compassion for the abductees' plight:

> How do I begin to understand who I am when I'm unwillingly blind to parts of my life? I guess I have to feel around to even just get a grasp on this whole phenomenon, which I'll never fully understand.

CHAPTER FOUR
Dissociative Disorders:

How [Not] to Tell if You've Been Abducted by Aliens

Making a list

As part of their support for one another, some abductees and abduction ufologists have been compiling lists of characteristics and recurring themes that occur in abductees' lives. These lists are thought to be indicators of abductions, and have been circulated in various forms.

One such list, posted to the Internet, is quite fascinating. It is located at www.anw.com/aliens/52questions.htm. They ask if you:

1. Have had missing or lost time of any length, especially one hour or more.
2. Have been paralyzed in bed with a being in your room.
3. Have unusual scars or marks with no possible explanation on how you received them, especially if you have an emotional reaction to them. (e.g. small scoop indentation, straight line scar, scars in roof of mouth, in nose, behind or in ears, on genitals, etc.)
4. Have seen balls of light or flashes of light in your home or other locations.
5. Have a memory of flying through the air that could not be a dream.
6. Have a "marker memory" that will not go away (e.g. alien face, examination, needle, table, strange baby, etc.).
7. Have seen beams of light outside your home, or coming into your room through a window.

8. Have had dreams of UFOs, beams of light, or alien beings.

9. Have had a UFO sighting or sightings in your life.

10. Have a cosmic awareness, an interest in ecology, environment, vegetarianism, or are very socially conscious.

11. Have a strong sense of having a mission or important task to perform, without knowing where this compulsion came from.

12. Have had unexplainable events occur in your life, and felt strangely anxious afterwards.

13. For women only: Have had false pregnancy or missing fetus. (Pregnant, and then not.)

14. Have awoken in place or position other than where or how you went to sleep (e.g. in your car, or upside down in bed), or don't remember ever going to sleep.

15. Have had a dream of eyes such as animal eyes (like an owl or deer), or remember seeing an animal looking in at you. Also if you have a fear of eyes.

16. Have awoken in the middle of the night, startled.

17. Have strong reaction to the cover of *Communion* or pictures of aliens. Either an aversion to or being drawn to it.

18. Have inexplicably strong fears or phobias (e.g. heights, snakes, spiders, large insects, certain sounds, bright lights, your personal security, or being alone).

19. Have experienced self-esteem problem much of your life.

20. Have seen someone with you become paralyzed, motionless, or frozen in time, especially someone you sleep with.

21. Have awoken with marks, burns, or bruises that appeared during the night with no explanation as to how you could possibly have received them.

22. Have had someone in your life who claims to have witnessed a ship or alien near you or has witnessed you having been missing.

23. Have had, at any time, blood or an unusual stain on a sheet or pillow, with no explanation of how it got there.

24. Have an interest in the subject of UFOs or aliens, are perhaps compelled to read about it a lot, or have an extreme aversion towards the subject.

25. Have been suddenly compelled to drive or walk to an out-of-the-way or unknown area.

26. Have the feeling of being watched much of the time, especially at night.

27. Have had dreams of passing through a closed window or solid wall.

28. Have seen a strange fog or haze that should not be there.
29. Have heard strange humming or pulsing sounds, and you could not identify the source.
30. Have had unusual nose bleeds at any time in your life, or have awoken with a nose bleed.
31. Have awoken with soreness in your genitals that could not be explained.
32. Have had back or neck problems, T-3 vertebrae out often, or awoken with an unusual stiffness in any part of the body.
33. Have had chronic sinusitis or nasal problems.
34. Have had electronics around you go haywire or oddly malfunction with no explanation (such as street lights going out as you walk under them, TVs and radios affected as you move close, etc.).
35. Have seen a hooded figure in or near your home, especially next to your bed.
36. Have had frequent or sporadic ringing in your ears, especially in one ear.
37. Have an unusual fear of doctors or tend to avoid medical treatment.
38. Have insomnia or sleep disorders that are puzzling to you.
39. Have had dreams of doctors or medical procedures.
40. Have frequent or sporadic headaches, especially in the sinus, behind one eye, or in one ear.
41. Have the feeling that you are going crazy for even thinking about these sorts of things.
42. Have had paranormal or psychic experiences, including intuition.
43. Have been prone to compulsive or addictive behaviour.
44. Have channelled telepathic messages from extraterrestrials.
45. Have been afraid of your closet, now or as a child.
46. Have had sexual or relationship problems (such as a mysterious "feeling" that you must not become involved in a relationship because it would interfere with "something" important you must do).
47. Have to sleep against the wall or must sleep with your bed against a wall.
48. Have a difficult time trusting other people, especially authority figures.
49. Have had dreams of destruction or catastrophe.
50. Have the feeling that you are not supposed to talk about these things, or that you should not talk about them.
51. Have tried to resolve these types of problems with little or no success.
52. Have many of these traits but can't remember anything about an abduction or alien encounter.

These are very specific characteristics, but it can easily be seen that many are not specific to alien abductions. For example, if someone has had sexual problems (#46), it may or may not be because of contact with aliens. (In fact, the presence of this trait in a list compiled by and for abductees might also be an indication of other psychological problems among this group.)

Numbers #44 and #45 are so dramatically different that one can hardly not be astonished by their inclusion. If anyone has in fact channelled messages from aliens, they would be certainly in the category of abductee or contactee. But simply to have been afraid of your closet when you were a child is not that unusual at all. The juxtaposition of the two questions automatically implies that one is related to the other, and this is not established in any real way. It relates normal childhood fears to something much more complex and indeterminable.

Number #48: a distrust of authority? Is this an indicator of abductions or simply a dissatisfaction with bureaucracy? Again, a common characteristic, but when combined with things such as seeing a hooded figure near your bed (#35), are we really getting a reading of someone's abduction-proneness, or just a series of unrelated concepts?

The point about having some of the traits but not remembering anything about an alien encounter is also curious. If someone doesn't have any memory about an alien abduction, it is because he or she can't remember being abducted. However, if a person *does* have some memory of an experience, does that mean the memory is false?

Abductees and "normality"

Are these traits really indications of abductions? Is it possible that they suggest something else entirely?

Debunkers sometimes claim that abductees suffer from some form of psychological disorder, although there is little formal research that supports this contention. In fact, abduction researchers counter this argument with results from studies that show the opposite: that abductees appear to be normal, functioning people with no signs of any psychopathology.

For example, Rima Laibow is a psychiatrist who has studied groups of abductees and published her results widely. In her reading of abductees, they are quite normal. In one study, she noted: "Patients who believe themselves to be UFO abductees are a heterogeneous group widely dispersed along demographic and cultural lines."

She further explains:

It is intuitively seductive (and perhaps comfortable) for us to assume that psychotic-level functioning will necessarily be present in a person claiming to be a UFO abductee. If this level of distortion and delusion is present, a patient would be expected to demonstrate some other evidence of reality distortion. Pathology of this magnitude would not be predicted to be present in a well-integrated, mature, and non-psychotic individual. Instead, we would expect clinical and psychometric tools to reveal serious problems in numerous areas both inter- and intrapersonally. It would be highly surprising if otherwise well-functioning persons were to demonstrate a single area of floridly psychotic distortion.... Well-developed, fixed delusional states with numerous elaborated and sequential components are not seen in otherwise healthy individuals. Prominent evidence of deep dysfunction would be expected to pervade many areas of the patient's life. One would predict that if the abduction experience were the product of delusional or other psychotic states, it would be possible to detect such evidence through the clinical and psychometric tools available to us.

This points to the first important discrepancy: individuals claiming alien abduction frequently show no evidence of past or present psychosis, delusional thinking, reality-testing deficits, hallucinations or other significant psychopathology despite extensive clinical evaluation. Instead, there is a conspicuous absence of psychopathology of the magnitude necessary to account for the production of floridly delusional and presumably psychotic material.

(Laibow, R. (1993). *Clinical discrepancies between expected and observed data in patients reporting UFO abductions: Implications for treatment.* Published on the Internet.)

In effect, Laibow completely negates the debunkers' argument. In her view, abductees are completely "normal."

In order to test this idea further, Laibow administered standard psychological tests to a group of abductees. An independent evaluator of the tests, unaware of the subjects' abduction experiences, found them to be all relatively intelligent and had "rich" mental lives but had weak sexual identities, impaired personal relationships, and tended to be paranoid, being wary and cautious of others. Laibow interpreted these results as showing no *significant* psychopathology.

While this is true (the abductees weren't violent or obviously catatonic), the comments by the evaluator might suggest they had, however, some need for counselling on a number of grounds. Laibow reported that the abductees' experiences could not be explained as fantasies unless they were pathological liars, paranoid schizophrenics, or severely disturbed individuals suffering from fugue states or multiple personality disorders. She noted "there is clinical evidence that at least some abductees are highly functioning, healthy individuals."

Laibow noted four reasons why abductions could not be explained as psychological problems:

1. The aforementioned absence of psychopathology.

2. The similarity of reports. Although the details of the abduction stories differ, there is a general thread that links them. Why aliens, for example? Why not the Wicked Witch of the West? Also, the stories are complex, but not as wildly rich as other fantasies produced by mentally ill persons. The aliens fly saucers, not teacups, and are grey, not polka-dotted.

3. Abductees resist being led or diverted in their storytelling by a hypnotist, implying they are not overly suggestive.

4. Abductees frequently show signs of Post-Traumatic Stress Disorder (PTSD), which normally results from events such as rape, abuse, or other violence. If abductees have not had such real-life experiences, why do they show such traits?

Laibow's second point is a good one. Why *do* abductees report aliens and not other creatures, for example?

One reason why this might be so is found in sociology, not psychology. Today, we have become sensitized to the concept of space travel and aliens. Hardly a TV commercial goes by without some reference, such as aliens abducting people for drinking the wrong brand of cola or UFOs leaving circles and chocolate in wheat fields. Nearly all television programs, from soap operas to comedies, have had UFO- or space-related episodes. Some of the most popular TV series include space operas such as "Star Trek" and "The X-Files," with all their associated spin-offs.

In 1996, while an American astronaut was spending half a year on board a Russian space station, hardly a word was mentioned by the press about her progress. We've become very used to space themes, and it's safe to say that aliens and spaceships are now part of our culture, at least in our imaginations.

Alien abductions have been with us roughly since the space race of the 1950s. UFOs, or what we believe are forerunners of UFOs, can be traced much farther back in time. In the late 1800s, people saw lights in the sky and interpreted them as balloons or airships. In the early part of this century, there were "mystery aeroplanes." It seems that mysteries, especially aerial ones, are explained in terms of popular beliefs relating to possible reality.

We can go back a bit more, actually, and see this in action throughout history. In the middle ages, it was fairies, witches, and dragons that were responsible for mysterious effects. During the Roman Empire, it was the gods. In other words, strange phenomena are interpreted by people as their current technological awareness allows. That's why flying shields flew over ancient Carthage and why flying saucers now fly over Gulf Breeze, Florida.

This could explain why it is aliens who are abducting abductees, but why would they be conducting medical examinations? Could it have something to do with the feeling of helplessness and distrust found in many abductees? Is it because there is a growing distrust of scientific and medical personnel that abductees personify such fears?

Laibow offered some advice for other health professionals confronted with an abductee:

> It is not within the area of expertise of the clinician to make an accurate determination about the objective validity of UFO abduction events. But it is certainly within his purview to assist the patient in regaining a sense of appropriate mastery, anxiety reduction, and the alleviation of the clinical symptomatology as efficiently and effectively as possible. This is best accomplished through an assessment the patient's actual state of psycho-dynamic organization, not his presumed state. In other words, in order to make the diagnosis of a psychotic or delusional state, findings other than the presence of a belief in UFO abduction must be present. In the absence of other indications of severe psychopathology, it is inappropriate to treat the patient as if he were afflicted with such psychopathology. It lies outside the realm of clinical expertise to determine with absolute certainty whether or not a UFO abduction has indeed taken place. Patients should

not be viewed as demonstrating prima facie evidence of pervasive psychotic dysfunction because of the abduction material alone nor should they be hospitalized or treated with anti-psychotic medication based solely on the presence of UFO abduction scenarios. Instead, they should be assessed on the basis of their overall psychologic state.

She insisted that just because a person thinks he or she is an abductee, there is no reason to assume there is anything "wrong" with that person. This is probably true, but is it possible that an abduction "memory" is a sign of a completely different problem?

Join the dissociation

Dissociation is defined generally as a psychological state in which a person becomes "removed" from reality. It is a "disconnection" from full awareness of ourselves and the world. Most of us have experienced a form of dissociation at some point, such as daydreaming, highway hypnosis (that trance-like feeling that develops as we pass endless numbers of telephone poles) or "getting lost" in a book or TV show. (Children are particularly susceptible to this latter form of dissociation, much to the chagrin of their parents.) These all involve a state whereby we "lose touch" with our surroundings and essentially "tune out" so that we lose track of time and where we are. Sometimes, it takes quite an effort on our part or by others to rouse us.

One kind of dissociation is what is known as "night terrors." In this normal and common state, you wake up feeling that you are paralyzed and unable to move, and are somehow under attack or otherwise very anxious. Folklorist David Hufford studied reports of this kind of experience and wrote a classic work titled *The Terror that Comes in the Night* (University of Pennsylvania, 1982). He found that such night terrors were widespread throughout our culture, and often included such elements as "hagging," in which a terrifying entity, looking like a naked, withered crone, hovers over a paralyzed victim's bed.

It should be emphasized that this kind of dissociation is *normal* and has to do with the way in which our brains function when we are concentrating, devoted to a particular task or in that twilight period between sleep and wakefulness. In the latter case, it is known that as we descend into sleep, our bodies "shut down" and we lose motor skills before we actually "turn off" our sight and hearing. So, being awake and realizing we are unable to move isn't that unusual. However, in severe cases, dissociation is a much bigger problem than simple sleep paralysis.

Dissociation is also one defence that our brains use to deal with trauma, particularly childhood trauma. When confronted by severe abuse, children will run away from their aggressors. When physical escape is not possible, psychological escape may be the only way out. In this way, thoughts, feelings, memories, and images of the traumatic event can be removed from the child's mind, allowing him or her to function relatively normally. It's a very effective survival technique — up to a point. If dissociation is used too often (for example, in a case of frequent abuse), it becomes a "natural" way of dealing with the world, even long after the abuse has stopped and there are no longer any threats.

So, if a person had been abused as a child and became used to using dissociation as a way of coping with the stress, as an adult, dissociation might be used involuntarily in a less appropriate situation. Chronic dissociation may lead to serious impairment in all aspects of life, including work, social activities, and interpersonal relationships. And, if dissociation continues for long periods of time, separate mental states may begin to exist independently, and these are the "multiple personalities" of which much has been written.

What are the symptoms of dissociative disorders? There are many, including: depression, mood swings, suicidal tendencies, insomnia, night terrors, sleep walking, panic attacks, phobias, substance abuse, compulsions, visual or auditory hallucinations ("inner voices"), eating disorders, headaches, amnesia, time loss, trances, and out-of-body-experiences. Furthermore, clinical psychiatrists also look for signs of blackouts, "possession," sudden changes in relationships, fluctuations in skills and knowledge, fragmentary recall of life history, spontaneous trances, enthralment, and rapture.

Many of these, of course, are also noted in the list for determining if one is an abductee! Does this mean that abductees are dissociative?

Now look at this other list:

Some common symptoms of Dissociative Identity Disorder:

- losing time/being in a new place or situation with no memory of how you got there
- feeling "little"/like a child
- sudden disorientation/feeling as if you missed something

- memories seen as happening to someone else
- memories available only sporadically, possibly including non-abuse and recent memories
- inadvertent use of the word "we" to refer to self
- frequent out-of-character actions that surprise even you
- actions that are overset with a haziness, as if you aren't really in control of what's going on; feeling removed from one's actions
- other people noting one or more of the above in you
- likewise, other people discussing with you things they say you did/said but that you yourself have little or no memory of, provided that you were not under the influence of any sort of drug at the time

It would be easy to compare the lists and declare that abductees and dissociative people are one and the same, but things are not that simple. People are only diagnosed as being dissociative if they have some of these symptoms *and* a psychiatrist can find that the patient has two or more distinct personalities, seems to have large gaps in memory, and has no signs of substance abuse. Only then can it be said that the person is truly dissociative.

Dissociation is thought to occur in as much as 1 percent of all adults. This is an astounding number of individuals, but it must be remembered that in mild cases, the dissociation might not be noticed. Perhaps, a mildly dissociative person would be viewed by others as a bit eccentric, obsessive, or "flighty."

Clinically dissociative people have documented histories of trauma (often life-threatening in nature) at an early age. Although child abuse is the most common cause, there are other sources of trauma that could be catalysts, including natural disasters, painful medical operations, war, and torture. So, unless abductees show signs of trauma in their lives, it might not be fair to diagnose them as dissociative. Yet, the symptoms of dissociative disorder are *so* similar to those of abductions, we must pause to wonder about a possible relationship between the two.

Among the diagnostic criteria for schizophrenia as outlined in the DSM-IV (the current diagnostic manual used by psychiatrists) are: delusions, hallucinations, disorganized speech, and catatonic behaviour. Auditory hallucinations, such as running conversations with a voice in your head or with someone/something that is invisible to everyone else, are bad signs. The manual also notes such effects as problems in dealing with or fitting in with the rest of society, including problems at work, interpersonal relations, and poor self-care. Given these generalized symptoms, it's easy to imagine how psychiatrists would view an abductee's story.

Another factor we must take into consideration is the existence of false memories. As can be seen from the case study of Angie, there do exist some concerns that some memories of child abuse and trauma may be spurious or "planted" by self-serving therapists. Although there is no question that abuse exists, organizations such as the False Memory Syndrome Foundation caution that the numbers of cases may be greatly exaggerated.

In a statement on the recovery of memories of sexual abuse, the president of the American Psychological Association noted that: "Human memories are not like fixed images in a family photo album. They can be shaped by a variety of influences at the time of the event and in later years." The APA also advised that memories can be influenced by questioning, especially in young children. They noted that memories "can also be influenced when a trusted person, such as a therapist, "suggests abuse as an explanation for symptoms/problems despite initial lack of memory of such abuse." And, what's worse, "repeated questioning may lead individuals to report 'memories' of events that never occurred."

If actual abuse cases are susceptible to therapists' biases and own beliefs, we absolutely *must* look askance at abductions. There is no doubt that some abduction therapists are driven by personal goals and are caught up in the intense media feeding frenzy for sensational stories. We have already noted that *anyone* can claim to have expertise in ufology, particularly abduction ufology. And, since there are no universally accepted standards for ufologists, there is no guarantee that an abductee can receive adequate care from within the ufological community.

CHAPTER FIVE
All in Your Head?

One of the most important experiments in the history of ufology was conducted in the 1970s by Alvin Lawson, a professor of English working with a group of California ufologists. Lawson asked an important question about UFO abductions, centred around the way abductees verbally describe their experiences. Because this was very early in the evolution of abduction ufology, it couldn't include the more recent spectacular cases that occurred after an increase in media exposure. However, the implications of the experiment are even more important now that we can look back in retrospect.

Lawson asked one simple question: Is there any difference between "real" abduction experiences and those that are deliberately created in peoples' imaginations? What he did was take a group of people who had not had an abduction experience, and a group of abductees. He hypnotized the non-abductee group to believe that they *had* been abducted by aliens, and then compared the recalled stories of the two groups. He wanted to know how the stories would differ; the idea was that if alien abduction stories are just stories, then the two groups would essentially be identical, and abductions would seem to be only fictions.

After all the subjects had been hypnotized and the elements of the stories compared, Lawson found that the abductees' and non-abductees' stories were basically the same. Both reported intense light sources as well as coloured and pulsing lights. There were humming sounds heard, a sense of floating, physical examinations by humanoid beings and messages that were imparted by the abductees' captors.

In effect, it appeared that abductions could be duplicated in the laboratory through the use of hypnosis. Not only could hypnosis be used to uncover hidden abductions, but it could be used to make them up entirely!

Lawson cited a similar experiment that involved a comparison between drawings of UFOs made by UFO witnesses and those sketched by those who had not seen any UFOs. Not surprisingly, there were no substantial differences, "indicating that anyone can sketch a UFO 'accurately' whether or not he/she has had a UFO experience." The fact that non-witnesses and non-abductees described identical aliens and UFOs prompted some soul-searching.

Lawson noted that the results

> make one wonder how much — if any — UFO witness testimony is ever "true." Further, researchers have determined that during REM or dream sleep, the human muscular system undergoes a mild paralysis (perhaps to prevent the physical acting-out of dreams). Close encounter witnesses frequently report a sense of paralysis at the first approach of a UFO and/or at other intense moments. But several imaginary abductees — and their enigmatic consistency is maddening — described feeling paralyzed at similar moments. If the paralysis means that UFO experiences are related to dreams, then how do we explain the imaginary abductees' reports of paralysis?

However, Lawson noted four reasons why he thought this still did not mean that UFO abductions were illusory. First, he observed that there exist multiple-witness abduction cases, even though it is unlikely that multiple hallucinations can occur. Second, he raised the issue of physical and physiological effects associated with some abductions. Third, hallucinating subjects do not immediately think their experiences are real, whereas abductees "are persuaded very early of the 'reality' of the event — however incredible they know it to be." Finally, Lawson pointed out that while the triggering mechanism for hallucinations and imaginary abductions can be determined, the stimulus for *real* abductions is unknown.

Today, though, we can challenge these four objections. We don't necessarily have to try to "debunk" abductions, but we have to make very sure that there are no alternative explanations for the phenomena before betting the farm. After all, the implications are rather significant.

It is *possible* that multiple witness cases are in fact spurious or unsupported, and that shared abductions are the result of dreams discussed between experiencers. For example, in one situation, two people immersed in New Age philosophy might be talking to each other about alien abductions each day. They might read the same books and discuss the abduction cases described therein. If one of them becomes an abductee, the other could subconsciously or consciously pick up on the other's experience and passively "share" the abduction. This isn't necessarily a case of shared hallucinations, but shared verbal and non-verbal impressions between impressionable people.

The issue of physical and physiological effects such as implants and scoop marks has already been discussed. They don't seem to be particularly good proof of anything, at this point, anyway.

What about abductees "feeling" that their experiences are "real?" Even in the relatively small sample of cases with which I have been involved, several abductees said they were confused because they could not tell whether or not their experiences were "real" or dreams. I don't think this is a consistent characteristic of abductions that can be relied upon to distinguish between hallucinated experiences and "real" abductions — unless we can accept that abductions are only hallucinations. Since this appears to be an unsatisfactory situation, we have to look a little further.

When memories are wrong

I had a rather humbling experience not long ago when I was shown that my memory of a particular event was in error. In 1978, I helped organize the first-ever science fiction convention in Winnipeg, called UN-CON. I was part of the sponsoring group, named Decadent Winnipeg Fandom (the name comes from a long story having to do with alcohol and the extroverted actions of some members).

Winnipeg is also the home to my good friend and mentor, Chester Cuthbert, a longtime fan and librarian of the original Winnipeg Science Fiction Society. His knowledge of science fiction as a genre, not just literature, is beyond comparison. Although Chester's SF collecting began when pulp fiction was wild and romantic, as a rule, he had never gone to see any "space operas" at movie theatres, not even *Star Wars*, which was a fine example of a thirties-style SF romance.

Not that we didn't try to take him to see one. And, during UN-CON, I remember taking Chester to see a private screening of a short film titled

The Ugly Little Boy, based on an Isaac Asimov story about a Neanderthal child brought forward in time and the touching relationship he had with a motherly doctor on a scientific team. In a science fiction publication, I wrote about how I and a few others coerced Chester into grudgingly agreeing to view the movie at the convention. I remember that he liked it and that I was also impressed with the plot, character development, and screenplay. It wasn't bad for a low-budget SF film in its time.

A few years ago, during the taping of a TV series about science fiction fandom, this particular event came up in a conversation on the set. I was one of the hosts, and for one show Chester was among the guests. I kidded him about dragging him off to the film, but Chester (who, incidentally, is forty years older than me) insisted that he did not see the movie as I remembered it. Of course, thinking that my more youthful memory was superior, I entered into a good-natured argument, since I could clearly recall taking Chester into the movie screening and that it occurred during UN-CON.

It was only recently, in 1999, when I found out how wrong memories can be. I dropped in on Chester for a visit, and after I sat down, he excused himself briefly then returned with some sheets of paper, browned with age. With a smile, he handed them to me to read, then sat back in his well-worn but comfortable chair.

I read them and immediately ate some crow. One item was a timetable of events for a conference on education, at which I and Chester were guests. Also on the program was the screening of *The Ugly Little Boy*. The conference occurred many months after UN-CON. The other item was his typed review of the conference, which described how he had finally been convinced to see a modern SF movie.

I was *so* convinced that Chester and I saw the movie at UN-CON that my mind fabricated a completely inaccurate, but *possible* series of memories to back up my belief. What's more, I could visualize each step of the non-event with great clarity. I'm not sure where my memory went astray, but this realization showed me that no memory is completely without fault. Of course, this brings up the obvious question: What *else* in my life have I only imagined?

Cause and effect

Getting back to Lawson's views on abductions, what about the physiological mechanism that may actually cause them? We know what may trigger false memories in some situations, but what are the stimuli for abductions?

We can get around this one easily, too. If some abductions are a psychological disorder of some kind, then they will have a resolvable cause.

This exercise in devil's advocacy is certainly not definitive. Either side can be argued at length, so we can only say that the line between abductions and imagined experiences is not as solid as we would like. We have to understand that abductions, above all else, are a subjective phenomenon, dependent on the perceptions, emotions, and mental states of the experiencers. If they really do have a physical (read: *extraterrestrial*) component, we have to look elsewhere for the evidence.

UFOs: The shocking truth

Although there is a social stigma associated with emotional and psychological problems, there is no reason to think that a person who displays symptoms of such problems is necessarily ill. This is because the human body can be affected by its environment, and the brain is a delicate organ that can be influenced by many external forces.

One of the most innocuous effects on our bodies is that of electromagnetism (EM). In severe cases, of course, an electrical shock can kill us, but more subtle EM radiation can actually be of some benefit. Electrical stimulation to help tissue and bone regeneration has been tried for many years, and electrical stimulation through acupuncture needles is gaining some ground even in traditional medicine.

On the negative side, certain kinds of EM radiation are definitely bad news. We are warned to check for leakage around our microwave ovens, and there is a great controversy centred around the possibility that television screens and computer monitors are linked to cataracts. Another controversy surrounds the concept that EM fields around power transmission lines are dangerous to our health and can contribute to increased likelihood of getting cancer.

Rock and roll

Natural phenomena have often been suggested as an explanation for UFOs. One main problem with this explanation is that UFO reports offer such a wide variety of characteristics that natural phenomena inevitably fall short of explaining all UFO traits. This hasn't stopped some people from explaining UFO reports as products of natural processes, however.

One theory that seems capable of explaining many UFO characteristics is based on a combination of various physical mechanisms and processes. This theory, called the Tectonic Strain Theory (TST), begins with the suggestion that rock under stress deep within the Earth can produce electromagnetic discharges. Basically, the crust of the Earth is composed of layers of rock that are pressing down upon one another, compressing the layers underneath. This pressure effectively causes the solid rock to creak and bend, and in doing so, releases electromagnetic energy. The amount of energy isn't very strong, but it is measurable, and in fact the detection of this energy is sometimes used to understand when earthquakes might be occurring.

This energy may manifest itself in one of two basic ways. One way is by it becoming visible as a moving spark or blob of light. The other way is by this energy affecting the human brain so that the observer will "believe" he or she is viewing a moving body of light or having a UFO experience!

Now, there's no real evidence that this is what is actually occurring in nature, but some statistical evidence has been presented in support of this theory. The numbers of reported UFOs in an area and the level of seismic activity in that area have been compared and found to be statistically related. Whether this is a "real" relationship or just coincidence is a matter of much heated debate. Other studies have attempted to show that variations in the Earth's magnetic field are also related to the number of UFO reports and other unusual phenomena.

The idea that UFOs are related to natural Earth processes was first presented by French ufologist Claude Poher in 1974, with limited success. The theory resurfaced in the context of the TST in the late 1970s and early 1980s. Papers dealing with certain aspects of the TST have been published in several journals, covering various disciplines. The proposed mechanism is interdisciplinary in nature, and carries with it some necessary qualifications to enable it to cope with one poorly understood phenomenon (UFOs) in terms of other poorly understood phenomena (earthquake lights and earthquake prediction).

The theory is best explained by its major proponent, Michael A. Persinger, a physiological psychologist at Laurentian University in Sudbury, Ontario:

Essentially ... normal geophysical processes applied in unusual space-time configurations are responsible for electromagnetic phenomena that have direct physical and biological consequences. These processes involve normal alterations in tectonic (structural) stresses within the Earth's crust and are mediated by piezoelectric-like effects. The primary natural analog of this putative phenomena would be earthquake lightning.... Whereas earthquake-related luminosities appear contingent upon large releases of structural strain (seismic activities), the luminosities and electromagnetic correlates of alleged close encounters with UFOs are associated with highly localized, less intense changes in crustal structures not necessarily involving major seismic activity. (Persinger, 1979b.)

In layperson's language, Persinger thinks that even if no earthquake is actually felt at the time of a UFO sighting, the energy from stressed rock deep within the Earth could still be responsible. In fact, in his major omnibus paper on the TST published on the Internet, he states very clearly that "UFO reports can occur anywhere" because underground stress is never nil. The TST therefore explains all UFO reports, no matter where they occur, and without any sign of or nearness to rock stress such as earthquakes or tremors. It also explains all *kinds* of UFO reports, from nocturnal lights to daylight discs and from landing traces to alien abductions. (Website: www.laurentian.ca/www/neurosci/tectonicedit.htm)

The TST draws upon several processes for its mechanism, each of them linked by scientific-sounding and logical arguments. The major steps involved are:

1) Strain is produced in the Earth's crust.
2) Strain produces an electromagnetic discharge.
3A) The electromagnetic discharge produces a spark or blob of light.
4A) The light is observed as a UFO.

Alternatively, steps 3A and 4A may be replaced by:

3B) The electromagnetic discharge affects a person.
4B) The person believes that he/she has seen a UFO or was abducted by aliens.

Evidence for the TST?

Earthquake prediction is a very hot topic in tremor-prone areas of the world. Earthquakes can occur without warning and do a great deal of damage. Seismologists are studying a variety of reported earthquake precursors on record, including the way the ground actually swells and "deflates" slightly as the stresses build up and decay, changes in the level of well water, and even the unusual behaviour of animals. (Some researchers are convinced that an increase in the number of "lost" pet ads placed in newspapers means that an earthquake is imminent!)

One earthquake predictor that has received some attention is the emission of electromagnetic energy from inside the Earth. For example, on March 31, 1980, electromagnetic pulses, essentially radio signals, were recorded thirty minutes before a powerful earthquake in Japan. Unfortunately, energy detected before earthquakes isn't always at the same frequency, and it's difficult to formulate a consistent theory for using the radio signals to warn of impending danger.

It has been known for some time that the rocks and minerals under pressure produce energy. The strongest bursts of energy come from minerals like quartz and other crystals, while rocks such as sandstone are almost inert. What actually produces the energy when rock is stressed isn't understood, although several theories have been proposed.

The term "piezoelectricity" comes from the Greek word "piezein," meaning "to press." Piezoelectricity is an electrical charge produced when crystalline material is subjected to pressure. An example is the crystal in a crystal radio; the scratching of a needle on the crystal's surface makes the radio work. (Another example is the luminous effect caused by biting down on a wintergreen candy or mint.) In nature, crystalline rocks such as quartz will have a certain amount of piezoelectric potential when they are stressed by rocks above them or below. Even though this can produce energy, there is some doubt that piezoelectricity can produce earthquake lights because it is short-lived and dies out quickly. But the piezoelectric field could also create "transistors" within the rock, using the layers of semiconducting minerals occurring naturally in the ore. These "transistors" could be coupled into "circuits," and energy might be amplified in the process. A burst of light might become visible to an observer, who might think it was a UFO.

However, even if visible light is produced, its nature is not well understood. This luminescence has been reported in the geophysical literature, especially in the form of "comet tails" detected on photographic film close to the rock undergoing fracture. In laboratories, some small, luminous bodies have been detected on a film of the fracturing of a core sample. They look like sparks, like when you hit a rock with a hammer, but these are believed to be fracture- and not impact-related. The theory is that such lights produced outside the laboratory will be much larger than those observed in the laboratory, perhaps reaching one metre or more in diameter.

If it is indeed possible that balls of light can be produced in nature by crustal stress, then it is likely that they would have been observed and reported. Are these what is reported as UFOs?

There are other rare, natural phenomena that appear as lights in the night sky. These include ball lightning and earthquake lights, both of which are still not fully understood by scientists, but progress is being made in unravelling their mysteries.

In general, earthquake lights are large domes of light, twenty to two hundred metres in diameter, seen about the time of an earthquake and with a duration of a few seconds to a few minutes. In addition, radio interference is reported when they are seen. A weird form of lightning, called ball lightning, has been reported occasionally, but enough cases are on record that some characteristics have been determined. It is generally spherical, with a diameter of about thirty centimetres, and may contain a large amount of energy.

Fields of dreams

The TST doesn't actually say that UFOs are caused by earthquakes, only that they are related. They have in common a strain field which is thought to be very broad and can stretch many kilometres across the surface of the Earth and also deep underground. An earthquake is an indication that such a field exists, as are UFOs.

Because an earthquake isn't an actual cause of UFOs, advocates of the TST say that a fracture (earthquake) might occur many kilometres distant and many days or even months separated in time and space from the point where the UFO was observed. But, since the two phenomena are related, an increase in earthquake activity means an increase in UFO reports. This relationship, however, only works well when UFO reports and earthquakes over a wide area and a long time period are included. The UFOs may be observed hundreds of kilometres from the epicentre of an earthquake and still be related. TST advocates have argued that a strain field may travel extensively, and be transmitted great distances through stable continental regions. In this way, for example, it has been claimed that the San Francisco earthquake of 1989 was linked to UFOs in Manitoba, more than 1,500 kilometres away. One logical question to ask, though, is why wouldn't the UFOs appear closer to where the earthquake occurs, where the most energy is concentrated and available for release?

Earthquake lights are sometimes seen about the same time as earthquakes, while according to the TST, UFOs can appear much before or later. Therefore, earthquake lights are probably not versions of UFOs.

In Britain, a slightly different version of the TST has been proposed, called Earth Lights (EL). Its main advocate is Paul Devereux. He and his associates carried out several experiments in which they crushed a specimen of rock and observed lights produced during the process. It was claimed they found "the best UFO-geology correlations yet published." For example, they found that many UFO sightings in Wales occurred within a few hundred metres of a fault.

Devereux, however, disagrees that piezoelectricity is the causative mechanism for UFOs, and prefers triboluminescence, the effect caused by mechanical friction upon mineral surfaces. The EL theory parallels the TST in many ways. A significant difference is that the EL theory restricts "Earth energy" effects upon human systems to distances generally less than one kilometre, whereas the TST involves faults and/or events up to two hundred kilometres away from an observer.

UFOs as effects of energy upon the human brain

It has long been understood that both electric and magnetic fields affect us in various ways. Weak fields can cause dizziness and irritation, whereas strong fields can cause drastic effects such as epilepsy. Basically, external EM fields interfere with electrochemical responses within the body, confusing the signals received from and sent by the brain. Some studies have suggested that headaches and fatigue are frequently reported by individuals exposed to electric fields for extended periods of time. Medical examinations of individuals exposed to electric fields have found changes in blood composition and cardiovascular function.

It is a natural progression, then, that if UFOs are caused by energy released within strain fields, UFO witnesses and field investigators may have an increased risk of cancer. This was actually proposed by Persinger in a scientific paper and presented as a warning to those at risk. The reasoning is that if an area where UFOs are observed is indeed bathed in

EM radiation from TST processes, then people living or working in the area for an extended period of time would receive large doses of this radiation. This is fundamentally similar to the debate over cancer risk in people living near power transmission lines, though the TST by definition is a natural rather than a man-made source of energy.

Humans can sometimes detect electric and magnetic fields. If you've ever had your skin prickle or the hairs on your body stand straight up, you've been near such a field. Magnetic fields are harder to detect, although the strength at which they can affect us may be as low as one gauss (a standard unit of measurement). For comparison, a typical light bulb radiates a magnetic field of about two gauss, while a more complicated appliance such as a coffee maker generates about ten gauss. It has been proposed that the detection of changes in natural magnetic fields might explain the abilities claimed by dowsers.

Finally, phenomena known as magnetic phosphenes are flashes of light sometimes observed by a person near an alternating magnetic field.

Temporal lobe experiences

The TST suggests that exposure to strong electromagnetic fields may cause drastic effects, such as temporary paralysis, a dreamlike state, out-of-the-body experiences (OOBEs), religious "awakenings" and feelings of "cosmic significance." Versions of these effects can be induced by stimulating certain parts of the brain with electric currents. Perhaps such stimulation may also induce "false" memories of dreamed events, making a person "believe" that he or she has experienced something that has not occurred. These "artificial hallucinations" would seem "real" to the individual thus influenced. In this way, aspects of UFO experiences such as seeing an alien entity, being abducted, being experimented upon, and conversing with an alien, might be explained as the effects of natural interference on brain functions.

The temporal lobe in the brain is very sensitive to EM radiation. TST advocates believe that all kinds of anomalous experiences can be ascribed to some sort of interference with the organ's function.

But does it create UFOs?

The TST is appealing to those wishing to explain UFOs in terms of known phenomena. While elements of the TST appear to include documented geophysical phenomena, the main thrust of the theory hinges on its unproved relationship with a controversial phenomena, namely UFOs. For a theory of its kind, the TST has received a large amount of publicity and a generally uncontested entrance into scientific literature. This situation has resulted in an apparent acceptance of the theory's "principles" without much scientific comment.

Although UFO reports have been collected for over fifty years (and much earlier, if we include pre-1947 reports), the actual case data is disappointing. Repositories of UFO case information such as a database called UFOCAT contain many reports with poor investigation or insufficient information due to the methods used in obtaining the data. For example, many entries in UFOCAT are from published articles or newspaper clippings, and not necessarily from an investigator's report, and are therefore merely anecdotes instead of factual data.

Problems with UFO data are found in all UFO report listings. It is details such as these which led one researcher, Allan Hendry of the Center for UFO Studies, to observe that UFOCAT is not useable for statistical studies of UFO data because of inherent flaws in its design. Yet several studies of the TST used UFOCAT as a source of data for its finding that UFOs and earthquakes were related.

There is no question that some of the ideas involved in the TST are sound. Rock under strain can indeed give off electromagnetic energy, earthquake lights exist, and most UFOs are lights in the sky. But the observation of UFOs in geographical regions where there are no earthquakes seems to invalidate the TST. Even a seismically quiet area such as the American Midwest is apparently not immune to TST effects, according to the theory's advocates. The Carman, Manitoba, UFO wave of 1975–76 was linked to a few minor earthquakes in southern Minnesota, hundreds of kilometres distant. Somehow, it is reasoned, the strain field wandered between the two points. Again, why the UFOs would not be observed closer to the earthquake epicentre is a question still in need of a proper answer.

Interestingly, this question is asked by Paul Devereux himself, originally critical of the TST:

> Why attempt to explain other, possibly more complex and perhaps unrelated mechanisms under the same conceptual umbrella?...This approach to the UFO problem cannot sensibly be conducted over the entire USA in any case — the area is so vast that untenable numbers of UFO events would have to be

involved. And how would one cope with the detailed geological data of such a continental area, even if it is available?

One of the few other criticisms of the TST, this time directed at Paul Devereux, was by Scottish arch-skeptic Steuart Campbell. He pointed out that since the United Kingdom is laced with geological faults, it is not surprising that many reports of British UFO sightings come from areas close to them. He cautioned that Devereux "should be as concerned with the UFO data as [he is] with geology" — since in his opinion, Persinger's database was flawed — and "the geological jargon conceals a poverty of hypotheses."

While the TST is very appealing in its description of UFO phenomena in terms of "terrestrial" rather than "extraterrestrial" phenomena, there is actually very little indisputable evidence that it actually exists. Using one poorly understood phenomenon to explain another using an unknown mechanism doesn't seem all that useful in ufology at the moment, but perhaps with time and more study, it can be accepted as an explanation for some small fraction of UFO reports.

The magic helmet

This background on the TST and Earth Lights was necessary to understand the theory that alien abductions are actually hallucinations caused by the Earth's own electromagnetic field. Since these fields can affect the brain, an assumption that memories of being abducted by aliens are false can use the TST as a convenient mechanism. If abductions don't really occur, then these bizarre experiences must come from someplace in the brain, and must be caused by a malfunction of some kind.

A number of years ago, so the story goes, Susan Blackmore was a psychic researcher. However, during the course of her studies, she became discouraged because her experiments in ESP and remote viewing were not at all successful. After much deliberation, she decided that such avenues of research were not worthwhile and became a harsh critic of psychical research. She joined the ranks of the skeptics, even becoming a CSICOP executive.

Such a turnaround in the attitude of a psychical researcher was viewed as a feather in the cap for debunkers. A former psychic investigator throwing in the towel and becoming an archskeptic? A powerful argument against the reality of psychic phenomena if there ever was one.

But then she read of Persinger's work.

As earlier described, there doesn't seem to be any strong reason to blindly accept the published findings concerning the seismic/UFO link. Some time ago, I did a study of my own, in which I compared the huge number of UFO sightings in the UFOROM UFO database, called MANUFOCAT, with Manitoba's seismic activity. Not surprisingly, since Manitoba doesn't experience earthquakes and is on the Canadian Shield in the centre of the continent, there isn't much to use as data. I published a note in a scientific journal, stating that the TST could not be true because it failed to explain the large number of Manitoba UFOs in the absence of any seismic activity. However, Persinger responded by finding high correlations between the UFOs in Manitoba and weak tremors up to seven hundred kilometres away from the UFO sighting locations and several months distant in time. In other words, observations of lights in the night sky near Winnipeg were therefore mathematically related to weak earth tremors in southern Minnesota.

There's no arguing with statistics, I suppose, but most of the MANUFOCAT sightings were actually airplanes and stars only misinterpreted as UFOs. In other words, the earthquakes were related statistically to random observations of things that were not UFOs, but the TST indicated this was somehow a relationship between underground rock stress and UFOs.

Anyway, back to Susan Blackmore. She travelled to Persinger's laboratory in Sudbury, where he impressed her with his research facilities, especially a device popularly known now as a "magic hat," which directs electromagnetic radiation inside a subject's brain. The device is used to study how external signals and fields can affect a person's perceptions and behaviour. Persinger has reported that the sensations reported by subjects in the laboratory are comparable with those of UFO abductees. Blackmore agreed, apparently.

Blackmore wrote about her trip to see Persinger for an article in the journal *New Scientist* (November 19, 1994). Its publication caused some controversy, and many researchers were asked for their comments. One person who responded was Australian ufologist Bill Chalker. In an Internet discussion group on November 23, 1994, he noted:

[The article by Susan Blackmore] largely focuses on the work of Dr. Michael Persinger, particularly his helmet device which sets up magnetic fields across a subject's head. The article argues that people with high levels of electrical activity in their temporal lobes are more prone to [abduction] experiences, and that such experiences can be explained by excessive bursts of electrical activity in the brain. Persinger's helmet device is intended to try and simulate the stimulation of the temporal lobe and thereby create such episodes. Dr. Blackmore reports that the method has yet to induce a full sensation of alien abduction ... the "magic hat" failed to produce anything *close* to an alien abduction. This is a point that should be emphasized.

I would argue that the diversity and detail of reported UFO experiences do not point to his theory as an ultimate explanation. It is *possible* that EM radiation plays an important role in altering our view of our immediate environment and *may* help to understand certain dissociative disorders. But there's an obvious problem: if EM radiation affects the temporal lobe that much to create abduction experiences in the minds of abductees, what about manmade EM radiation in the environment? How about abduction experiences brought on by *cellular phones*? computer terminals? electric blankets? Surely these are more intense sources of EM radiation and would cause *more* effects!

Basically, my objection to the reported correlation between abduction accounts and the temporal lobe effects is that the former are very detailed, descriptive narratives of coherent experiences, whereas the latter are vague sensations. Now, it's possible that with a skewed belief system, dissociation and fantasy-prone personalities, EM effects *might* induce an abduction fantasy. But that's a long way from an explanation for abductions.

Yet, Persinger's arguments are highly appealing to those who would seek an answer to the mystery of UFOs in what is ostensibly a scientific theory without any reference whatsoever to aliens or other paranormal phenomena. It's much easier, for some, to think in terms of natural radiative processes making people imagine they have seen a UFO, been abducted, or heard messages from the dearly departed.

My own view, however, as drummed into me through my scientific training, is that any theory needs some decent evidence before it can be accepted as fact. In my opinion, the TST fails in this regard for a number of reasons.

With specific reference to alien abductions, Persinger's "magic helmet" is said to replicate the experiences of abductees. There are two problems with this claim that I can see. First of all, if the helmet recreates a natural phenomenon, one could ask why the phenomenon selects certain people who are in their beds inside grounded, Faraday-cagelike metal structures (a "container" that shields its contents from electromagnetic radiation — it's why your radio can't pick up some stations clearly when you're inside a metal-framed building, for example), which should dampen any electromagnetic effects. Why would it also only affect the temporal lobe and not other electronic devices in the same room, such as televisions, radios, cellular phones, or digital watches?

The second problem is the most interesting. Does the helmet *really* duplicate the effects?

The haunted house

Don Hill is a writer and musician. He recently produced a series of radio documentaries about his quest to learn the "truth" behind some strange experiences he and family had in their house along the Bow River in Alberta. He turned the radio series into a television special that elaborated upon why he believed that Persinger's theory explained their experiences.

Basically, his house was haunted. Shortly after he and his family moved in, they noted

> inexplicable knockings.... Household fixtures and pictures seemed to be always off kilter, and the general atmosphere about the place was oppressive; it felt like a heavy weight had descended on all of us. Even the pets were uneasy.... There [were] some intense spots in the house. And they were at the back of the house — like a cold spot.

They also heard:

> this loud banging at the door — like somebody had a baseball bat pounding the door. The dog was barking. We woke up, jumped out of bed, ran to that door, opened it, and there was absolutely nothing there....

Later,

> ... several electrical appliances went wonky, and electronic devices — computers and the like — konked out for no apparent reason. Light bulbs switched themselves on-then-off, or

individually surged up and down in brightness (despite being on a shared circuit that wasn't turned on); some even exploded....

This led him to conclude: "I realized we had a presence in that house. It was there. And it was vocal." After a little over a year, he and his wife felt that they were being "drained" of their energy because of some bizarre, unnatural force in the house. They showed signs of depression and extreme anxiety. They called in shamans to perform purification ceremonies and even tried to exorcize the demons with holy water. Nothing worked.

However, even after they moved, their experiences themselves seemed to haunt them. Hill admitted that he had become "obsessed." He sought answers from mystics, theologians, and psychologists, one of whom suggested that Hill was a "synaesthete" — a person whose brain operates differently than others and is able to "see" music and "hear" colours, for example.

He searched throughout the world for answers, visiting researchers in Canada, the United States, and Europe. He was most impressed with Persinger's view that his "haunting" was the result of natural electromagnetic phenomena. So impressed, he volunteered to sit in Persinger's temporal lobe stimulation chamber wearing the "helmet."

Once Persinger had applied the "juice," Hill reported:

a tingling ... a dryness in my throat. And I have to report too that I'm feeling tense. There's something behind, a kind of tension. Behind my shoulders.... A distinct feeling of being watched. Unpleasant. My guard is up. A feeling something dreadful is about to unfold. Fear.... Brief flashes of white light, a muted soapstone colour; smudges; mere shadows.... I see architecture, Gothic-looking stuff. A cathedral-like entrance way.... I'm rushing. Shaking.... A rush of cold! Whew!!! And also visual effects like a green pulse.... My shoulders are very tense, up towards my ears right now.... Panic. Discomfort. Twitching. And lapses of focus.

He concluded: "This is close to the experience I had in the house! ... I think I found what I was looking for."

In his opinion, Hill's sensations while under the influence of Persinger's magnetic field were identical to those which he experienced in the "haunted" house. If such magnetic fields were capable of duplicating these effects in everyone, then we have another way of explaining paranormal experiences.

There are some cautions, however. It turns out that not everyone experiences the same kinds of effects while subjected to electromagnetic fields. In fact, some people report virtually no effects at all. Jay Ingram, the host of a Canadian television science program, agreed to be a guinea pig during a segment featuring Persinger's temporal lobe experiments. He reported he did *not* have much in the way of experiences, even though he was looking forward to them. He said that during the experiment, he sensed someone was touching or pulling his limbs, and at one point he saw a wallpaper effect of small, doll-like faces, but he didn't see a ghost or have an abduction experience.

Charles Tart is a psychologist and professor emeritus at the University of California at Davis. He told Hill that his reaction was dictated by his own beliefs because he

> went into that laboratory with an expectation, a very strong expectation that this would cast light on the experience you had in that house. Now, I don't know how much the actual laboratory procedure affected your brain; it might have done it a little bit, it might have done it a lot. But you went in with a strong psychological set to then shape things. So it's quite possible that what happened in the laboratory to you produced some genuine effects in your brain. But what those were are very hard to separate out from the construction you then made out of it because of your expectations.
> (Hill, Don. (1998). "Haunted house, haunted mind." [Transcript]. CBC Radio, Ideas, October 30, 1998.)

I would have to agree. If a person is predisposed to the possibility that he or she will have an abduction experience while wearing a device said to duplicate such an experience, then it is likely one will be perceived.

Susan Blackmore also volunteered to have her temporal lobes manipulated in Persinger's laboratory. She reported:

> Nothing seemed to happen for the first ten minutes or so. Then suddenly my doubts vanished. "I'm swaying. It's like being on a hammock." Then it felt for all the world as though two hands had grabbed my shoulders and were bodily yanking me upright. I knew I was still lying in the reclining chair, but someone, or something, was pulling me up. Something seemed to get hold of my leg and pull it, distort it, and drag it up the wall. It felt as

though I had been stretched half way up to the ceiling. Then came the emotions. Totally out of the blue, but intensely and vividly, I suddenly felt angry — not just mildly cross but that clear minded anger out of which you act — but there was nothing and no one to act on. After perhaps ten seconds, it was gone. Later, it was replaced by an equally sudden attack of fear. I was terrified — of nothing in particular. The long-term medical effects of applying strong magnetic fields to the brain are largely unknown, but I felt weak and disoriented for a couple of hours after coming out of the chamber.

She felt something pulling her body and distorting it, and several EM-produced intense emotions, but not much beyond that. No aliens, no ghosts, no gynaecological examinations. She rationalized these differences by suggesting:

> ... what would people feel if such things happened spontaneously in the middle of the night? Wouldn't they want, above all, to find an explanation, to find out who had been doing it to them? If someone told them an alien was responsible and invited them to join an abductees' support group, wouldn't some of them seize on the idea, if only to reassure themselves that they weren't going mad?

This is a possible scenario, but as we have seen, most reported abduction accounts are much more detailed and vivid. They are more than simply panic attacks and vertigo.

Other factors are certainly the personality and belief system of the witness. One could argue that a person who is "into" UFOs and has read the abduction literature will be more likely to extrapolate alien intervention if he or she is subjected to a magnetic field. But this raises another question.

If the sensations (but not the memories) of an abduction experience can be reproduced in a laboratory, how possible is it that such things can occur in nature? How possible is it that one particular person in a well-grounded apartment building would be affected by a weak, virtually undetectable natural electromagnetic field and have a nightmarish abduction experience, but no one else on the block would have any effects?

The TST, as an explanation for abduction experiences, requires that rock stress, deep underground, generates EM fields which travel many miles to the surface, even in geographical regions where there are no reported earthquakes. These fields must also overcome the ambient fields in our homes, already affecting us, given off by televisions, hair dryers, computer monitors, and cellular telephones. These fields must then affect a person who is already mentally willing to imagine an abduction experience, perhaps psychologically sensitive, and be combined with a vivid dream which will be coloured by half-remembered media presentations on UFOs and weird phenomena.

We could also note that the TST could be an explanation for the rare instances where entire families report unusual phenomena, thus explaining multiple-witness cases. And, cynically, we could note that perhaps the effects of technological EM radiation, such as from televisions and cellular phones, could explain certain bizarre behaviour in the general population, including random violence, severe depression, and addiction. Persinger has even suggested that religious fervour is possibly explained by EM effects. Even love isn't safe. One UFO expert (Lorgen, 1999) has recently offered her opinion that alien abductors control our relationships, bringing people together for their own purposes. Since love is a strong and intense emotion, perhaps the TST can explain it as well.

CHAPTER SIX
Without a Prayer:

The Religion Connection

Gimme that New Age religion

When one considers obsessive behaviour as it relates to UFOs, the parallel experience of religious ecstasy must also be mentioned. How would alien contact be interpreted within a context of religious fervour? Perhaps the following case can give us some idea.

On Sunday, May 2, 1976, Mr. and Mrs. F. and their four children were travelling near Carman, Manitoba, Canada, which happened to be the centre of a major UFO flap at the time. A deeply religious man, F. was pondering some grave concerns as he drove. He later published a tract about their experience, and it gives some insight into what actually took place.

F. wrote that as he drove near Carman, he thought:

> What is this world coming to? Why is everybody after money so much and so few have time to read and study the Bible; instead, they have to be with the worldly lusts. How long can this go on?

Something gave him the impression that they would see something as they travelled further that would help him answer his questions. Approximately 3/4 of a mile north of Carman, F. noted that "a small cloud appeared in the sky west of us, very bright and strange." He drew his family's attention to the cloud, and as he drove, one of his children commented that the cloud appeared to have rainbow-coloured stripes.

When he next looked up, the cloud "opened up" with a noiseless explosion. F. pulled the car off the road, and together they gazed upward. A "big, colourful war" was taking place, with armoured horses running to battle in the west, and in the east "quite a few white angels, each surrounded by pillars of fire." After a few minutes, the tableau disappeared and they got back in the car and continued home. Suddenly, their ten-year-old boy said that a big, red dragon was in the sky, and F. stopped the car again to look up.

He saw:

> a very bright, colourful funnel upside down over the whole car, two great big hands coming down underneath the car and felt as if we were lifted up into the Heavens.

He went on to describe his impressions:

> While we were lifted up our feelings disappeared, our weight was gone and our flesh had disappeared, felt as though a little gust of wind could blow us anywhere.... I looked up again and saw an angel up above as if it were the sun, two hands saying, "COME, COME, COME".... Sitting and watching the Heavens, very bright and colourful pillars of fire still burning around us, a very bright star started falling from right above us, falling towards the north and as it came to the pillars of fire, they opened up. There was no flame over the path of the falling star. The star fell to the black horizon and disappeared. We [were] still sitting and watching the Heavens, [and saw] another star come from the north with terrible speed, going south.

At one point, F. looked over his shoulder to see if his family were alongside him, and found that they were still there. One of his children cried in alarm that the car was dangerously careening towards the ditch, and he had to take some evasive action. His other children, joining him in his excitement, repeatedly called out that they could also see images in the sky, but of a somewhat more secular nature: a lion, a deer, an eagle, and a witch.

F. published his tract shortly after his experience, and he expounded his belief that he and his family had witnessed a vision of God's power and glory. He wrote: "Without the LORD, we are nothing. His power is way beyond mankind." He explained that the visions could be found in the Bible (Revelations: 4, 10, and 12).

What is most interesting is that he describes how other traffic on the road seemed to ignore the wondrous sight, failing to stop and watch the event with them. It did not occur to F. that the vision was personal, and probably could not have been observed by anyone else not suitably "tuned in." Indeed, there is some evidence in his tract that others in the car did not share his experience at all, but were concerned at his rapture.

The experience of religious ecstasy has been documented by many writers. Historians recording the lives of various saints often cite their having episodes of spiritual ecstasy during periods of deep meditation. The experiences of Ste. Bernadette, during which she spoke with the Virgin Mary, are examples of similar incidents. It must be noted that some researchers consider apparitions of the Virgin Mary to be analogous to UFO sightings, and, while a literal definition of "UFO" might allow such categorization, the two phenomena appear to be quite different on other levels. Nevertheless, it would be difficult not to classify the experience of F. as something other than a religious vision. The "falling stars" seen after the main experience were possibly just that, though they could also have been aircraft. Shortly after their experience, the F.s went to live as missionaries in South America. It is not known if they have had any further UFO experiences.

Todd Jumper

Another case which shows how abductions can be viewed as highly spiritual and religious experiences is that of Todd Jumper. Raised as a Mormon, this young man had a series of UFO-related experiences which he firmly believed were due to satanic aliens invading our planet and negatively affecting our spiritual well-being. Jumper was compelled to witness (in the strict religious use of the term) so that we may all know the "truth" and be able to put on our Christian armour for protection against these evil elements.

Jumper disseminated his story throughout the Internet, and was thus able to reach many more people with his message than most other religious messengers. His web page is at www.eagle-net.org/mce. I would encourage readers to visit his large website to get a better appreciation of his philosophy and experiences.

Jumper's life story reveals his difficulties in dealing with his UFO experiences, and how he has been viewed by church authorities. Needless to say, their lack of understanding regarding Jumper's unusual and aberrant claims is not surprising. In effect, Jumper has created his own sect of the Church of Latter-Day Saints, incorporating his own beliefs into that faith.

Jumper's treatise describes his persecution by church officials, and implies a comparison of himself with the founders of other great religions. This might, to some, be an immediate indication of delusions of grandeur and a detachment of reality. However, such an attitude is precisely his point; is Jumper exactly the kind of person who would found a new faith?

Jumper's first memory of an alien encounter dates back to when he was four years old and living in a trailer park. One day while taking a nap, he had a dream about

> being near the pond with my friend Mark, he was crying. I then saw this monster about as big as me with big black eyes, a skinny grey body and it had a green light about it. At first I thought it was some kind of swamp monster from the pond. I was so scared that I couldn't move. I tried to scream and my friend just stood there. It walked up to me and pointed at the pond where the creek fed into it and I saw a little boy floating in the water. I then woke up out my bed and it was night time. I heard a loud buzzing beside my head and saw what I can only describe now as a large ball of yellow light beside my head. I ran out of the room and into my mom and dad's room and woke up my dad and said that I saw a giant bee beside my bed, I thought it was a giant bee because it was buzzing. After that night I never saw it again.

Here we can see elements of other abductees' experiences: being unable to move and then waking up in one's own bed, disoriented and afraid.

In later years, Jumper says he became very fearful at bedtime, sensing "somebody was in my room," much like the experiences of Louis, for example. During this time, he and his parents were active within the Mormon community and he became immersed in a deeply religious culture.

This religious upbringing is certainly important when considering Jumper's next evocative experience. When he was about twelve years old, he had just received the Aaronic priesthood within the church and had gone into a wooded area to pray. He was expecting a "sign" of some kind to be given to him from above, and indeed heard a voice in his head telling him that he was selected to be a great religious leader.

During his youth, Jumper had a number of UFO sightings, including a large black triangle hovering over his house and a large black circular object lingering near the site of a car accident. These experiences led to an obsession with UFOs; he talked with friends about them, read many books, and found a drawing of a grey alien very much like the one he had seen in his dream. He noted that the drawing "shocked me so much that I immediately closed the book and left the library."

His feelings of being "watched" continued and intensified. He couldn't sleep at night because of the fear, and then, when he did sleep, he would wake up at night and see balls of light floating in the room but he was paralyzed, unable to move. One night, when he got up to go to the bathroom, he saw the face of an alien in a second-floor window, causing him to panic and run back to his bed.

Then Jumper did something that seems an unusual method of dealing with alien attack, but perfectly understandable given his religious upbringing: he prayed to God for intervention. One night, a green light appeared in his room and he found himself unable to move.

When the green light entered the room, my body was paralyzed. I tried to call upon Heavenly Father to cast it out of my room but I could not speak, my jaw was really tight. So I prayed in my head when all of a sudden I saw that the woodgrain on my bedroom door appeared to be forming into the face of man with a beard and long hair; I thought it was Jesus Christ. Then a bright white light came from above me and chased the green light away. As soon as this happened I had control of my body and I immediately pulled the covers over my head; I had no idea that God would actually do such a great thing. I then heard a voice which was so calm and loving saying to me "You are safe now Todd, you may go back to sleep." And I peeked through the blankets and saw a man in white clothes standing beside my bed. I was still a little frightened but I felt peace and that the terror was over ... for now.

Here we have the most unusual combination of religious phenomena and popular ufological images. Jumper was convinced that Jesus came to drive away the alien "demons."

During this time of his life, Jumper began questioning his church's teachings. While he was a firm believer in Jesus Christ and His power, he noted:

There were times when I doubted my beliefs in the church, feeling that it was inadequate and that if it was the true church of

God then it would be able to tell me what aliens were, but I continued to search myself for the meaning of it all.

He had more vivid dreams about the end of the world, seeing cities on fire, wars, and a "darkness upon the lands."

Over the next several years, Jumper had many visions. He was visited by Jesus, who embraced him and encouraged his prophecy and leadership. Angels met with him and talked with him, giving him insight and telling him secrets that he still cannot reveal to the world. He believed he was destined to be a great prophet and share his revelations with the world.

Then, he had another UFO encounter that was nothing short of extraordinary. In 1992, he had been at his grandmother's house and remembers that on a particular night, they talked about aliens. That night, a noise woke him up and he found his room bathed in green light. Once again, he found himself paralyzed but looked out his window to see a menacing, black-eyed alien staring at him. He found himself being drawn out his window, but started praying to God for deliverance. He suddenly found himself on the ground outside his house, in the company of an angel. He saw that the evil alien was still at his window, and in a fit of anger, ran up to the alien, grabbed it by its neck and strangled it to death. The angel apparently approved, and accompanied him into his house where they encountered more evil beings whom he dispatched with well-directed punches. Jumper believed that this vision experience was an indication that it was his mission to help rid the world of satanic aliens.

What can one say about such an account? It can be read on many levels — from a purely religious perspective, in which Jumper was literally battling demons, to a more physical approach, where extraterrestrials were caught in the act of their nefarious intentions through the actions of Jumper and assisted by "ultraterrestrials" in the form of an angel and other cherubim. This is a fascinating version of fundamental Christianity mixed with popular ufology. One can wonder if Jumper's strong religious beliefs were in conflict with popular culture and myths, giving him a great deal of angst and anxiety. Or, are angels and grey-skinned aliens simply different kinds of entities existing in our universe? Or, perhaps a more cynical question, are they both simply manifestations of our minds?

Jumper later noticed a "scoop mark" scar on his neck and believed it to be proof of his struggle with the aliens. He was convinced that, unlike Jacob, he had been wrestling with not an angel but a devil. When he told a church official about his encounter he was assured that UFO aliens were indeed "Angels of Satan."

Jumper's ideas of alien intervention borrow heavily from popular ufology and what is known as "ancient astronaut" theory, in which ancient writings, myths, and ruins are interpreted as being our ancestors' records of meetings with aliens. In Jumper's version, some angels came to Earth and "became wicked," having sex with women and creating hybrid aliens. This host of fallen angels live inside the Earth where they use their extraordinary powers of "satanic science" to wreak havoc on humanity. (This is nearly identical to the stories of the "Deros" and "Teros" of early contactee literature, actually pre-dating the modern flying saucer era. These creatures were said to be aliens living inside the Earth and using special ray guns to make people do things against their will.)

Since then, Jumper has had several more experiences, but he is content that he has learned to deal with the aliens through his power of prayer and the assistance of angels in overcoming the forces of darkness. He warns us to be careful in dealing with the enemy.

What is most interesting is that Jumper's experiences are not *that* far removed from other abductees' accounts. We have the classic bedroom visitations, the paralysis, and the waking up in bed following a vivid encounter. What is different is that his intense religious feelings have crossed over into popular UFO culture and given him a unique way of coping with his experiences. Whereas many abductees complain about their powerlessness at the hands of aliens, Jumper has found an effective mechanism for dealing with them — and he deals with them effectively. In fact, his greatest struggles appear to come from within the church itself, which finds Jumper's teachings problematic, to say the least.

Body, mind, spirit

The religious interpretation of abductions is not a trivial issue. Michael Persinger has suggested that religious experiences can be induced by the action of magnetic fields upon the brain. In particular, he points to conversion events as indications of alterations in brain function.

> Beliefs that dominate a person's life are considered delusions only when they deviate extremely from culturally acceptable concepts. Psychologically, there is no difference in the belief that God protects a person from harm and the conviction that Omnipotent Space Creatures are spiritual custodians.

He notes that dissociation, a common process, often occurs during intense personal events such as divorce, death, and job changes. Periods of missing time and memories may change to the point where there are buried deep within our subconscious.

> When this occurs the concept of self is sometimes changed; in more religious traditions the period coincides with conversions.... During periods of personal stress, these dissociated memories, modified by beliefs and expectancies, occur as experiences that are perceived as originating "outside" of the self. These experiences are perceived as real and are frequently ascribed to religious or mystical intervention. The consequent conversion in cognitive structure alters the perception of the self and the sense of purpose.

From Heaven above: saved by the aliens

Of the many different cores around which a cult can form, possibly the most curious is the phenomenon of UFOs. Fanatical UFO belief is basically an anti-science movement. It rejects the scientific evaluation and rational explanation for UFOs in favour of a more mystical and religious view. It becomes cult-like when adherents become closed to any interpretation of UFOs as conventional phenomena. Further, fanatical UFO believers often alienate themselves from other UFO buffs, who are interested in a search for "the truth" but do not "know" the truth as fanatical followers claim.

There are two basic forms of such fanatical groups:

1) spiritual/religious UFO cults; and
2) obsessive UFO belief cults.

The spiritual UFO cults embrace omnipotent beings known often as the "Space Brothers," closely akin to deities. They are always much more advanced than humans, and their levels of advancement are such that they almost always have apparently magical or mystical powers, often including ESP and other psychic abilities. In some cases, they are also more "spiritually attuned" than us.

They are extraterrestrial in the same sense that God is "not of this world," and come from distant planets. Each sub-cult names a different planet of origin for their alien brothers and sisters, including Clarion,

Korendar, and Zanthar. In UFO cult mythology, for example, Clarion is said to exist "on the other side of the Sun." Some groups select planets within our solar system as their aliens' homes, including Mars, Jupiter, Saturn, and Venus, although some have located their aliens on or inside the Earth.

The belief-based cults usually have no spiritual relationship with the Space Brothers, but simply believe that extraterrestrials are visiting Earth. They reject scientists' explanations of UFOs, and often insist that there is some sort of grand cover-up of the knowledge that aliens are among us.

One of the early, well-known spiritual UFO cults was the Aetherius Society, founded in Britain by George King in March 1954. One day, King said that he heard a voice from heaven, telling him: "Prepare yourself; you are to become the voice of Interplanetary Parliament."

Eight days later, King said a man in white robes walked through a door into his room and delivered the aliens' message that mankind is spiritually unwell. King was advised he was to become the terrestrial representative of the Interplanetary Parliament, which meets regularly on Saturn. He was told to prepare himself for his important duties by practising yoga and leading a healthier lifestyle.

A few months later, King was contacted again, this time by the aliens' leader, Master Aetherius. Aetherius was from Venus, where an advanced civilization rules the Solar system. King's body was taken over and controlled by Aetherius, who began proselytizing as he was the "primary terrestrial channel." His mission was, simply, to "alert the world."

King attracted a considerable number of followers. His meetings usually took the form of a public channelling display. King went into a trance and began speaking as a "lesser agent," telling of upcoming natural disasters as well as happier occasions such as sightings and landings of flying saucers. Then, Aetherius himself would get channelled, and inform the gathered crowd about esoteric teachings, describing "cosmic energies" and the need for more "positive ions" in the world.

Occasionally, another entity would get channelled, including such individuals as Jesus Christ. Jesus explained that He had been born on Venus and had come to Earth in a flying saucer that was disguised as the Star of Bethlehem. Jesus is now on Mars, where He continues His teachings. Channelled, Jesus recited from the New Testament and led the group in prayer.

King commended that his followers needed to "charge" mountains in order to prevent cataclysms. He would often lead groups into various mountainous regions where they would pray in circles, thus charging "energy batteries" that could be used by the aliens to prevent disasters.

Another UFO cult leader was George Adamski. His mission on Earth began on November 20, 1952, at 12:30 p.m., near the town of Parker in the California desert, when he and some friends saw a UFO apparently land nearby. He instructed his friends to remain with their car while he went to investigate.

Adamski said that he came face to face with a space being who had human features and long, light-coloured, shoulder-length hair. (Later, such aliens were called "blonds.") Communicating in sign language, Adamski learned that the visitor was from Venus. Later, he was told that the Space Brothers were very displeased with human behaviour and had enlisted Adamski to carry their message of peace and goodwill to all mankind.

Adamski published three books describing his encounters with the aliens and their messages. They each were financial successes, allowing him to travel widely and attract a huge following. He referred to himself as "Professor George Adamski," and claimed that he lived and worked at Mount Palomar Observatory. In reality, he ran a small cafeteria halfway up the mountain road leading to the astronomical institution. He did have a small portable telescope, through which he took several photographs of aliens and their spaceships hovering nearby, all of which were out of focus or of dubious heritage. One widely published photograph, showing a close-up of a flying saucer with portholes and ball-like objects underneath, has been dismissed by skeptics as the top part of a vacuum clear, a bottle washer, or a chicken brooder.

Adamski's followers formed groups in many cities around the world, including Canada. Adamski died in 1965, but his groups continued meeting as recently as the late 1970s.

George Van Tassel founded the "College of Universal Wisdom" in 1953. Van Tassel is best known as the organizer of the Giant Rock Flying Saucer Convention, which was held annually for nearly two decades on a desert airfield near Giant Rock, California.

The night of August 24, 1953, Van Tassel was sleeping with his wife and woke up at about 2:00 a.m. to find a man standing at the foot of his bed. The human-appearing entity said that his name was "Sol-ganda" and insisted that Van Tassel come with him aboard his spaceship. Van Tassel noted that his wife was in a deep sleep, Sol-ganda said was brought on by a "spell." Outside, Van Tassel saw a bell-shaped craft that was powered by an "antigravity beam."

Van Tassel didn't receive any direct message from his alien contact, but simply was shown things that he interpreted as directions and information to pass on to others. For example, during one of his later contacts, he was visually shown the true history" of the human race, as observed by aliens. Typically, Van Tassel would go into a trance at a meeting and channel information from Sol-ganda or other aliens.

Van Tassel was often attacked by skeptics, and one of the most memorable incidents was the action of a lawyer who set out to show that Van Tassel's stories were hoaxes. He sent Van Tassel faked UFO photos, which Van Tassel quickly adopted as true and proof of his own experiences. When both the lawyer and Van Tassel appeared together on a popular UFO-related radio talk show, the lawyer revealed the photos as his fakes.

Despite such damaging evidence, Van Tassel remained popular and his Giant Rock convention attracted many thousands of devotees and contactees annually. Near the convention site, he built the Integratron, a wooden, dome-shaped temple, from plans he said were supplied by the Space Brothers and similar to Solomon's Temple from the Old Testament. The Integratron was designed for "rejuvenation" of the human body, through "omni-beams" directed from above.

In September of 1944, *Amazing Stories* magazine editor Ray Palmer received a letter from Richard Shaver. Shaver detailed how he had learned of an "ancient alphabet" from a lost race that had once thrived on Earth and had battled evil aliens. Palmer had his reservations, but he published the letter and was surprised to receive hundreds of requests for more information.

Shaver replied with a long story titled: "A Warning to Future Man," which Palmer edited and rewrote as "I Remember Lemuria." (Lemuria is a legendary continent that sank or otherwise disappeared.) It was published in March 1945. The piece received an unprecedented response from the magazine's readership. More than 50,000 letters flowed in from people who praised the work but also added their own personal experiences that supported the story.

Basically, Shaver's story relied on "racial memories" about a race of subhuman creatures called deros (detrimental robots) living in underground cities within the Earth. The deros had once been slaves of an advanced civilization that existed on Lemuria, but which perished during the cataclysm that destroyed Atlantis.

Deros had control of the Lemurians highly advanced technology, including mind-rays, which they directed at humans on the surface of the Earth, causing mental, emotional, and physical problems. Other devices caused earthquakes, volcanoes, and droughts. Their sole pastime was to annoy and persecute the human race. Occasionally, they would kidnap humans and torture them, sometimes returning them to the surface, but most often hiding them forever, such as the cases of Jimmy Hoffa and Judge Crater.

Ray Palmer continued to publish the Shaver stories as fact, which eventually led to his firing from *Amazing Stories*. He then began his own science fiction pulp magazine, first called *Other Worlds*, then *Flying Saucers from Other Worlds,* and then finally *Flying Saucers*. The stories continued being published until the 1970s.

Mark-Age is a quasi-religious group that still exists today. Its basic set of beliefs is that mankind was once part of an interplanetary spiritual communications system, but has turned away from spiritual matters. Because of this, the Hierarchical Board of the Solar System "drew the veil" over our consciousness. However, some of the aliens, being benevolent, are trying to increase our spiritual consciousness — using mental communications with certain members of our society, projecting their own bodies, or actually making themselves seen in their flying saucers.

Mark is the chief contact for Earth, and has been assigned to make mankind "space-conscious" and ready to meet other life forms. Mark-Age devotees believe that God is helping the United States space program because it is defined as "one nation under God." The Soviet Union was not given such help because it was in their opinion atheistic.

According to the Raelians, aliens are really the "Elohim" referred to in some biblical teachings, meaning literally, "those from the sky." They created humans in a laboratory on their own planet and put us on Earth. We accidentally gained intelligence through interbreeding, and became self-conscious. The aliens left us to our own affairs, but they occasionally send messengers to check on us, such as Jesus, Mohammed, and Buddha. The latest alien messenger is Rael, born as Claude Vorhilon, who has been to their home planet and met all the other messengers there.

Raelians believe that all of the miracles and visitations recorded in the Bible were performed or caused by aliens and their UFOs. They have about 10,000 members worldwide, based in France but with satellite groups in other countries including the USA and Canada.

Robert Barry founded the Twentieth Century UFO Bureau in the late 1960s. He stressed that the public had been lied to by the government about the existence of UFOs and aliens on Earth. Basically, his was an anti-cover-up group. Barry also taught that UFOs were spaceships piloted by angels, although a few were driven by Satan and his forces. The angel-piloted UFOs assisted the Israelis in their battles in the Holy Land. In the 1970s, Barry held public meetings in a number of cities and towns, promoting himself in "Bible belt" areas such as Steinbach, Manitoba, and in Pennsylvania.

As discussed earlier, the experiences of Olive are most interesting with regard to religious interpretations of UFOs. She was born in 1933 in Fredericton, New Brunswick. When she came out of her mother's womb, she had a caul on her face, considered a lucky or fortunate omen. She claimed that at age 7, she died from pneumonia, but "rose again on the third day" after sulfa drugs were administered to her. At age 10, she walked into another dimension and began having visions.

In 1968, space creatures took her in their craft to other planets, and even inside the Earth. While on board during one of her journeys, they used an x-ray device to look inside her body. They found several tumours and operated on her with such advanced surgical techniques that they left no scars.

Olive says she was chosen by beings from the fourth dimension to carry their message of peace and sanity to the world. She was directed to help convince mankind to stop pollution, cease atomic testing, and repent to God. She was interested in educating children in the aliens' message through UFO comic books and TV shows.

In 1975, a "scout craft" burned a cross into a field in New Brunswick. No snow stayed on the cross, which remained warm to the touch all winter. In spring, no grass grew. A spring nearby turned reddish, then cleared, but

Olive began holding religious ceremonies at the site. She claimed that people could be healed by water from the spring, and her "services" were attended by many devotees who were healed of ailments such as arthritis, lameness, and blindness.

However, some local residents who were skeptical of the activities attempted to put an end to them by hiring a bulldozer to plow the cross over. Olive and her group made a public demonstration of solidarity by laying in front of the bulldozer and stopping the plan. But, as Olive noted, the bodies of those who wanted to plow over the cross were found soon after at the bottom of a lake, with many bones broken. She said that this showed that bad things would happen to those who got in the way of the plans of Space Brothers.

Olive said she could sense "vibrations" emanating from the UFOs flying overhead, and also from radiation left behind after they took off from their landing sites.

The Society of Unarius was directed by Ruth Norman (Archangel Uriel) for several decades until her death in the 1990s. The group owns dozens of acres in California where each year they await the mass landings of spaceships that will save selected spiritually attuned individuals. They believe that Earth needs to become the thirty-third member planet of the Interplanetary Confederation. Jesus, Mohammed, and Einstein were channelled by Norman, giving further teachings to the Society's followers. The Society holds parades and meetings for which members dress up in costumes representative of other planets in the Confederation.

We can see recurring themes present in most of these groups:

1) Mankind's spiritual awareness is missing or weak.
2) Space Brothers are trying to coax us back onto the path of spiritual understanding.
3) There will be a Second Coming.
4) Salvation is possible.

It appears that, for the most part, UFO religious cults and groups are all concerned with the welfare of the human race. They are trying to spread the teachings of their "masters" in hope that mankind will be saved from itself.

Therefore, they are basically "normal" religious groups that simply replace God with a physical being from another planet. They reject science's dismissal of UFO reports, and in doing so, adopt an anti-science attitude that is impressed on their followers.

In 1997, Marshall Applewhite and his followers committed mass suicide in California as a result of a prediction that Comet Hale-Bopp was the harbinger of spiritually-enlightened aliens ready to "process" humans ready to "move on" to a better life. (However, the Heaven's Gate cult used technology itself to spread and interpret spiritual and mystical teachings, an interesting combination of beliefs.)

The groups usually receive instructions directly from their "masters," usually through channelled missives. Unfortunately, this sometimes led to many "unauthorized" readings and messages by individual members, since there was no control over the depth to which members could become immersed in the particular group's ideology. This sometimes led to their own contacts with the alien masters, distorting the original teachings. Since individual members could themselves become "in tune" with the aliens, they could obtain their own ego-enhancing, spiritual "high."

But as we have seen from the Heaven's Gate incident, there are personal dangers in becoming too involved in one's faith. In 1982, two people waited in their car for more than a month in North Dakota. They spent the entire time in their car, waiting for a spaceship to arrive. They were drawn by a "higher power" as they sat in below-freezing temperatures, snowbound in their vehicle. Eventually one of them died of a combination of hypothermia, dehydration, and starvation, which spurred the other to seek help. (Source: *Winnipeg Free Press*, November 19, 1982.)

Some UFO-based religious groups' concepts probably reflect anxieties about our present society and more specifically, the possibility of nuclear war or the general angst felt by those oppressed or otherwise "left out." Other themes are the role of religion in a technological society, the need for peaceful international, relations, and the possibility of extraterrestrial visitation.

According to most groups, the Space Brothers come from planets free from war, poverty, and need. They also have achieved immortality through an emphasis on spiritual matters. In short, they exist in idyllic paradises much removed from terrestrial problems. The Space Brothers also have come to Earth to stop arms proliferation and to prevent further war. Many early UFO religious cults were anticommunist but were paradoxically socialist in their structure. This was ironic, because both the FBI and CIA monitored the groups because they were deemed "dangerous," often infiltrating the groups in order to keep watch on them.

Cult members' fear of death is lessened or eliminated by the belief that the aliens will prolong their lives or reincarnate them on another planet. The groups often make Jesus a spaceman, but still define him as a true messenger who died trying to teach us truth and love.

Since Earth is not "ready" yet, the groups have to have human leaders to act as go-betweens. All groups share their mission to educate mankind in order to save us from destruction. Hence, they seek public exposure in order to transmit their leaders' messages.

Furthermore, it should be noted that UFO cults almost always promulgate a "Christian" philosophy of love, peace, and reconciliation. Most have taught that we should be kind to one another, respecting all life and caring for the Earth. Many have strong environmental convictions.

However, by shifting their omnipotent deity from a spiritual God to a more technological entity, UFO cults place humans at par with their saviours. If only we knew enough science, we could be like the aliens. This path to enlightenment is one that is much easier than spiritual development, which requires somewhat more complicated things such as honest introspection, altruism, and love for all.

Bo and Peep (or Te and Do) first formed the Christian Arts Centre in Houston in 1972 to promote religious artistic activities. Only three years later, the families of twenty people were panicked when they received postcards from their children informing them that they were "leaving this Earth" and would not see them anymore. Police investigation uncovered the cult commune in Oregon. It was learned that at that time, dozens of people had left their jobs, families, and even their children to follow "The Two."

That was in 1975. In 1997, we learned that the cult was still operating, with tragic consequences. Their message was the same, and people still were being recruited into its membership. We know that in 1997, thirty-nine people died. In 1975, dozens of people joined the cult, and many were never heard from again.

CHAPTER SEVEN
What to Do About the Abduction Phenomenon

Three cases

I've often wondered about the different categories of abductees and how they interrelate. Some abductees seem to have only vague memories of dreams concerning lights in the sky, while others are adamant they have had vivid "real" experiences and terrible traumatic encounters with aliens in the flesh. Some abductees are more like contactees, now set on a mission to tell the world about their revelations, while others are fearful of anyone knowing about what happened to them, to the point they will seek legal action against anyone leaking their story. Some abductees report a profound spiritual awakening following their encounters, becoming obsessively religious, but others speak only in terms of nuts-and-bolts spaceships from other planets.

Three cases which came to my attention several years ago illustrate these differences well, and raise some important questions for ufologists.

The first person called me in August 1995, requesting my help in dealing with her abduction experiences. She had been repeatedly dreaming about aliens coming into her bedroom and a paralyzing beam of light emanating from the ceiling. Her story was very similar to others who had approached me for help over the years, and had a familiar ring to it. What was slightly unusual in this case was that she had been keeping accurate records on her computer and drawing realistic pictures of her encounters. She even kept a diary beside her bed for when she woke up from her "dream abductions." The aliens also had described to her future events and given her other esoteric knowledge. The revelations included information that she was in training for the Rapture, during which time only abductees would be saved.

Most curious was the fact that this woman was educated enough to know that, as she told me, "this couldn't possibly be real, but it *seemed* real!" She had a degree in psychology and so knew something about the workings of the human mind; she was willing to accept that her dreamlike experiences were imaginary, but she felt they seemed far too real for ordinary dreams.

It was the second caller who got me thinking about abductions and formulating some questions. This woman told me a very similar story to the first woman's experience (the "usual") and also wanted help in dealing with it. But there was a difference.

She explained that she had told her family physician about her experience. The doctor had referred her to a psychiatrist. The woman claimed that the psychiatrist had listened to her story and her recall of the dreams and promptly diagnosed her as schizophrenic. This was because by her own admission, she could not tell if her dreams were "real" or not. She was technically unable to distinguish fantasy from reality. As a consequence, she spent several months in a psychiatric institution.

Finally, a third case presented another variety of abductee. A man described to me (in a matter-of-fact manner) how an entity or entities had contacted him and were helping him make decisions in his life through their recommendations and cautions. He would sometimes wake up in the middle of the night to find an entity with him in his room, telepathically conversing with him and warning him of what he might expect the next day. This was all done benevolently, of course.

What I began pondering were the differences between the three cases. Were all three "legitimate" abductions? For that matter, what constitutes a "legitimate" or "real" abduction? Was it possible to distinguish this?

I also wondered if a person who doubted the reality of his or her own apparent abduction by aliens was in some ways different than others who accepted that aliens ruled their minds. Which ones were coping more effectively with their experiences? Indeed, what was the best course of action for me to recommend?

This was a long way away from the reports of disk-shaped objects or lights in the sky which had been the mainstay of my early days in ufology. Things were so much simpler then. Now, with aliens in people's bedrooms and channelled messages from Reticulians, UFO research was taking on new dimensions — literally. Forget angels; if only I had an alien on my shoulder to help guide me in my research.

The Hamlet defence in ufology

Is a person who thinks he or she has had a nighttime abduction experience schizophrenic? If so, what about the person who is unsure of the reality of the experience? If you're consciously aware that something was possibly imaginary, are you schizoid? On the other hand, what can we say about people who are absolutely convinced that aliens are conversing with them regularly?

Abductees are, by some definitions, schizophrenic. This is *not* to say that they all have some kind of psychological problems. What this does mean is that abductees have had experiences that were surreal, yet were somehow perceived as real to them. This inability to distinguish reality from apparent fantasy is one symptom of clinical schizophrenia.

However, ufologists are placed in a very precarious situation because of this. Abductees and contactees will certainly not stand for any suggestion that they are schizophrenic or delusional. To them, their experiences are "real." Some admit to having internal conflict because they "know" that alien abductions are impossible yet they have an overwhelming sense that they had an encounter of some sort.

Added to this are complications such as false memory syndrome, alleged ritual abuse, screen memories and outright lying. (For completeness, we can also include people who have mental problems, although Meerloo and others examined mental institutions and found virtually no patients displaying abductee/contactee symptoms.)

I asked one medical professional who is familiar with the abductee phenomenon for his opinion on the relationship between Alien Abduction Syndrome and psychiatry:

> There *are* some schizophrenics who, in addition to their other problems, incorporate abduction experiences into their hallucinations. (I have met some.) They are identifiable by other signs and symptoms besides the abduction account. *On the other hand*, it makes no sense to diagnose someone as schizophrenic simply on the basis of abduction experiences. In general, if someone presented abduction experiences as the *sole* symptom, and he was able to deal with them through supportive

counselling and psychotherapy (not necessarily including hypnosis), I would see little reason to medicate him and no reason at all to hospitalize him.

Do psychiatrists have enough background in this phenomenon to deal with it effectively? Probably not, because most have no training or familiarity with treating paranormal experiences. Those few involved in transpersonal psychology are probably an exception to this. But what constitutes "effective" management is still open to debate, because the nature of the experience is still unknown. Also, we don't know whether there are multiple causes for a reported abduction experiences (sleep disorder, schizophrenia, dissociative disorder, TLE, and then the "real" abduction experiences, whatever that means).

I am not convinced that most "abduction therapists" have enough background to deal with the problem effectively, either — or that what they do is in the long run safe or effective. There are no outcome studies on this question. Generally, abduction experiencers fall between some pretty wide cracks in the health care system, and in society.

So, then, given that psychiatric view of abductions, what are the implications for ufology? Can a ufologist *ethically* advise/counsel/treat an abductee without a referral to a professional psychologist or psychiatrist? Probably not. It would seem that it might be unwise to counsel abductees because of the possibility that they may have underlying psychological problems, and most ufologists are not trained to deal with this. Certainly some of the people who have come to me with abductee/contactee experiences have had such problems, and I would suspect that it is more pervasive than is usually acknowledged.

The reason for this is that it is not "politically correct" to suggest abductees/contactees have *not* had alien experiences unless one is an ardent skeptic or debunker. For a ufologist to question whether or not an abductee has actually had an alien encounter is tantamount to heresy.

Think about it. If a person claims an abduction experience, a ufologist usually tries to fit the experience in with his or her perceived notion of alien visitation, not question the view of the experiencer.

The problem is whether *either* approach is appropriate.

Since I know that some abductees/contactees I have spoken with may be reading this book, I would like to clarify my position lest it be misinterpreted (if it hasn't been already).

I *do not* believe that all abductees/contactees are schizophrenic or have some mental problems. What I *do* believe is that abductee/contactee experiences *can* be compared with dissociative or delusional experiences reported by some schizophrenics. I have met and spoken with many abductees/contactees and have found most to be rational, earnest, and fully functioning in society. Many have approached me for help in coming to terms with their apparently real experiences given their surreal nature. My question to the psychologists and psychiatrists is, "Does this mean that abductees/contactees are schizophrenic, or does it mean that they are reacting 'normally' to unusual stimuli?"

The abductee problem

One of the strongest arguments against abductees "really" being in receipt of direct (and often physical) alien contact is the greatly conflicting nature of the experiences they recall. In very few cases are the aliens described exactly alike (with identical planets of origin, identical spacecraft, identical medical instruments, identical relayed intent, etc.). Admittedly, some abductee researchers are attempting to identify matching symbols observed by some abductees on board the ships, and there are some cases that have some similar characteristics, but for the most part, each abductee case possesses some unique facets. This may be partly explainable due to differing recollections by disparate abductees and deliberate interference by the aliens themselves, but these could be considered arm-waving exercises. (One ufologist even has suggested that, because the abduction stories are so bizarre and incredible, abductions are proof that aliens have their own warped sense of humour.)

Although most abductees seek help from ufologists, it is increasingly apparent that ufology is ill-prepared to deal with them. An abductee case is far more complicated than an ordinary sighting of a UFO. Even though abductions are often considered the fourth category of close encounters, they are extremely different from the lesser three categories and should be placed in a category or series of categories of their own.

It is usually recognized that UFO investigators do not investigate UFOs, but the reports made by the witnesses themselves. Already, ufology is once-removed from pure scientific investigation and could be considered more analogous to memorate studies by anthropologists. Abduction cases are even more humanistic; there is often no definite "time" of an event, and it might not "take place" in a precise location.

They are extremely subjective and may represent something beyond our investigation.

This is why psychologists are more suited to abduction studies. Researchers often have found that abductees have emotional and psychological problems that may or may not be directly related to their experiences. Some appear to have a history of sexual or domestic abuse, and others exhibit symptoms of stresses within their lives. (It has been suggested that it is *because* of such backgrounds that they are "chosen" or otherwise sensitive to abduction-like encounters, or that lifelong abductions are the *cause* of the psychosocial problems.) Regardless of the cause and effect, however, an abductee seeking help from a UFO buff is asking for trouble. Simply put, few ufologists have the therapeutic tools and expertise required to properly unravel an abductee's experiences within a framework of personal problems.

Alien Abduction Syndrome (AAS)

I've stopped counting how many people have come to me asking for help or guidance in understanding their abduction experiences. Not only that, I've come to identify the "usual" story: "I had this dream, well at least I *thought* it was a dream, that these little creatures were in my room and I could understand them even though they weren't really talking and it hurt when they touched me and then I seemed to be floating somewhere not in my room and they told me some things I couldn't understand and then I was suddenly back in my room. But I think they are still around."

I've read John Mack's epic case study *Abductions* and I tend to see the points of many of his critics. Far from the aliens preparing his clients for some future use and teaching them about ecology and spirituality, I think some of those in his group have problems in dealing with our reality.

Not that that's such a bad thing, mind you.

Now, I'm not a psychologist by training, nor a psychiatrist, so I'm sure my diagnosis is going to draw some flames. But I think that what we have here is *Alien Abduction Syndrome.*

For some reason, certain people appear to *think* they have been contacted by aliens. This could be because of various contributing factors: dissatisfaction with life; stress; domestic problems; family problems; peer pressure; rape trauma; chemical imbalances; or child abuse. Perhaps any one of these or any combination of them. I believe that thorough studies might help to understand AAS. (It's even possible that aliens are actually doing some abductions, but that's another matter.)

Skeptic Kevin McClure has a slightly more cynical view of the abduction phenomenon. He writes and produces *Abduction Watch*, an online ufozine, following and critically analyzing the latest developments in the field. As he noted:

> If I'm right, and there never has been a single, physical, enforced act of abduction of a human being by an alien, non-human being, the belief in abductions has left some very confused people out there.... They will be depending on an alien presence for love, support, care, even rescue. Even if they feel that they have been abducted and used for physical, sexual purposes, and have minimal control over what is happening to them, they will have faith in the good intentions of their unseen benefactors. A sort of Stockholm Syndrome with invisible captors.
> (*Abduction Watch*, Number 6, January 1998.
> www.magonia.demon.co.uk/abwatch/aw6.html.)

McClure says that abductees have changed their lives because of their belief in aliens' control over their destinies. They expect to be abducted again and again, and their relationships within society are molded to accommodate their use, and indeed, abuse, by the aliens. He adds:

> those whose lives are being affected and interfered with by their belief in their abduction experience are victims of abuse. Not, maybe, abuse that is committed or caused deliberately, but abuse that arises from the strong, utterly mistaken, personal beliefs of those who propagate the abduction myth.... I think we would be right in seeing "alien abductees" as victims, whom we have a duty to inform and assist.

He cautions abduction researchers and issues a dire warning for ufology:

> Despite all the adverse publicity, some investigators, researchers, and therapists may still not know the important facts about seeking recall through regression. They may not realize what they are doing. For me, the first tenet of therapy, of helping people in any way, is: "Above all, do no harm," but great harm is being done. There is clearly a great need to stop the abduction mythos

causing any more damage to those it has already taken in, and to prevent it taking in any more than is absolutely unavoidable. Then, beyond that, there is the important task of enabling those who have become convinced they have been abducted, with all that entails, to realize that they have been misled. To enable them to realize that, simply, they are not abductees, and that they don't have to deal with those problems any more. And nor, as investigators, do we.

Let me backtrack, however. First of all, I don't think that all people who report such experiences have AAS. Secondly, in most cases, AAS is not a "problem." (This is another example of the 90 percent rule in action.)

The real issue, though, is how to deal with such cases. Most ufologists are woefully inadequate as abduction therapists/counsellors. Investigating a nocturnal light and counselling an abductee are two very, very different things. You just don't "file" an abductee case away as you would a daylight disc case. Furthermore, ufologists are not trained as psychologists (generally), though John Musgrave published a paper in the late 1970s or the role of the UFO researcher as a counsellor and healer. It was ignored at the time.

However, there's another side to this issue, and more questions. Who *is* appropriate and/or adequate as a counsellor/investigator of abductee cases? What relationship should there be between a clinical psychologist and a UFO researcher?

These questions began concerning me as a result of some calls I received during the past several months. I regularly get calls from people about UFO experiences, fireballs, sasquatch, ghosts, and UFO abductions. The abductees are often of the "usual" variety, and their stories seem not to vary much. Roy Bauer and I have been meeting with them on an *ad hoc* basis, sometimes referring them to others.

It's very difficult to deal with, sometimes; because of an altruistic streak, I feel compelled to help people plaintively asking for assistance in understanding their experiences. But who to send them to for further assistance? I can only handle so many "clients."

In some cases, abductees have gone with me to clinical psychologists, hypnotherapists, and other kinds of counsellors (most have gone on their own). Not surprisingly, the quality of the "professionals" varies considerably.

One memorable session was at the office of a "qualified hypnotherapist" who did regressions as part of therapy. I was allowed to sit in with an abductee who wanted to unlock the memory of a certain night during which she and her sister were *both* abducted simultaneously. The therapist put on a tape of waves crashing amidst some flute music, set a large crystal on the table, and informed the abductee that she shouldn't worry because he was going to do some Huna chanting and send spiritual energy to her if she got afraid.

I worried. She worried, too. Then, halfway through her regression, she said, "You know, that taped music is annoying." Needless to say, the session was a failure.

The beginning of a backlash against self-certified abductee therapists is appearing in ufology, thankfully. Slowly, researchers are realizing that abductees must be treated with a great deal of compassion, ethics, and straightforward care, rather than vague mysticism and neo-spiritualism to help them cope with alien control. John Velez, a ufologist and an experiencer himself, noted:

> Abduction research must be taken out of the hands of amateurs and para-professionals. Not so much for the sake of the research itself — there are many "amateurs" [who] can do as competent if not [a] better job than some pros — but for the sake of the well-being of those individuals reporting.... It is my firmly held opinion that unless and until abductees begin reporting their experiences to mainstream professionals such as family physicians, trusted counsellors, etc., we will never get the attention and the serious investigation that we need.
> (*UFO Updates*, October 14, 1997.)

Velez posted his concerns because of details of an abduction case investigation posted to *UFO Updates* a few days earlier which shocked and horrified many readers. An abductee researcher, in a simple attempt to share information about an ongoing case investigation, described how two 16-year-old girls came to her with details of some dreams that contained abduction elements. They had the dreams following the sighting of an "orange glow" nearby their home. The abduction investigator interviewed the girls and then told them that in her opinion

> the visitation was by an actual craft with humanoids, because this is consistent with similar incidents taking place around the world ... [and that they] could expect a phantom pregnancy, but that it

would be ended with another visitation... the purpose of all this
was to make hybrids....

She also told the girls they

could also expect some of a wide range of known paranormal
effects like clairvoyance, clairaudience, astral travel, OOBEs
[out-of-body experiences], levitation, or long-striding.
(*UFO Updates*, October 12, 1997.)

The girls were described as being very frightened, and this caused
their mothers concern.

Readers were concerned as well, and angered that the investigator
had told the girls they would become pregnant and then lose their babies.
Even though the investigator thought she was acting in their best
interests, her approach made readers realize how problematical the issue
of abduction therapy is in reality.

Others' views

I often receive comments from people who express their own opinions
about what is really happening with regard to abductions and UFOs.
One person pointed me to a note posted to alt.alien.visitors, describing
why abductions could not be so easily dismissed by skeptics:

From alt.alien.visitors Fri Sep 9 15:02:16 1994
From: flreynolds@aol.com (FLReynolds)
Subject: Arguments against abduction as psychological
phenomenon

Arguments against abduction phenomenon as simply a
psychological phenomenon:

POINT 1: Repeatable and clinically testable phenomenon:
under hypnosis a subject recalls a detailed description of
events involving the subject and a second individual. When
informed of this fact in the abstract, being careful not to
reveal any more detail than this, either from the physician or
the first subject, the second individual strenuously denies

any involvement. However, when the second subject is taken under hypnosis, the second subject recalls the events and independently corroborates the detailed description of events as described by the first subject.

POINT 2: This phenomenon occurs in children under the age of three.

POINT 3: This phenomenon only occurs in tight association with the UFO phenomenon.

No psychologist has ever addressed all of these points taken together as a whole, in an attempt to explain them away as a psychological phenomenon, since any such contention is clearly pseudo-scientific and unsupported by any work of clinical psychology. In general, the psychological community is exceedingly silent on this matter, for which they are being subject to considerable heat for being unable to explain away. Witness the attack on the discipline of psychology as whole and its well-established use of hypnosis in trauma cases. If psychologists could come up with an even half-way justifiable way to dismiss Mack's work as a whole, it would have been immediately forthcoming, considering the intense pressure they are under to do so.

I would observe, however, that Reynolds' three points are not necessarily proven fact. There are only a handful of cases whereby one abductee has corroborated another's testimony, and these are viewed with suspicion by some researchers. As for abductions occurring in children as young as three years old, I can only note that in my own experiences with three-year-old children, I have found they can come up with some really imaginative things.

For example, when I asked my three-year-old what he had for lunch, I could easily convince him that he had a grilled-cheese sandwich, when he really had eaten spaghetti (and vice-versa). Sometimes, he even gave me a wrong answer without any prompting. So, I personally have to doubt whether or not the testimony of a young child in recalling an alien abduction is very accurate. Yet, Mack has described abduction experiences in even *younger* children:

A two-year-old boy that I interviewed said that he was taken into the sky by a man who bit his nose. A not-yet-three-year-old boy said that owls with big eyes (it is common for children to remember the alien beings disguised in animal forms) take him up to a ship in the sky, and he is afraid he will not be able to get back to his mother.

(Mack, John. (1992). Why the abduction phenomenon cannot be explained psychiatrically. PEER. Website: www.peer-mack.org/mit92.html.)

Finally, as for abductions occurring in close association with the UFO phenomenon, I'd say no, again. I have had a number of abductees come to me with their stories without any prior UFO sightings and without an associated UFO observation on the night of the abduction.

On the topic of abductions, I received a review copy of an excellent fortzine titled *The Anomalist*, edited by Patrick Huyghes and Dennis Stacy (of MUFON fame). *The Anomalist* has quickly earned a place as the most interesting and informative zines I have seen, and one I will willingly read. Stacy and Huyghes have done an admirable job of gathering some of the best names in Fortean literature and produced a twice-yearly zine that covers everything from UFOs to bigfoot to remote viewing experiments and the infamous face on Mars. It's a quality production, it's well-written, and it's good.

Anyway, one of the feature articles was by Robert Baker, the arch-nemesis of abductee experts who is convinced that virtually all abduction cases can be explained. He pointed out that the psychological literature has been chock full of descriptions of abduction-like experiences, all in the context of sleep disorders and hallucinations. He suggested that abductees counselled by abductee therapists recall alien encounters, whereas those who present with the symptoms of bedroom paralysis, visits from floating entities and missing time and are seen by psychotherapists familiar with sleep disorders are diagnosed with recognized elements of sleep disorders. He presented a convincing argument in a contrary vein to most abductee literature and his comments outlined the "other side" of the abduction debate.

My own interpretation of the abduction phenomenon leads me into some other territory. Researcher Roy Bauer recently suggested that UFO abductions, ritual abuse and past-life regressions may all be fields where memory is a poor diagnostic tool. There is no physical evidence for any of the three in most cases that are uncovered through hypnotic regression.

Furthermore, there can be conflicting evidence found which seems to rule against the reality of the recalled event. And all three situations can involve screen memories that can block the original traumatic event.

Are they, then, delusions or fantasies? If so, what is the trigger that produces the trauma? How can such complicated fantasies be woven by otherwise normal human beings? I would tend to think that even if UFO abductions do not represent alien intervention, there is plenty of fuel for psychological and sociological studies, well beyond the labelling of such cases as "dangerous," as noted by debunker Philip Klass.

One of Klass's arguments against abductions is that, technically, abductions are criminal acts. He believes that abductees should report their experiences to the FBI, who specialize in such major crimes. Obviously, with the resources available to the FBI, the data and information they would gather towards solving the case would be impressive indeed. However, it would be difficult for the FBI to investigate an abduction case after the victim was returned and, furthermore, how would an FBI office really view a citizen's report of this kind?

Diametrically opposite to Klass is Eve Frances Lorgen, who not only believes that aliens are abducting humans but that she understands their purposes. Beyond simple things such as implants and hybrids, Lorgen is convinced that aliens control our emotions and virtually all aspects of our lives. She views "alien-orchestrated human bonding dramas" in abduction accounts as evidence that aliens manipulate our relationships. She says "the aliens play the role of the mythical Cupid and his arrow," forcing abductees to be attracted to one another, destroying any existing marriages or relationships and then manipulating the rest of their lives. How else, she asks, can we explain such passion and obsession displayed by abductees? (See her web pages at http://users1.ee.net/pmason/el.html)

Another radical view is held by Austrian ufologist Helmut Lammer. He notes that

> some UFO abductees have reported that they have also been kidnapped by military intelligence personnel and taken to hospitals and/or military facilities, some of which are described as being underground.
> (Lammer, H. 1997. Preliminary findings of Project MILAB: Evidence for military kidnappings of alleged UFO abductees. www.alienjigsaw.com/milab.html.)

Lammer asserts that "most abductees report interaction with military personnel" and that some abductees' stories sound a lot like mind control experiments. He thinks that military doctors examine abductees for implants and are perhaps studying how brainwashing techniques can be used on an unsuspecting populace.

Perhaps the most important information in Lammer's work, however, is his discussion of terrestrial implants already in use around the world. He notes that millions of animals have already been successfully implanted with transponders manufactured by various companies. The transponder is activated by a low-frequency radio signal and allows tracking of animals at great distances. The smallest one in use so far is about the size of a grain of rice. As early as 1989, a patent was filed for an implantable homing device for humans.

The argument is that if such devices are commercially available on Earth, imagine what the military might have in its secret spy catalogues, and what advanced alien scientists might have produced. Unfortunately, the bits of metal and glass removed from abductees so far have looked so unlike electrical devices, it is hard to see any connection with terrestrial manufacture. However, terrestrial companies would certainly be repositories of knowledge regarding the nature and biomedical implications of implants, and the thorough study of this information would be an excellent research project for abduction researchers to tackle.

Tempered with this, however, is the fact that sometimes people are convinced they have implants when none are present. Some of the most curious cases of this kind are dental implants. There is a large body of anecdotal literature about people whose braces or fillings cause them to "pick up" radio stations and TV broadcasts. But there are also many cases of people whose delusions cause them to believe they are being tracked and controlled by secret forces through transmitters in their teeth (Brown and Lambert, 1995).

Advice from Down Under

Australian ufologist Pony Godic has pointed out that some abduction accounts are very similar to initiation rites of aboriginal medicine men. He notes that memories such as contact with entities and missing time are found in both contemporary UFO abduction stories as well as stories told by tribal initiates.

But Godic's serious studies of Australian abductions led him to some conclusions that seem to be excellent summaries and delineations of the abduction problem. Godic notes:

> The [abduction] controversy can be largely resolved into three camps:
>
> 1. The experiences are possibly objectively real.
> 2. The accounts are hoaxes or misinterpretations.
> 3. The experiences are largely of a psychological nature.
>
> [The third] hypothesis received its strongest lift from the fascinating work of Macall and Lawson with "imaginary abductees." ... The correspondence of "imaginary" and "real" abduction and "interrupted journey" experiences are impressive and indeed the similarities with other types of "journeys" and experiences ("out of body experiences," "pseudo death" accounts, etc.) are food for thought.

This leads Godic to suggest a course of action for researchers in their work with abductees:

> The perspectives, given by the wide ranging arguments for and against the validity of these types of cases, require the researcher should:
>
> I) Approach these types of cases with an open mind and, at first attempt, gain as much information as possible on that part of the experience which is extant in conscious recall. We could do no better to gain a good perspective of these types of cases by familiarizing ourselves with the available literature.
>
> II) If a "time loss" is highlighted, care should be undertaken in the way in which we approach it. [Leo] Sprinkle has provided an excellent starting point for those who are considering hypnosis and similar methods of "memory" retrieval. The quality of technique is paramount importance here. An experienced practitioner, who should be qualified, accompanied by an experienced investigator, well steeped in the shortcoming of hypnotic regression technique, and a qualified psychologist, is

desired. Interpretation of the information gained under such investigation should be cautious and well-considered.

These types of investigations should be supplemented with as much supportive information as possible. Sprinkle again indicates certain things that can be undertaken ("lie detection" through polygraph testing and psychological assessment). The controversial use of psychological stress evaluation (PSE) has been suggested as also worth trying.

However, it can be seen that, while "interrupted journey" accounts may offer some opportunities for assessing the interactions with the UFO phenomenon, sorties by investigators into this "murky field" should be undertaken *only* if they are fully aware of the total picture. This area of information retrieval brings us into the domain of the human mind's ability to articulate interactions with apparently inexplicable manifestations. It is the experienced UFO researcher, well versed in this field, who is best able to evaluate the type of information gained through this type of information retrieval. Only time will tell whether it will give us more insights into the human mind or into the UFO phenomenon. Could it be that it will do both?

Preventing and/or avoiding alien abductions

In a pragmatic approach, several abductees have speculated that it might be possible to prevent the aliens from abducting humans through subtle intervention. For example, Lorne Goldfader suggested:

If you suspect an attack is in progress (it can last anywhere from 2–5 days), and you display all of the symptoms but are unable to defend yourself or find the resources to do so, try to mingle with a large crowd of people (to wash out your brain wave trace signals). Get away from the area where you are having a problem. Get a magnetic map and go to a LOW intensity area of field strength (the Greys sometimes manipulate surrounding available energy resources as offensive weaponry).

However, the best and by far the most effective method is to mentally construct a shield of protective light around your body. The electromagnetic frequencies and nerve impulses of your brain will respond to these thoughts in a material sense. Imagine that the armament possesses a reflective surface so that anything coming your way bounces off. Now, direct this incoming energy to travel exactly in reverse back to its originating source and order it, with 100 percent conviction, to fulfill its intended purpose on the transmitter. Ask for help from the highest levels of intelligence and love which is your greatest defence. There are always forces on your side. If you keep on working for the good you may become like them some day.

Soon-Yi's doctors, who were skeptical she really had been abducted, simply told her to "Pull yourself together." Not particularly pleased with their flippant attitude, she noted:

> There is nothing they can do now. Scars can be seen but there's no way of telling how they got there. Basically, [my doctors] have been absolutely no help at all, albeit I haven't said it was "aliens," I have just given them the symptoms and they say "take a pill." And that is literally! So far, I've been given Migraleve for the headache, sleeping pills for the nights, Valium (or something like it) for the nerves. And I was sent two young women to help teach me relaxation techniques and try to get me out of the house.

But what *can* be done?

Because abductions are very personal and individual experiences, any solution or technique for dealing with such encounters probably won't work for everybody. Goldfader's version of building self-confidence in order to combat the evil forces isn't a bad idea in principle, since many of us need to muster courage to face everyday life. Others will likely find that the power of prayer would be an answer. In the case of Penelope, she found that through complete co-operation with the aliens, she was better able to function and cope with her nightly experiences. Soon-Yi found she could handle her fears and emotions with a proper regimen of medications. Still others found great solace in speaking with other abductees, as a way to gain reassurance that they weren't "crazy."

These methods assume that the aliens really are here, however. If abductions are products of overactive imaginations, societal difficulties, or electromagnetic effects, then some of the abductees' suggested methods might not be appropriate.

Jerry Clark, editor of the *Encyclopedia of UFOs* and a well-respected authority, has noted that there are two distinct types of abductees: those who are psychologically "normal" and those who show "signs of mental disturbance." He suggests one experimental approach to abduction ufology:

> Here were have all sorts of opportunities to test hypotheses. Here's one testable hypothesis: The first group are more likely to report abduction experiences for which there is some degree of independent evidence, including multiple participants, the second group significantly less so.

As to why this is occurring, he cautions:

> What is happening, clearly, is that as abductions attain a high profile in popular culture, paranoids and other disturbed people use them as focuses of fantasy, just as during the Cold War such folk fantasized that Russian spies were persecuting them. That didn't mean, of course, that no Russian spies existed, just that there weren't nearly so many as reports had it.
> (*UFO Updates*, October 9, 1997.)

I would add my own caution, however. While it may be true that two groups of abductees exist, the search for independent evidence has so far been very elusive. Even if multiple witnesses were claimed for a particular case, the dubious nature of abduction case investigation and the bias of researchers would make such witnesses suspect, to say the least. And that's not even mentioning the problems with physical evidence such as implants and scoop marks.

A recognized expert in multiple personality disorder recalled one case which involved alien intervention and which had serious implications for the medical treatment of delusional individuals:

> There was always doubt about the reality of the stories Margaret told. For instance, one of her alters had a clear memory of aliens coming into her apartment, impregnating her, coming back months later to remove the fetus, then returning years later to show her the half-human, half-alien child they were raising among the stars. This alter was mortified when I raised the possibility that the aliens were possibly not literally real; she said I had ruined the therapy

and her chances of recovery forever by doubting her.... Many [abductees] probably have complex dissociative disorders, but many appear to be otherwise normal."
(Ross, Colin. (1994). *The Osiris Complex: Case Studies in Multiple Personality Disorder.*)

This raises two problems. First, just because an MPD patient has abduction images in one of her personalities does not mean that all abductees have MPD. However, it does warn us that a person who presents as an abductee may have a personality disorder. Further, anyone who says that no abductees show signs of mental illness is obviously wrong. The second point is that by doubting a patient's belief system, resistance to recovery is hindered. Therefore, how many clinicians will simply allow the belief to continue unabated?

Skeptic and Fortean researcher Rebecca Schatte suggests that abduction cases should be handled by a case management team. She notes:

Research, in my opinion, is best left to the professional, such as a medical professional. However, investigation could be done by a ufologist. These two factions would have to work together and the needs of the "client" would come before any investigation.... Anyone who is not a medical professional or under the direct supervision of a medical professional should not be performing hypnosis on abductees.

And to whom should an abductee turn for help?

I like the idea of going to one's family physician. Who better to assess the health, mentally and/or physically, of a patient? I would think that with the support that abductees tend to lend one another, the task of going to the family physician could be made easier.
(*UFO Updates*, October 15, 1997.)

Of course, the cynic in me has to point out that few family doctors are at all versed in abduction ufology, and they would be completely at a loss as to what to do with their patients in these situations. Also, many abductees tend to be loners and may not have seen the same doctor regularly in some time. Visiting a new doctor "cold" with this type of case would be rife with problems.

There also is a trend in ufology where the rush to embrace abductions has surpassed actual case investigations. Kevin McClure and others have cautioned that UFO investigators appear to be willing to forego detailed case investigations if there is any whiff of a witness's confusion of time, location, and facts and if he or she has had any history of odd experiences or dreams at any point in life. "Hard" ufology and its search for explanations of sightings seems to have slipped out of vogue, and has been greatly overshadowed by abduction ufology. This is rather unfortunate, because statistical studies of UFO reports and basic case investigations of simple nocturnal lights are the foundation upon which all ufology rests. If these cornerstones are ignored, then the rest of the edifice may crumble.

CONCLUSIONS
What's Really Going On?

We have seen that abductees come in many shapes and sizes, and with many varying styles and content within their stories. A host of abduction "experts" have put forward explanations with equally varying content, and many are completely convinced of their particular approach to the exclusion of all others.

During more than a decade of working with abductees on a one-to-one basis, I have learned one thing for sure: every case is different. While I do recognize that there are some similarities between the individual encounters, the details vary greatly, and it would seem that abductions are very complex phenomena.

Some of the abductees with whom I have worked or whom I have otherwise studied have seemed completely well-adjusted, confident, and at ease. On the other hand, there have been some individuals who have come to me showing rather pronounced signs of paranoia, schizophrenia, and/or dissociation. I am not convinced by the claims of those experts who insist that no abductees have histories of abuse or that they all come from well-adjusted, content families. Even a cursory examination of abductee case histories shows otherwise.

I also do not agree with those who claim a certain "agenda" for the aliens. I do not see any consistent and reliable information which points to either a plan for genetically breeding a new race of hybrids or to exterminate the humans infesting Earth. I don't see that aliens are in a concerted effort to raise our collective or individual spiritual consciousness. Certainly, some abductees and contactees claim mystical revelations and rapport with religious overtones, but others, particularly those who have sexual relations with aliens, appear much more secular in nature.

The possibility that aliens are attempting to warn of impending doom if we continue our destruction of rain forests, nuclear proliferation, and warlike behaviour is a hopeful one. Indeed, it would be wonderful if this particular message was heard. Alas, the messages of the various aliens reported by the myriad of abductees and contactees are so vague, so verbose, and often so contradictory that they do more to undermine any confidence we might have in the supposedly advanced and highly intelligent extraterrestrial civilizations. From abductee to abductee, the aliens' descriptions of their home worlds vary greatly, and while some of this can be attributed to a plethora of inhabited planets within our galaxy, it's rather odd that there have been only one or two contact cases with the same alien from the same planet.

Depending on which abductees you talk to, it's either the Reptilians or the Greys who are the "good" aliens. Maybe it's the Nordics or Blonds. There are Pleiadeans, Reticulians, Korendarians and aliens from the planet Clarion. Some are merely from a "higher vibrational state," which has no meaning at all in physics but seems to make sense to those immersed in certain New Age philosophies. The aliens are willing to impart metaphysical insight about the nature of reality (and surreality), but either don't seem to know the answers to some of our most burning questions ("How do we trisect an angle?", "What is the cure for the common cold?", "Does the refrigerator light really go out?", etc.), or simply don't want to.

Despite the flood of books and articles about abductees and the television specials that purport to reveal the "truth" about the aliens' intentions, it seems rather obvious that we simply don't know enough about the aliens to say anything one way or another. Even by some abductees' own admissions, they were told explicitly by the aliens that they are deliberately being fed "disinformation" just to confuse us. If that is true, then how can any one theory be held over another?

This is, of course, if aliens are really in the picture. The sad truth is that we still don't have any incontrovertible evidence that aliens are indeed visiting Earth. Circumstantial evidence, some would say, but nothing concrete. Yes, there are well-documented, well-witnessed reports of UFOs performing aerial manoeuvres impossible by terrestrial craft. But does this *automatically* mean aliens are involved? Unfortunately, no.

On the other hand, dismissing all abduction accounts as products of disturbed minds seems rather inappropriate, too. While it's easy to point fingers at some of the more outlandish stories, there are some cases in which the abductees seem to be quite "normal" in comparison with the rest of humanity. (Which, admittedly, isn't saying much.) There are some curious and thought-provoking cases, such as that of the nurse who was visited by white bulbous-headed entities and who was not one to make up stories.

Simply saying that all abductees are imagining their experiences is not adequate. Why would they "remember" stories that have some similar patterns? Why are they about aliens, in the first place? Why not historical figures from the Civil War? Why not Buddha? Why not Claudia Schiffer or some other supermodel? Why not Eric Braden or some other stud? Why has the archetypal *alien* been figuring so prominently in people's vivid dreams?

Some researchers with good backgrounds in psychology who have studied abductees insist that test results show them to have "no overt psychopathology." In other words, abductees are "normal" in any sense of the word. Yet, when I was working with Louis in conjunction with clinical psychologists, even though his MMPI scores were "normal," the psychologists had some concerns. Some psychological problems do not necessarily show up in standard tests, and extreme caution must be taken when working with individuals. "No overt pathology" simply means that the person in question isn't a belligerent sociopath or completely psychotic, yet may have some quirks that might be of some concern.

Let's face it; most abductees function fairly well in society. Most are rational, level-headed individuals with good jobs and some kind of family unit. Many are divorced, but compared with the general population, that's not that unusual. Many have histories of abuse, but some feminist studies have shown that as many as 50 percent of all women are abused in relationships. Some abductees have trouble holding down jobs — but so do many non-abductees. Many abductees don't feel they "fit in" with others here on Earth. Well, given world crises and personal strife, that's not unusual, either.

Some abduction experts claim that most abductees have Celtic ancestors or even have First Nations blood in their heritage. Since everyone's bloodlines are intermingled to one degree or another, this isn't particularly surprising. Besides, if you were to ask someone if her or she had any particular racial lineage, chances are that person would name a distant relative that had that connection.

We can indulge in endless speculation about the purposes of aliens abducting hapless humans: genetic interbreeding, scientific curiosity, societal manipulation, or simply alien recreation. The stories are fascinating and seem to satisfy people's thirst for amazement and Fortean delight. But do we really understand what's going on?

No.

At this point, I would charge that there simply has not been enough serious, unbiased, reproducible, and adequately supported research into the abduction phenomenon to support any one theory. It appears that each researcher is working independently, in isolation from one another, and without much sharing of data and certainly without any decent peer review. No one theory completely explains alien abductions, whether it be one that suggests *they* are really here for evil breeding experiments or that abductions are nothing more than fantasies. This is not surprising, because the foundation of abduction ufology, namely UFO case investigation, is largely being ignored. Many researchers assume that alien abductions exist because there are many UFO sightings reported, and because UFO sightings imply alien visitation.

The reality is that dedicated studies of UFO reports themselves show major problems in the collection and analyses of UFO case data. Since 1989, I have co-ordinated national studies of UFO reports and have published the results and presented my findings at various conferences. I have found that there are, indeed, well-witnessed and well-documented UFO cases for which there are no explanations, but these are few and far-between, and represent a very small minority of cases. In fact, even these cases do not imply alien visitation — they only show that there are some cases that are puzzling. Most cases, including those witnessed and reported by people insisting their observations of distant lights in the sky definitely were of alien spacecraft, are unimpressive to say the least.

After more than ten years of studying alien abduction stories and working directly with abductees, I can only state that there is a great paucity of true and incontrovertible scientific data upon which to build any useful theories. I believe that the scientific community has fallen very short in its view of the phenomenon. If there is no physical phenomenon here, then at the very least there is one that has components within the fields of sociology and psychology. In any case, alien abduction accounts should not be dismissed. Enough people are affected by Alien Abduction Syndrome that it is time for science to overcome its stigma of avoiding UFO witnesses and abductees. It is no wonder that UFO buffs and abductees take no notice of scientists' and debunkers' flippant attitudes. Why should they?

I have great compassion for abductees. During the course of my research, I have met many fine people, outstanding individuals who are genuinely bewildered by their experiences. They have sought help because they are having trouble coping with their memories and emotions, and have received a scattershot response from clinical professionals unfamiliar with the phenomenon and unsure of diagnoses, procedures, and methodology. In the absence of clinical assistance, abductees have turned to self-proclaimed experts in a variety of fields who really have no more answers than anyone else. The creation of cultish groups acting independently and reinforcing abductees' fears and anxieties does little towards helping those in need.

My advice for abductees is: Don't give up. There *are* some dedicated and sincere individuals out there who are willing to listen. Social workers, counsellors, and medical professionals are slowly becoming aware that AAS is a real problem. You're not alone.

Above all, don't believe everything you read.

APPENDIX
Alien Incompetency Theory (AINT):

A Unified Theory to Explain UFO Phenomena, Including Abductions

(Note: A version of this theory was originally published in the *Swamp Gas Journal*, Special Issue #4, Spring, 1996)

One of the most significant issues in ufology today is the attempt to explain the wide variety of conflicting, confusing, and bizarre elements of the UFO phenomenon. In every subfield of ufological studies, there are aspects which strain the logic of even the most seasoned researcher and cause one to doubt the rationality of the genre.

To this end, a new theory has been developed by members of Ufology Research of Manitoba (UFOROM) that appears to explain most, if not all, of these baffling elements. The theory, labelled AINT, is the Alien INcompetency Theory, and describes how all the confusing aspects can be explained by assuming one simple tenet: aliens are incompetent.

To illustrate the theory, one need only to look at examples from within the phenomenon itself, including its outlying subfields. First, let us look at alien abductions.

One of the basic premises of alien abductions is the conscious recall by abductees of their experiences aboard alien spacecraft. Nearly all abductees report that during their ordeal, the aliens create some sort of mental block within their minds so that they cannot remember what has occurred. Yet, as evidenced by the huge number of abduction accounts published and under investigation, these mental blocks are ineffective.

This is odd, considering the advanced technology and knowledge reported to be held by the aliens. Some abductees report that their captors claim thousands of years of development beyond our own, yet they, too, have failed to produce a lasting memory screen that can withstand our feeble efforts to unlock it via simple hypnosis techniques duplicable by any charlatan or stage magician. Why would this be?

Vladimir Simosko, a UFOROM associate and noted Fortean researcher, has suggested some alternatives. Aside from sheer incompetence, he notes two other possibilities:

1) aliens have a wacky sense of humour; and
2) they want us to remember, despite the pretense of intending us to forget.

Another curious observation is that nearly all abductees report aliens with roughly humanoid shapes and comparable sizes, but with different origins and purposes. Some aliens tell their victims they are from Venus, some from the Pleiades, and others from Zeta Reticuli. Since space science has learned Venus cannot support life, this is obvious misinformation. As for the Pleiades, these are stars much younger than our Sun and without hope for planets with suitable living conditions at this time.

Some aliens claim their home planet has deteriorated from misuse and pollution, and wish to warn us about our own disruption of our planet. Others suggest they need our biological material to breed new life (literally) into their gene pool, perhaps to regain such things as emotions or other human characteristics. It is interesting that these scenarios imply that the aliens have somehow caused their own demise and that without our help they are lost. In other words, they made some serious mistakes. It is not too much of a stretch to suggest they were incompetent in managing their resources!

Of course, some aliens are said to claim that they are superior to us and have their own agendas. This is precisely the claim an incompetent person would say to cover his or her mistakes in order to keep from being embarrassed.

The "implants" recovered from abductees' bodies are also evidence of incompetence. Every one of the implants recovered so far has been different in size, shape, material, and the location where it was implanted. Clearly, the aliens are mysteriously poorly versed in proper scientific methodology and the logical use of tracking devices. While there is a trend for some to be found in abductees' noses, others are found in feet, shoulders, wrists, and knees. Surely, if the aliens are conducting a scientific test, their methodology would be consistent. In fact, the implants appear to be little more than chunks of metal or calcified plastics rather than microtransmitters. Perhaps the alien doctors don't know what they are doing. It is astonishing that they would accidentally implant abductees with inert pieces of glass, metal shavings, and wood splinters instead of transceivers and transponders, as might be expected of extraterrestrials wishing to monitor the activities of their victims.

We can look at other aspects of abductions for further evidence. One abductee studied by John Mack described how she woke up one morning after her abduction wearing lavender underwear. This was baffling to her because she didn't own any underwear of that colour. Mack quickly interpreted this to mean that the aliens had somehow made a mistake on board their craft during a busy mass-abduction, and mixed up abductees' clothing. Other abductees have reported returning from their abductions with slippers on the wrong feet and other items of clothing either missing or improperly fastened. In a case studied by Budd Hopkins, an abductee's earrings were found to be in backwards after her ordeal on board a craft.

This all speaks to one explanation: the aliens were incompetent. One would hope that superior beings who have been watching humans for many years would have easily picked up nuances such as the colour of our clothing and the way jewellery is fastened to our bodies.

Simosko would again note that this could be a display of an alien sense of humour, or perhaps an "intelligence test" of some sort. Regarding further refinements of AINT, he offers four postulates:

1) If the aliens are intervening to "help us along," they are incompetent because it isn't working out too well; humans remain relatively unsophisticated and not very "tuned-in" to the universe.

2) If the aliens are intervening by holding us back, it isn't working all that well, either, since although an overwhelming majority of humans are tuned-out, there are a number who are attempting to raise the level of consciousness: Mother Theresa, the Pope, Sun Ra, the Dalai Lama, Sharon Stone, etc.

3) If the aliens are trying *not* to intervene, they're even more incompetent than the other postulates would indicate.

4) If there are several different groups of aliens, some helping and others preventing our advancement, this is proof of incompetence because they cannot "get their act together."

Another aspect of the UFO phenomenon is crash/retrievals. Associated with the idea that some alien ships have crashed on Earth is the concept that Terran government or military bureaucrats have failed to keep the crashes secret, allowing some documents to be leaked to UFO researchers. (More on this later.)

The most famous crash story is that of the Roswell incident, in which a flying saucer apparently crashed during an electrical storm in New Mexico in 1947. While researchers have spent many years tracking down witnesses and speculating as to where the ship might have gone down, the obvious question has never been asked: Why did it crash in the first place?

One only needs to consider accidents of terrestrial vehicles in order to realize the answer: pilot or driver error.

It would be truly remarkable to consider that an alien pilot who has navigated his (or her or its) craft through interstellar space using highly advanced technology and propulsion would be unable to maintain level flight through a mere thunderstorm. There is only one reasonable and possible explanation: the pilot was incompetent. Considering the large number of saucer crashes now claimed by researchers, it would seem that many aliens have difficulty flying their vehicles. Surely this could imply that many are incompetent.

We can look to crop circles as further support for AINT. Allegedly, crop circles constitute a form of "communication" between aliens and ourselves. It is implied they are trying to warn us of or prepare us for some upcoming fateful situation through the creation of "agriglyphs," consisting of complex mathematical patterns and obscure symbols. Why would they attempt to communicate with us in such a fashion? Why not just send a radio message or write something in English or Japanese on a sheet of cardboard? Why not hundred-foot-wide Mayan lettering in marketable durham?

Obviously, their communication skills are less than exemplary, especially since researchers cannot come to an agreement as to the exact messages (other than something about impending "Earth changes"). The aliens must be, of course, incompetent.

What about the infamous Men in Black (MIBs)? They are described as human in appearance, though possessing some characteristics that give them away. Their facial pallour is often olive or grey in colour and their eyes are wide and staring. Their movements are jerky and their speech stilted. They may ask people unusual questions or otherwise show an unfamiliarity with Terran customs. For example, in response to the query, "Hey, buddy! What you lookin' at? You want a knuckle sandwich?", a MIB might say, "Yes, please, with some mayonnaise." Such actions easily show they are not humans at all; if their purpose is to mimic humans, their imperfections show that they are, again, incompetent.

Contactees often will share their imparted knowledge from their alien mentors. Unfortunately, practically all contactees claim contact with different aliens from different planets and with different messages to humankind. (They are similar to abductees in this way.) When pressed to ask their channelled entities for more palpable proof of their claims, or perhaps a useable prediction or two, the contactees are told by the aliens that Earth is "not ready" for the knowledge or, instead, give a vague diatribe about "parallel vibrational states" or "temporal matter disruptions."

An examination of other channelled material finds many other examples of alien double talk and bafflegab. Rather than accepting the channelled information as revelations from higher beings, the lack of content of the messages suggests something else: the aliens themselves don't know the answers or lack the information as well. Again, we can ask how an incredibly advanced civilization would not be able to give one single example that would prove their superiority. Could it be that they do not know the answers, despite their reputed intelligence?

One can also ask why aliens would choose to abduct people from lower castes or social status rather than those in positions of authority. Why don't they land on the White House lawn? Perhaps they don't know to do so.

How could they not know this? They are incompetent.

In all of these examples, it is possible to interpret the aliens' actions as being far from superior. In fact, they seem rather ridiculous. But, if the aliens are really superior beings from an advanced civilization on a distant planet, why are they acting in such an illogical manner? We can point to a parallel situation here on our own planet. Why, given our own relatively advanced technology and level of knowledge, is bureaucratic infighting delaying the construction of the space station? Why is NASA nearly bankrupt?

We can also look at examples in areas other than space science. Why would politicians lobby for tighter controls on cigarettes because of cancer dangers, but pass bills that would subsidize farmers to grow tobacco? Why do bureaucrats create subcommittees to investigate wastes of time and taxpayers' money? Why would politicians sponsor a covert activity to break into a psychiatrist's office in a hotel? (For that matter, why would people vote for politicians, knowing their track records for honesty and integrity?) Why can't my subscription to a magazine get renewed, even when I send the check in four months before the subscription expires? And why are 60 percent of all automobiles recalled by the manufacturer during the first year they are on the road?

The answer, of course, is incompetence. Bureaucratic bungling, political wrangling and general ineptitude are responsible for most of the problems in the world today. Politicians and bureaucrats create such confusion that it is clear they themselves have no idea what they are doing.

Now, imagine a highly evolved technical civilization on a distant planet. Its society functions well, with the exception of a comparatively small number of its population. These would no doubt be their most ineffective politicians and bureaucrats. What better way to remove them from the general gene pool and work force than to send them off on interstellar voyages that, with relativity, would return them many, many years later, if at all?

Because they are incompetent, they would be confused as to their mission. They would be clumsy pilots and navigators and, because they lack the true knowledge of their society, they would be unable to tell anyone anything about their purpose or scientific capability with any degree of understanding or common sense.

As evidence that this is true, a cursory study of the terrestrial government cover-up of UFO crashes shows incompetence as well, but this time with regard to human bureaucrats. The presence of a vast number of leaked documents shows that the government (even a "shadow" variety) cannot function effectively because it is, after all, still a government (which, by definition, is incompetent).

Therefore, we can observe that bizarre aspects of the UFO phenomenon are explained best by assuming the aliens are incompetent. More to the point, they must be the most incompetent examples of their race, namely the bureaucrats. The Alien Incompetency Theory is borne out by an examination of the available observations and claims of witnesses, and can finally explain what is going on. An understanding of this situation will certainly change the way ufologists approach their subject.

BIBLIOGRAPHY

_____. (1994). "Doc sued in 'alien' implant." *Winnipeg Sun*, 14 May 1994, p. 2.

_____.(1998). Dissociative identity disorder/Multiple personality disorder: Frequently asked questions (FAQ). *Published on the Internet*: http://members.aol.com/BoyyM/FAQ.html.

Black, Jerry. (1999). Jerry Black's challenge to Whitley Streiber. *UFO Updates*, 2 January 1999. http://www.ufomind.com/ufo/updates.

Blackmore, Susan. (1994). "Alien Abduction: The Inside Experience." *New Scientist*, 19 November 1994, pp. 29-31.

Brown, E. Sherwood and Lambert, Michael T. (1995). Delusional Electronic Dental Implant: Case reports and literature review. *Journal of Nervous and Mental Disease*, V. 183, No.9, pp. 603-4.

Cameron, Vicki. (1995). *Don't Tell Anyone, But ... UFO Experiences in Canada.* General Store Publishing House, Burnsdown, Ontario.

Campbell, Steuart. (1983). "UFO Data." *New Scientist*, 15 December 1983, p. 799.

Cashman, Mark. (1997). Re: Abduction. *UFO Updates*, 13 October 1997, http://www.ufomind.com/ufo/updates.

Chalker, Bill. (1994). Temporal lobe lability and UFOs. *Published electronically in alt.alien.visitors*, 23 November 1994.

Clark, Jerome. (1976). "UFO Abduction in North Dakota." *Saga UFO Report*, V. 3, No. 3, August 1976.

Clark, Jerome. (1997). UFO Abductions. *UFO Updates*, 9 October 1997, http://www.ufomind.com/ufo/updates.

Colombo, John Robert. (1988). *Mysterious Canada.* Doubleday, Toronto.

Colombo, John Robert. (1991). *UFOs over Canada.* Hounslow, Toronto.

Conway, Graham. (1989). "Alien Abductions in British Columbia." *Flying Saucer Review,* V. 34, No. 1, March 1989.

Conway, Graham. (1996). [Comments on Dorothy Izatt], *Published on the Internet:* www.manari.com/experts.htm.

Dean, Jodi. (1999). *Aliens in America: Conspiracy Cultures from Outerspace to Cyberspace.* Cornell University Press, Ithaca, NY.

Devereux, Paul. (1982). *Earth lights: Towards an Uunderstanding of the UFO Phenomenon.* Turnstone Press, Wellingborough, England.

Fenwick, Larry. (1995). "Implant probed in Canada by Scanning Electron Microscope." *CUFORN Bulletin,* V. 15, No. 1.

Fox, Phyllis. (1979). "Social and Cultural Factors Influencing Beliefs about UFOs." In: Haines, Richard F., ed., *UFO Phenomena and the Behavioral Scientist.* Scarecrow Press, Metuchen, NJ, pp. 20-42.

Golman, Daniel. (1994). "Miscoding Seen as Root of False Memories." *New York Times,* 31 May 1994, pp. C1, 8.

Hall, Celia. (1997). "Recovering Memory is Banned by Psychiatrists." *London Daily Telegraph,* 1 October 1997, p. 6.

Hendry, Allan. (1979). *The UFO Handbook: A Guide to Investigating, Evaluating and Reporting UFO Sightings.* Doubleday, Garden City, NY.

Hill, Don. (1998). *Haunted House, Haunted Mind.* [Transcript]. CBC Radio, Ideas, 30 October 1998.

Hopkins, B., D. M. Jacobs, and R. Westrum, (1992). *A Report on Unusual Experiences Associated with UFO Abductions, Based Upon the Roper Organization's Survey of 5,947 Adult Americans.* Intruders Foundation, NY.

Hufford, David. J. (1982). *The Terror that Comes in the Night: An Eperience-Centered Study of Supernatural Assault Traditions.* University of Pennsylvania Press: Philadelphia.

Ingram, Jay. (1996). "Aliens and the Sudbury Connection." *Toronto Star,* 14 January 1996.

Izatt, Dorothy. (1998). Manari: The Dorothy Wilkinson Izatt Experience. *Published on the Internet:* www.manari.com.

Jacobs, David. M. (1997). *The Threat: Revealing the Secret Alien Agenda.* Fireside, NY.

Jumper, Todd. (1997). My UFO Experiences. *Published on the Internet:* http://www.eagle-net.org/mce.

Klass, Philip J. (1981). "Hypnosis and UFO Abductions." *Skeptical Inquirer*, V. 5, No. 3, pp.16-24.

Laibow, R. (1993). Clinical discrepancies between expected and observed data in patients reporting UFO abductions: Implications for treatment. *Published electronically in alt.alien.visitors* on 8 January 1993.

Lammer, Helmut. (1996). Preliminary findings of Project MILAB: Evidence for military kidnappings of alleged UFO abductees. *Published on the Internet:* http://www.alienjigsaw.com/milab.html

Lawson, Alvin. (1980). "Hypnosis of Imaginary UFO 'Abductees.'" In: Fuller, Curtis G., ed. *Proceedings of the First International UFO Congress*, Warner, NY, pp. 195-238.

Leslie, Melinda and Mark Williams. (1996). Are you an alien abductee? 52 indicators of UFO encounters or abductions by aliens. *Published on the Internet:* http://www.anw.com.aliens/52questions.htm

Loftus, Elizabeth. (1997). "Creating False Memories." *Scientific American*, September 1997, pp. 70–75.

Lorgen, Eve Frances. (1998). Alien implant removals. *Published on the Internet:* http://users1.ee.net/pmason/el.html.

Lorgen, Eve Frances. (1998). Points of view. *Published on the Internet:* http://www.soft.net.uk/staffs/ufoesp/pov.html.

Lorgen, Eve Frances. (1999). The love bite: Alien orchestrated human bonding dramas. *Published on the Internet:* http://users1.ee.net/pmason/el_bonding.html.

Mack, John. (1992). Why the abduction phenomenon cannot be explained psychiatrically. *Published on the Internet:* http://www.peer-mack.org/mit92.html.

Mack, John. E. (1994). *Abduction: Human Encounters with Aliens.* Charles Scribner's Sons, NY.

Matheson, Terry. (1998). *Alien Abductions: Creating a Modern Phenomenon.* Prometheus Books, Amherst, NY.

McClure, Kevin. (1998). Alien implants — a chiropodist speaks. *Abduction Watch*, No.15, November, 1998. *Published on the Internet:* http://www.magonia.demon.co.uk/abwatch/aw15.html

McClure, Kevin. (1998). Recovered memory and hypnosis special. *Abduction Watch*, No. 6, January 1998. *Published on the Internet:* http://www.magonia.demon.co.uk/abwatch/aw6.html.

Meerloo, Joost. (1967). "Le Syndrome des Soucoupes Volantes." *Medecine et Hygiene*, No. 794, September 1967, pp. 992-996.

Musgrave, John. (1976). "The UFO Investigator as Counsellor and Healer." *Canadian UFO Report*, V. 4, No. 2, pp. 15–17.

O'Brien, Barbara. (1976). *Operators and Things: The Inner Life of a Schizophrenic.* Signet, NY.

Persinger, Michael A. (1979). "Possible Infrequent Geophysical Sources of Close UFO Encounters: Expected Physical and Behavioral-Biological Effects. In: Haines, Richard F., ed. *UFO Phenomena and the Behavioral Scientist.* Scarecrow Press, Metuchen, NJ, pp. 396-433.

Persinger, Michael A. (1988). "Geophysical Variables and Behavior: LIII. Epidemiological Considerations for Incidence of Cancer and Depression in Areas of Frequent UFO Reports." *Perceptual and Motor Skills,* V. 67, pp. 799-803.

Persinger, Michael A. (1998). The tectonic strain theory as an explanation for UFO phenomena: A brief history and summary, 1970 to 1997. *Published on the Internet:*
http://www.laurentian.ca/www/neurosci/tectonicedit.htm

Persinger, Michael A. And Derr, John S. (1985). "Geophysical Variables and Behavior: XXXII. Evaluations of UFO Reports in an Area of Infrequent Seismicity: The Carman, Manitoba, Episode." *Perceptual and Motor Skills,* V. 61, pp. 807-813.

Polanik, Joseph. (1999). Abduction Researchers: The Good, the Bad, and the Ugly. *UFO Updates,* 7 February, 1999,
http://www.ufomind.com/ufo/updates

Priscu, Virgil. (1997). Re: UFOR: Skywatch: UFOR: Bedouin "alien" murder. *UFO Updates,* 14 August 1997,
http://www.ufomind.com/ufo/updates

Ross, Colin A. (1994). *The Osiris Complex.* University of Toronto Press, Toronto, p. 149.

Rutkowski, Chris. (1993), *Unnatural History.* Chameleon Publishing, Winnipeg, Canada.

Rutkowski, Chris. (1994). "The Falcon Lake Case: Too close an Encounter." *Journal of UFO Studies,* N.S., V.5.

Rutkowski, Chris and Del Bigio, Marc. (1989). "UFOs and cancer?" *Canadian Medical Association Journal,* V. 140, pp. 1258-1259.

Sandow, Greg. (1998). "The Threat: A review." *UFO Updates,* 6 January 1998, http://www.ufomind.com/ufo/updates.

Schatte, Rebecca. (1997). Re: Researching abduction cases. *UFO Updates,* 15 October 1997, http://www/ufomind.com/ufo/updates.

Schnabel, Jim. (1994). *Dark White: Aliens, Abductions and the UFO Obsession.* Hamish Hamilton, London.

Sherman, Harold. (1946). "The Green Man." *Amazing Stories,* October 1946.

Sherman, Harold. (1979). *The Green Man and His Return.* Amherst Press, Amherst, Wisconsin.

Sims, Derrel and M.J. Florey. "Evidence for, and Implications of, Medically Unexplained Implants in Abductees." *HUFON Report,* September 1994, 6-8; January 1995, 3-5; February 1995, 6-8.

Stark, Todd I. (1993). Hypnosis research overview. *Published electronically in alt.hypnosis,* July 1993.

Stollman, Gary. (1996). Gary Stollman. *Published electronically in alt.alien.visitors,* 16 December 1996.(And also:
http://www.fringeware.com/anathema/AR/mail/stollman.html.)

Strieber, Whitley. (1987). *Communion: A True Story.* Beach Tree, NY.

Vallee, Jacques and Torme, Tracy. (1996). *Fastwalker.* North Atlantic Books, NY.

Velez, John. (1997). Researching abduction cases. *UFO Updates,* 14 October 1997, http://www.ufomind.com/ufo/updates.

Velez, John. (1997). Possible x-rays of "implant." *UFO Updates,* 4 September 1997, http://www/ufomind.com/ufo/updates.

Velez, John. (1999). Re: The verdict on the "implant" x-rays. *UFO Updates,* 4 March 1999, http://www.ufomind.com/ufo/updates.

Warren, Donald I. (1970). "Status Inconsistency Theory and Flying Saucer Sightings." *Science,* V. 170, 6 November 1970.

Watson, Nigel. (1999). "Loving the Alien." *Fortean Times,* No. 121, April 1999, pp. 34-39.

Wright, Dan. (1990). "Commonalities and Disparities: Findings of the MUFON Abduction Study Project." In: Andrus, Walter H., Jr., ed. *MUFON 1995 International UFO Symposium Proceedings,* MUFON, Seguin, TX, pp. 164-203. (And also:
http://www.debshome.com/abduction_studies.html.)